CRITICAL INSIGHTS

Midnight's Children

CRITICAL INSIGHTS

Midnight's Children

Editor
Joel Kuortti
University of Turku, Finland

SALEM PRESS
A Division of EBSCO Information Services, Inc.
Ipswich, Massachusetts

GREY HOUSE PUBLISHING

Library of Congress Cataloging-in-Publication Data

Midnight's children / editor, Joel Kuortti, University of Turku, Finland.
-- [First edition].

pages : illustrations ; cm. -- (Critical insights)

Includes bibliographical references and index.
ISBN: 978-1-61925-389-6

1. Rushdie, Salman. Midnight's children. 2. Rushdie, Salman--Criticism and interpretation. 3. Postcolonialism in literature. 4. India--In literature. 5. Nationalism in literature. I. Kuortti, Joel, editor of compilation. II. Series: Critical insights.

PR6068.U757 M553 2014
823/.914

First Printing

Contents

Resources

About This Volume

This anthology on Salman Rushdie's award-winning novel *Midnight's Children* (1981) introduces a seminal work in postcolonial literature. It is Rushdie's fundamental take on India, which has functioned as a lighthouse for a generation of Indian and other postcolonial writers. As an introduction, the volume opens with this brief explication of the texts in the collection. It is followed with an overview of the main thematic issues in the novel. These themes—together with other topics—are then discussed in more detail in the main articles. The introductory part also includes a brief outline of Rushdie's career. Born in 1947, Rushdie is still an active writer, so this biographical sketch is by nature open-ended and—through future hindsight—subject to many changes in the years to come.

The collection consists of thirteen original essays, and it is divided in two main sections. In the first section, there are four articles that outline the contextual parameters of *Midnight's Children*. The second section, then, comprises nine critical readings that tackle various aspects of the rich and complex novel.

First of the articles in the first section is John J. Su's "Rushdie's Global Modernism," which analyzes both the narrative itself and Rushdie's novel in general by applying the concept of genealogy. Genealogy is one of Rushdie's central narrative strategies and, therefore, relevant for the discussion of the novel. The novel itself, then, Su argues, is a progeny of global modernism and has a genealogy of its own. In her article, "*America, the Great Attractor, whispered in my ears*': From Bombay to New York: Mapping Geopolitical Shifts in Rushdie's Fiction," Marianne Corrigan looks at Rushdie's oeuvre in general terms. She considers the geographical settings of Rushdie's various novels and considers the geopolitical significance in the postcolonial contexts of globalization, migration, and consumerism.

vii

Joel Kuortti's contribution deals with the critical reception of *Midnight's Children*. Since its publication, *Midnight's Children* has evoked a lot of interest from various quarters, and the article delineates the developments within criticism and looks into possible new critical avenues. Finally, in the article by Anuradha Marwah, the topic is approached from a comparative perspective. "From Salman Rushdie to Arundhati Roy: Issues of Continuity in Indian Fiction in English" discusses Rushdie together with Arundhati Roy's *The God of Small Things* (1997). Whereas *Midnight's Children* was Indian writing's first breakthrough into the global literary scene, Roy's novel marks the entrance of a new generation onto that scene. Marwah compares the two literary celebrities as phenomena in their own time and how they both were a part of the commodification of Indian/postcolonial literature.

The articles in the critical readings section approach *Midnight's Children* from a variety of critical angles. The first two consider, among other things, language from ethico-philosophical and translational points of view. Tuomas Huttunen initiates the section with his article "Nasal Connections: The Possibility of Ethical Deconstruction in *Midnight's Children*." Here, ethical issues are considered in the cosmopolitan, postcolonial context. The crucial question concerns the possibility of ethical agency in a narrative. Jenni Ramone continues the discussion of narrative in relation to various translation principles in "Faithful Versus Free: Padma and Saleem as Competing Translators." Furthermore, she considers the ways in which postcolonial novels can or cannot fit into the genre of *Bildungsroman*: it is a question of finding—or rather *not* finding—a society to fit in.

The next four articles enter the field of history and politics. Both Ágnes Györke in "Topographies of Nationalism in *Midnight's Children*" and Raita Merivirta in "'A Collective Fiction': The (De) construction of Nehruvian India in *Midnight's Children*" discuss the issues of nation and nationalism so prevalent in criticism of *Midnight's Children*, as Rushdie's novel has often been read as a national allegory. Györke takes up the Midnight Children's Conference as an allegory of the split between contradictory ideals about independent India, and its dissolution as an indication of the lost Nehruvian ideal. Merivirta, then, concentrates especially on the Nehruvian secular idea of India, and discusses the allegorical potential of Saleem to encapsulate the state as imagined in optimistic tones. This optimism is eventually shattered during the Emergency, and both the Conference and Saleem disintegrate.

Madan M. Sarma's "Indian Oral Narrative in Postmodern Historiography: A Reading of *Midnight's Children*" further engages with the discourse of the nation as it takes up the idea of metafictional historiography. This is one of the basic approaches to the novel, and Sarma applies it to an analysis of the use of Indian oral traditions in the narrative. He discusses how, through this operation, the novel plays with the idea of historical knowledge and suggests a more impartial understanding of the history of the nation. Lotta Strandberg's "Bombay in *Midnight's Children*", then, situates the novel in the metropolitan city of Bombay and discusses the importance of the city itself for the narrative and its significance for the nation-state and representations of it.

The three remaining articles discuss the questions of identity and gender—often seen as problematic in Rushdie's works. Liani Lochner's "Fictions of the Self: The Reader, the Subject, and the Text in *Midnight's Children* and *The Satanic Verses*" combines the discussions of language and nation through an examination of the concept of subjectivity. As much as the social subject is constituted through language, the power relations are present in the makeup of individual identity. In Jūratė Radavičiūtė's article, "The Play with the Connotations of Sexuality in *Midnight's Children*," the construction of identity is investigated through the use and subversion of synechdoches, especially those bodily elements— namely nose, voice, and hair—that have sexual connotations in the novel. Through the provocative use of these, the novel undermines the structures of hegemonic historiography. The final article is Celia Wallhead's "The Role of the Women Characters in the Nature/Nurture and Optimism/Pessimism Questions in *Midnight's Children*." It is a detailed analysis of some of the main female characters in the novel and how the falsely constructed family ties reflect on the views—

either optimistic or pessimistic—about the society, nation, and life in general. Women are central in the protagonist Saleem Sinai's life, and the discussion of the status of women throughout the social spectrum reflects the novel's critical stance towards the way Indian society had been developing.

The volume concludes with a chronology of Rushdie's life, as well as a bibliographical list of Rushdie's major works and a select general bibliography of criticism on Rushdie and, in particular, *Midnight's Children*. All in all, the articles and other materials of this volume evoke the richness of Rushdie's enchanting, enchanted world. We hope that the book offers intriguing entries into this increasingly evolving, literary magical reality that has captured millions of people all over the world for more than thirty years. The 'open sesame' or 'abracadabra' allowing entrance to this world is to be found in the beginning of *Midnight's Children*: Once upon a time…

THE BOOK
AND
AUTHOR

Midnight's Children: More Useful than the Facts

Joel Kuortti

A Perfect Work?

A novel was born in London ... once upon a time. Well, that's not enough. One needs to be more precise: Salman Rushdie's second novel was published by Jonathan Cape in London in 1981. When was that? That is also important. All right, it was in February 1981. And the title ... With the publication of Salman Rushdie's *Midnight's Children*, the reviewers joined palms in respectful greeting to pay homage to the arrival of a new age. There were gasps from the crowds to record how the destiny of a novel became indissolubly chained to the development of literature. For the next decades, there was to be no flight.

For many readers, *Midnight's Children* has become a must-read on India: a perfect introduction into the past of an ancient civilization and the present of a young nation. The Indian partition literature scholar Rituparna Roy calls it undeniably "a singular achievement" that is "a watershed" within Indian literature (Roy 89–90). The Indian novelist and critic Amit Chaudhuri describes it even further as "a gigantic edifice that all but obstructs the view of what lies behind" (Chaudhuri, *Huge, Baggy Monster* 113; *Picador Book* xxiii). Here, I will discuss how 'perfect' it may be and what sort its 'perfection' might be when I look into the novel's main features and themes and contextualize its relevance in view of the wider Indian and postcolonial discourse.

Unlike the birth of the protagonist of *Midnight's Children*, Saleem Sinai, the grand arrival of Rushdie into the global literary scene was not prophesied. Nor had Rushdie's earlier venture into fiction—the publication of *Grimus* in 1975—paved the way for the recognition of his voice. Never before had Indian literature received such an international acknowledgement, even though Rabindranath Tagore (1861–1941) had won the prestigious Nobel

Prize for literature in 1913, and writers like Premchand (or Dhanpat Rai, 1880–1936); Mulk Raj Anand (1905–2004); R. K. Narayan (1906–2001); Raja Rao (1908–2006); Kamala Markandaya (1924–2004); and later, Anita Desai (born Anita Mazumdar in 1937) had established careers in India and had reputations extending beyond the subcontinent.

Within India, the twenty-two currently official (called 'scheduled') Indian language literatures—together with numerous other non-scheduled language literatures—have thrived and have produced writers with large readerships within their language communities. Some have work that has reached beyond the wider Indian scale. However, it was only in English, either in translation or originally written in Indian English, that Indian literature began to reach the Goethean scene of world literature. This is not an evaluative statement on the literary value of English, but an observation of how the history of Indian literature has evolved around the time of independence in 1947 and after, when Rushdie "heralded a new era in the history of Indian English fiction" (Naik and Narayan 38).

The sizeable Indian diasporic community has produced hundreds of authors, for whom English is the first language of expression—whatever the mother tongue might be (Sailaja 15). Rushdie, an Urdu speaker by birth, was educated in English in India and completed his studies in England. The position of the English language in the Indian literary scene (as well as in politics) has been a contested one. An indication of this is that the highest official literary establishment—the Indian National Academy of Letters—the Sahitya Akademi has a problematic relationship with English (Sadana 94, 102). While the Akademi began granting its awards in 1955, English (together with some other non-scheduled languages) literature only got its first Award in 1960 with R. K. Narayan's *The Guide* (1958)—after the Akademi had changed the policy concerning its view on which languages to acknowledge, making exceptions for other Indian languages and especially for "literary productions in English by Indian nationals" (Rao 58; Orsini 83–85).

Midnight's Children, then, would not have qualified for the Akademi Award, as Rushdie was no longer residing in India—

although he was still an NRI, a non-resident Indian. However, for various reasons, it became a novel that transformed the way in which India was to be seen in the global media and in the eyes of readers all around the world—except for critical voices in India. Firstly, it presented India in a language that was unusual in literary usage. It used English in a form that was not Queen's English, but a bastardized form of Indian English, with structures and expressions only in use in India. Similar language could be found already in G. V. Desani's (1909–2000) novel *All About H. Hatterr* (1948), but Rushdie brought the vernacular to a new level of recognition.

Secondly, the multiplicity explicit in *Midnight's Children* exposed India as a conglomeration of a myriad of different population segments rather than a politically unified state: there were language riots, religious clashes, caste inequalities, social disparities, alongside natural beauty, cultural richness, and individual courage. Thirdly, the novel introduced several persistent themes into postcolonial literature, many of which feature in earlier works, but find a form in *Midnight's Children* that would linger long in the literary criticism of Rushdie and many other authors: themes like history, memory, identity, fictionality, and the postcolonial nation.

I Language: All-India Radio

Initially, language in its various meanings is perhaps the most noticeable feature in reading *Midnight's Children*, or, indeed, criticism of the novel. In her discussion of the status of Indian writing in English in the 1970s, the distinguished Indian literary critic Meenakshi Mukherjee comments that "the most significant challenge is the task of using the English language in a way that will be distinctively Indian and still remain English" (Mukherjee, *Twice Born Fiction* 165). That Rushdie's "linguistic risk" with English a few years later was timely (Kothari 50) is evidenced by the popularity of the novel, as well as by the influence it has had in other writers. In her commentary on the postcolonial status of English, the Indo-Canadian critic Uma Parameswaran—one of the first to write extensively on Rushdie—applauds Rushdie with whom, she argues, "all was changed, changed utterly. No more glossaries, no more explications, just an exuberant mélange of coinings and compound words" (Parameswaran 354). Also Mukherjee comments on Rushdie's "daring to translate idioms and puns mediated by no apology, no footnote, no glossary" (Mukherjee, *Rushdie's Midnight's Children* 10). While this is not the view of all critics (see e.g. Khair 109–110; Trivedi 81), Indian writing in English had gained a new, strong trend.

Considering the post-Rushdie Indian novel, Chaudhuri warns against the tendency "[t]o celebrate Indian writing simply as overblown, fantastic, lush and non-linear" (Chaudhuri 116). For him, this would mean a simplification and—rather than a turn for a new—a return to mimetic representation, "surely an old colonialist prejudice" (Chaudhuri 116). That there is a space and call for such a word of warning indicates that Rushdie enjoys a special position within (that) literature.

With regard to language, Rushdie employs several strategies and techniques. One of the most crucial strategies is the first person narrative, which implies an authentic perspective. This concept will be discussed more in relation to history and politics in the next section. Another central strategy is elaborate, intertextual, fragmented, and delayed narration that echoes both postmodern narrative constructs and works like Laurence Sterne's *Tristram Shandy*, published in nine volumes between 1759–1767 (Pesso-Miquel 18). Rushdie calls this type of hybrid, pluralistic writing 'mongrelization.' For example, he describes how "*The Satanic Verses* celebrates hybridity, impurity, intermingling, and the transformation that comes of new and unexpected combinations of human beings, cultures, ideas, politics, movies, songs. It rejoices in *mongrelization* and fears the absolutism of the Pure. […] It is a love song to our mongrel selves" (Rushdie [1990] 1991, 394; emphasis added).

It is not only on the level of narration, however, that Rushdie's text is involved with hybridity. While undeniably English, the novel is very much also not-English. The functional allegory in this respect is Saleem's telepathic connection with the one thousand other midnight's children, the *All-India Radio*, or, as the broadcaster's voice announces the Indian national radio broadcasting company in Hindi: "*Yé Akashvani hai*" (Rushdie, *Midnight's Children* 166, further references preceded by *MC*). At first, Saleem has problems understanding because of the multiple languages—the "polyglot frenzy" that is going on inside his head: "The voices babbled in everything from Malayalam to Naga dialects, from the purity of Lucknow Urdu to the Southern slurrings of Tamil" (*MC* 168). Only later does he find a way to bypass the limiting particularity of individual languages onto an underlying level where "language faded away, and was replaced by universally intelligible thought-forms which far transcended words" (*MC* 168).

Circumventing or finding a way around the problem of language multiplicity is a fundamental question for a nation consisting of multiple language communities, such as India. In more general terms, it is also a burning issue for translation—and especially for cultural translation. Such an in-between territory of cultures within a culture, or as the eminent postcolonial critic Homi Bhabha defines it—a "space of the translation of cultural difference within *the interstices*" (Bhabha 224; emphasis original)—requires a language that does not privilege the center nor any given margin, but negotiates between them.

Rushdie's novel functions within such negotiation, so much so that the literary critic Gillian Gane problematizes its self-evident Englishness by asking: "What *is* the language of the novel?" (Gane 570; emphasis original). In his perceptive analysis, the writer and critic Tabish Khair contrasts Raja Rao's and Rushdie's style of language use and concludes that while neither of them uses language in the way it is actually spoken in the streets of India—Rao, on one hand, being too Sanskritized, Brahminical, ritualized, and textualized, and Rushdie, on the other, being too cosmopolitan, stylized, and manufactured (Khair 107–109). He concedes, however, that "Rushdie is mostly trying to appropriate a kind of Indian English that his characters are supposed to speak while Rao is *mostly* translating the vernacular spoken by his characters. Rushdie's reality is predominantly anglophone [sic], while Rao's is largely 'vernacular'" (Khair 110; emphasis original).

When English functions as the telepathic medium that transcends words, the question of authenticity so often evoked in discussions of the novel is not resolved easily through analysis of the linguistic features. These features are, however, very interesting and significant, and Rushdie has even lent this particular usage a name: 'chutnification' (*MC* 459)—a blending of (even improbable) ingredients as in the pickling process, and he has been credited for enabling "the novel in English to go *jungli*," the Hindi term for "going 'native'" (Wong 200; Talib 25). Among the out of the ordinary linguistically informed techniques Rushdie uses, we can list, for example, the use of the following:

- vocabularies or lexis from Indian languages (mainly Hindi and Urdu—'cheroot,' MC 12; 'dharma-chakra', MC 122)
- interjections ("Hai Ram!", MC 143; "Allah-tobah," MC 81; "Yara", MC 16)
- unconventional grammar ("Eat, na, food is spoiling," MC 24)
- unconventional similes ("like a mad plantain," MC 13; "like an empty pickle jar," MC 19)
- Indianized idioms ("Sistersleeping pigskin bag from Abroad," MC 20)
- Indianized word order ("their ears also," MC 366)
- reduplication ("what-what," MC 20; "joke-joke" MC 101)
- rhyming reduplication ("writing-shiting," MC 24; "pumpery-shumpery", MC 242)
- list compounds ("intertwined lives events miracles places rumours," MC 9; "the hartal of pamphlet mosque wall newspaper", MC 33)
- oxymorons ("gigantic dwarf", MC 307)

For more categories and examples of Rushdie's language usage, consult Sisir Kumar Chatterjee (148–150), Gillian Gane (576–587) and Sarala Krishnamurthy (14–23). Many of the mentioned techniques make use of code-switching, cultural translation, and imaginative inventiveness. As I have discussed, none of these should, however, be taken as simplistic avowals of authenticity or groundedness. As developed further in the next section and summarizing the Indian critic T. Vijay Kumar's idea, in its internationality, Indian English literature does not simply represent the whole of India, and the 'vernacular,' only a fragment of it (Kumar 325).

One further specific linguistic aspect in *Midnight's Children* and in much of Rushdie's subsequent writing remains to be mentioned, that of cinematic language. Even though Rushdie's approach is very literary and intertextual, he uses also a lot of expressions, particularly from the field of cinema. For example, Florian Stadtler, who has studied Rushdie from the filmic point of view, comments that "Rushdie uses Hindi cinema's visual culture to articulate in [*Midnight's Children*] a vision of post-independence India that finds its echoes in Indian popular cinema" (Stadtler 124). Indeed, Saleem claims that "nobody from Bombay should be without a basic film vocabulary" (*MC* 33), and he adopts technical vocabulary, cinematic imagery, and perspectives, as well as intermedial references to various films—even the notorious concept of an "indirect kiss" (*MC* 142). In this respect, it is relevant to note that the novel was adapted into film in 2012 by the Indo-Canadian director Deepa Mehta. The film is not discussed in this volume in detail, as the focus is literary, but comparative studies of the novel and the film, as well as those of the film and other films, are emerging. What is perhaps most remarkable is the shift from the fragmented narration in the novel—which could be seen as a cinematic technique—to a more linear one in the film.

Politics: Handcuffed to History

Language is not a separate issue in *Midnight's Children*. It is very much connected with the historico-political setting as well. After India gained its independence, the unity of the young nation-state—"the new myth—a collective fiction in which anything was possible" (*MC* 112)—was challenged by the language question. The Indian Constitution had secured the position of Hindi as the national language and that of English as a link language. The other major languages were listed as scheduled languages. The southern Dravidian language-speakers were not content with the hegemony of the Indo-Aryan Hindi, and other major languages felt that they needed to safeguard their languages. In her analysis of the significance of cinema in the formation of Indian nation, the film scholar Ajanta Sircar comments on the language debate, indicating that it signaled how the idea of nation was different in the colonies than it was in the West. Sircar also notes that the way in which internal boundaries were drawn in India, "along linguistic lines [...] is testimony to the fact that there were many other competing narratives of community prevalent in the country. Hindi was only *one* among many such conceptual worlds" (Sircar 32). The ideal unity of India was threatened by linguistic partition, such "heteroglossia is collisional" (Srivastava 229). The threat was real and erupted in violence.

In Bombay, language riots were ignited in 1956, demanding separate states for the Southern Marathi speakers and Northern Gujarati speakers. This is recorded by the first person protagonist Saleem in the novel in the following way: "Language marchers demanded the partition of the state of Bombay along linguistic boundaries—the dream of Maharashtra was at the head of some processions, the mirage of Gujarat led the others forward" (*MC* 167). Later on, Saleem witnesses the result of this political campaign:

> *Language divided us*: Kerala was for speakers of Malayalam, the only palindromically-named tongue on earth; in Karnataka you were supposed to speak Kanarese; and the amputated state of Madras— known today as Tamil Nadu—enclosed the aficionados of Tamil. Owing to some oversight, however, nothing was done with the state of Bombay; and in the city of Mumbadevi, the language marches grew longer and noisier and finally metamorphosed into political parties, the Samyukta Maharashtra Samiti ('United Maharashtra Party') which stood for the Marathi language and demanded the creation of the Deccan state of Maharashtra, and the Maha Gujarat Parishad ('Great Gujarat Party') which marched beneath the banner of the Gujarati language (*MC* 189; emphasis added.).

The irony does not escape the reader—rather than uniting, *language divided us*. While Saleem is an unreliable narrator (Rushdie, "Errata" 1992), his contention is that if one does not get beneath the particularity, the result is a breakdown into conflicting, fragmenting political divisions. Saleem's own bodily fragmentation, another allegorical feature, is evidence of this, although he claims that he is "not speaking metaphorically" (*MC* 37). Not only the political history is relevant here, either, but the fact that Saleem, "mysteriously handcuffed to history" in birth (*MC* 9), takes the blame (if not credit) for having been "directly responsible for triggering off the violence which ended with the partition of the state of Bombay, as a result of which the city became the capital of Maharashtra" (*MC* 192).

One of the recurrent charges against Rushdie in criticism is that *Midnight's Children* is a pessimistic novel, that it drains hope from the Indians, and the Indian nation. This issue is, indeed, one of the central ones in the novel, and the concluding paragraph does end in a desperate note about the midnight's children being "both masters and slaves of their times, […] unable to live or die in peace" (*MC* 463). Here, the political criticism of the novel is at its sharpest, as it recounts the Emergency period in Indian history (June 1975–March 1977). Rushdie's unsympathetic critique of Prime Minister Indira Gandhi—disguised thinly in the novel as the Widow—also led to a court case as he was obliged to remove a (an allegedly) libelous sentence from the novel—although the case was dismissed, as Gandhi was assassinated in October 1984 before a court ruling was made.

The novel's initial optimism with the Nehruvian secular ideal is surmounted by the utter nihilistic machinations of the government during the Emergency. There were violent and oppressive measures taken against the insurgents in the aftermath of the Indo-Pakistan war of 1971 that had lead to the secession of East Pakistan and the formation of Bangladesh. The extreme measures taken by the government meant restrictions for civil rights and political activities, as well as unaccounted for confinements and—particularly significant for *Midnight's Children*—forced sterilizations. A symbol for the sterilizations is the free transistor radio that was (deceitfully) promised to those who "volunteered" for the operation (*MC* 167)—the topic is further developed in Rushdie's short story "The Free Radio."

The optimism that had been "growing like a rose in a dung-heap" was countered, as Saleem recounts, by "the Widow's finest, most delicate joke: instead of torturing us, she gave us hope" (*MC* 437). The hope—and the optimistic bug disease epidemic fever virus (all epithets used in the novel for the phenomenon)—I understand, is in the multiplicity of the Midnight's Children's Conference, the plurality of India, the sheer uncontrollable "annihilating whirlpool of the multitudes" (*MC* 463), whereas the other option signified by the Widow means taking hope away. Yet, Saleem's "optimism, like a lingering disease, refused to vanish" (*MC* 298), at least for a while.

This is the political gist of *Midnight's Children* in its crudest form: that India was depleted of its hope, its noisy teeming crowd, and ayah Mary Pereira's ditty "You kin be just what-all you want" (*MC* 383). In the allegorical universe, this implies hope not only for Saleem but for all of India. When the government begins the enforced vasectomies in the name of family planning, the hope nurtured by Saleem is drained not only (or even predominantly) metaphorically but very much physically. Such 'ectomy,' a cutting out, which in medicine has multiple forms—"appendectomy tonsillectomy mastectomy tubectomy vasectomy testectomy hysterectomy"— finds the most irrevocable form in the Widow's annihilation of any hope: "Sperectomy: the draining-out of hope" (*MC* 437).

Postcoloniality: Now, Suddenly, Independence

Without claiming to have covered all critical aspects of *Midnight's Children*—perhaps some of the more pertinent ones at best—one last topic will be discussed here, namely the postcolonial framework. *Midnight's Children* did not only herald Indian English literature into a new era, but it paved the way for other postcolonial literatures to reach global readership—and the international literary market. The postcoloniality of *Midnight's Children*, then, is not a separate topic but very closely linked to the previous topics of language and politics.

As has been discussed in the previous sections, the variety of English that is known as Indian English is not a consistent one, nor does it have fixed features (Sailaja 14). The postcolonial call for Indianization of English, suggested already by the early Indian English novelist Raja Rao in his preface to the novel *Kanthapura*— "We cannot write like the English. [...] We can only write as Indians" (Rao 5)—means in Rushdie's parlance, 'the empire writing back with a vengeance' (Rushdie, "Empire Writing..." 8). What Rushdie brought into discussion was precisely that unashamed stance towards the supremacy of the language of the colonial center. Even if Rushdie's intentions and success in this has been disputed, it is incontestable that he made his mark not only in postcolonial literature but also in theory. The most illustrative example of this is the title of the key text of postcolonial studies, *Empire Writes Back* by Bill Ashcroft, Gareth Griffiths, and Helen Tiffin published in 1989. It both acknowledges Rushdie's position and the counter-writing tendency inherent in much of postcolonial writing.

The explicit exclusion of discussion—and the metafictional comment "but excusably so"—of Mahatma Gandhi's part in the independence struggle in *Midnight's Children* (*MC* 112) is curious, all the more so because, as Saleem recounts the time around the Jallianwala Bagh disaster, "this is India in the heyday of the Mahatma, when even language obeys the instructions of Gandhiji" (*MC* 33). Apart from that, he is present only when he is assassinated in January 1948. The news is broken to Saleem's family when they are in the movies, watching the first 'indirect kiss'—a kiss exchanged between the male and female leads by the means of an object: an apple, a cup of tea, a sword, a mango—in the film *The Lovers of Kashmir* (*MC* 142–143). The unreliability of Saleem is emphatically underlined as he confesses that he has got the death date of Mahatma wrong and that he has no way of amending the story so that it would be correctly dated. Therefore, "in my India, Gandhi will continue to die at the wrong time" (*MC* 166). Together, the relative absence, willing suspension, and the false attribution of Gandhi's death create an aura of reverence within the otherwise highly irreverent narrative.

The setting of the novel in the onset of independent India already marks it for critical commentary, and the description of the boatman Tai as "[a] watery Caliban, rather too fond of cheap Kashmiri brandy" (*MC* 11)—with its reference to William Shakespeare's colonial allegory *The Tempest*—invites a postcolonial reading. The narrative further takes issue with some (but by no means all) of the more burning events in the anti-colonial history of India, most notably the Jallianwala Bagh massacre in April 1919 (*MC* 32–36). This tragic carnage was one of the decisive moments that turned public opinion in India and abroad against the British colonial power and sped up the process leading to independence. When the British finally agree to leave India and, at the same time, Pakistan in the hands of the people, it is a hasty decision, as the representative of the colonialists, William Methwold comments: "Hundreds of years of decent government, then suddenly, up and off. […] And now, suddenly, independence. Seventy days to get out" (*MC* 96). In the proper reserved discontentment of his manners and stature, Methwold stands in for the colonial power: in his ironic representation of the British, the benevolent master who had "built your roads. Schools, railway trains, parliamentary system, all worthwhile things" (*MC* 96).

In parting, he indulges in one more of his power games. He is selling the property, four villas of the Methwold Estate, inexpensively to Aadam Aziz and three others on two conditions: that they should be bought as is, together with all that was in them, and that they should be intact until the moment of transfer on the hour of India's independence. He implores, or rather dictates, Aadam to accept this generous offer, and to "permit a departing colonial his little game? We don't have much left to do, we British, except to play our games" (*MC* 95).

The irrationality of the request pains Aadam, who during his studies in Heidelberg, Germany had "learned that India—like radium—had been 'discovered' by the Europeans", and the decisive thing estranging him from his friends Oskar and Ilse was "this belief of theirs that he was somehow the invention of their ancestors" (*MC* 11). Such an Orientalist perception has not been scarce in colonial history, but for Aadam, it comes as a shock, all the more so, as he has benefitted from Western medical education, which is perceived both as suspicious (in Tai's eyes) and beneficial (by Ghani the landowner). The transaction is, however, so lucrative that Aadam persuades his wife to play Methwold's game. So far, the ironic focus has been on Methwold, but during the weeks prior to the transfer, the Estate begins to change the new tenants: they observe the cocktail hour only just introduced to them by Methwold, and, when he comes for a visit, "they slip *effortlessly* into their *imitation* of Oxford drawls" (*MC* 99; emphases added). The future postcolonial subjects are here portrayed in Bhabha's terms as mimic men whose "colonial mimicry is the desire for a reformed, recognizable Other, *as a subject of a difference that is almost the same, but not quite* (Bhabha, "Of Mimicry and Man" 86). Both Methwold's game and the Indians' patient waiting for the transfer of power are mocked, here, and all the while "Methwold, supervising their transformation, is mumbling under his breath. [...] 'Sabkuch ticktok hai,' mumbles William Methwold. All is well" (*MC* 99). While the subalterns excel in imitating the proper English, the soon-to-depart Brit speaks Hindi. This is illustrative of the critique that was often directed at those who attained power after the independence of former colonies—that for the majority, things did not change.

Conclusion: To Tell the Truth, I lied

Rushdie's texts are *writerly* in the sense that Roland Barthes defined the term in *S/Z:* flexible, plural, open, infinite in their languages (Barthes 11). The inclination for plurality is, accordingly, perhaps the most defining characteristic of *Midnight's Children*. As I have argued, this is true in the linguistic, political and postcolonial aspects of the novel.

The 'simple' event of Saleem's birth generates a multitude of births, and the emergence of two independent nations. While on one hand, Saleem's life is configured in terms of fragmentation, the growth of the fetus in Amina's womb (that is actually Shiva), on the other hand, is powerfully described in very basic linguistic terms: "What had been (at the beginning) no bigger than a full stop had expanded into a comma, a word, a sentence, a paragraph, a chapter; now it was bursting into more complex developments, becoming, one might say, a book—perhaps an encyclopaedia—even a whole language" (*MC* 100). The ensuing swap of the babies, Saleem and Shiva, complicates hereditary allegiances. At the same time, this arbitrariness of ancestry parodies the way in which independent India (just like any nation-state) had been created as "the new myth—a collective fiction in which anything was possible" (*MC* 112).

The motto of the Indian Republic—Satyamev Jayate (truth alone triumphs)—is emblazoned in the national emblem in Devanagari script. Throughout *Midnight's Children*, the concept and attainability of truth is questioned through the convoluted genealogies of people, the sheer multiplicity of individual truths, the contested foundations of the nation, and the integrity of its guardians. In the novel, then, Rushdie puts forward another kind of a maxim that is based on the rhetorical validity of the "writery" (as Padma calls Saleem's enterprise, in a mock-Barthesian way): "in autobiography, as in all literature, what actually happened is less important than what the author can manage to persuade his audience to believe" (270–271). Without making a blanket dismissal of history or other factual writing (Rushdie himself having a university degree in history), Saleem is, nevertheless, adamant in his declaration that this could be the motto of the Midnight's Children's Conference, or the magicians' colony: "Sometimes legends make reality, and become more useful than the facts" (*MC* 47). The memory's truth that Saleem mediates is not the last say on the matter, however, because no mentally stable person trusts somebody else's story (*MC* 211). The overtly romanticized—and counterfactual—description of Emergency as a long midnight, the unverifiability of the forced ectomies, the inescapable faults in chronology, all these become understandable and useful in the realm of stories. *Midnight's Children* shows us that it is in the stories, legends, tales of the Thousand and One Nights, and in the chatter of the teeming crowds that we encounter realities, which can be bleakly pessimistic or enthusiastically optimistic.

Works Cited

Ashcroft, Bill, Gareth Griffiths, and Helen Tiffin. *The Empire Writes Back: Theory and Practice in Postcolonial Literatures*. New York, NY & London: Routledge, 1989.

Barthes, Roland. *S/Z*. Paris: Editions du Soeuil, 1970.

Bhabha, Homi K. "How Newness Enters the World: Postmodern Space, Postcolonial Times and the Trials of Cultural Translation." *The Location of Culture*. Homi Bhabha. London & New York: Routledge, 1994. 212–235.

_____. "Of Mimicry and Man: The Ambivalence of Colonial Discourse." 1984. *The Location of Culture*. Homi Bhabha. London: Routledge, 1994. 85–92.

Chatterjee, Sisir Kumar. "Rushdie's Use of Language in *Midnight's Children*." *Studies in ELT, Linguistics and Applied Linguistics*. Ed. Mohit Kumar Ray. New Delhi: 2004. 146–162.

Chaudhuri, Amit. "Introduction." *The Picador Book of Modern Indian Literature*. Ed. Amit Chaudhuri. London: Picador, 2001. xv–xxxiv.

_____. "Huge, Baggy Monster: Mimetic Theories of the Indian Novel after Rushdie." *Clearing a Space: Reflections on India, Literature and Culture*. Amit Chaudhuri. Oxford: Peter Lang, 2008. 113–121.

Dwivedi, O. P. "Linguistic Experiments in Rushdie's *Midnight's Children*." *Transnational Literature* 1.1 (Nov. 2008). Web. 3 Jan. 2014. <http://dspace.flinders.edu.au/jspui/bitstream/2328/3244/1/Dwivedi.pdf>.

Gane, Gillian. "Postcolonial Literature and the Magic Radio: The Language of Rushdie's *Midnight's Children*." *Poetics Today* 27.3 (2006): 569–596.

Hai, Ambreen. "From a Full Stop to a Language: Rushdie's Bodily Idiom." *Making Words Matter: The Agency of Colonial and Postcolonial Literature*. Ambreen Hai. Athens: Ohio UP, 2009. 204–264.

Khair, Tabish. *Babu Fictions: Alienation in Contemporary Indian English Novels*. New Delhi: Oxford UP, 2001.

Krishnamurthy, Sarala. "The Chutnification of English: An Examination of the Lexis of Salman Rushdie's *Midnight's Children*." *CONTEXT: Journal of Social and Cultural Studies* 13.1 (Mar. 2010): 11–28. Web. 7 Jan. 2014.

Kumar, T. Vijay. "Sharing Nation Space: Representations of India." *Shared Waters: Soundings in Postcolonial Literatures*. Cross/cultures: Readings in the Post/colonial Literatures in English, 118. Ed. Stella Borg Barthet. Amsterdam & Atlanta: Rodopi, 2009. 323–334. Ebrary. Web. 6 Jan. 2014.

Mukherjee, Meenakshi. *The Twice Born Fiction: Themes and Techniques of the Indian Novel.* 1971. New Delhi: Arnold-Heinemann, 1974.

_____. "Introduction." *Rushdie's Midnight's Children: A Book of Readings.* Ed. Meenakshi Mukherjee. New Delhi: Pencraft International, 2003. 9–27.

Naik, M. K. & Shyamala A. Narayan. *Indian English Literature 1980–2000: A Critical Survey.* New Delhi: Pencraft International, 2001.

Orsini, Francesca. "India in the Mirror of World Fiction." *New Left Review* 13 (2002): 75–88. SOAS Research Online. Web. 3 Jan. 2014.

Pesso-Miquel, Catherine. "Clock-ridden Births: Creative Bastardy in Sterne's *Tristram Shandy* and Rushdie's *Midnight's Children*." *Refracting the Canon in Contemporary British Literature and Film.* Eds. Susana Onega Jaén & Christian Gutleben. Amsterdam & Atlanta: Rodopi, 2004. 17–52.

Rao, D. S. *Three Decades: A Short History of Sahitya Akademi, 1954–84.* New Delhi: Sahitya Akademi, 1985.

Rao, Raja. Foreword. *Kanthapura.* Raja Rao. 1938. New Delhi: Oxford UP, 1989. v–vi.

Roy, Rituparna. *South Asian Partition Fiction in English: From Khushwant Singh to Amitav Ghosh.* Amsterdam: Amsterdam UP, 2010.

Rushdie, Salman. *Midnight's Children.* 1981. London: Picador, 1982.

_____. "Empire Writes Back with a Vengeance." *The Times* 3 Jul. (1982): 8.

_____. "The Free Radio." 1982. *East, West.* London: Jonathan Cape, 1992. 33–58.

_____. "Errata: Unreliable Narration in *Midnight's Children*." 1983. *Imaginary Homelands: Essays and Criticism 1981–1991.* London: Granta, 1991. 22–25.

_____. "In Good Faith." 1990. *Imaginary Homelands: Essays and Criticism 1981–1991.* London: Granta, 1991. 393–414.

Sadana, Rashmi. *English Heart, Hindi Heartland: The Political Life of Literature in India.* Berkeley: U of California P, 2012. Flashpoints Ser., 8.

Sailaja, Pingali. *Indian English.* Dialects of English. Edinburgh: Edinburgh UP, 2009.

Sircar, Ajanta. *Framing the Nation: Languages of 'Modernity' in India.* New York, London, Calcutta: Seagull, 2011.

Srivastava, Neelam. "Languages of the Nation in Salman Rushdie's *Midnight's Children* and Vikram Seth's *A Suitable Boy.*" *Ariel: A Review of International English Literature* 36.1–2 (2005): 201–231. Web. 7 Jan. 2014. <http://www.ariel.ucalgary.ca>.

Stadtler, Florian. "'Nobody from Bombay should be without a basic film vocabulary': *Midnight's Children* and the Visual Culture of Indian Popular Cinema." *Salman Rushdie and Visual Culture: Celebrating Impurity, Disrupting Borders.* Routledge Studies in Twentieth-Century Literature. Ed. Ana Cristina Mendes. London: Routledge, 2012. 123–138.

Talib, Ismail S. *The Language of Postcolonial Literatures.* London: Routledge, 2002.

Trivedi, Harish. "Salman the Funtoosh: Magic Bilingualism in *Midnight's Children.*" Midnight's Children: *A Book of Readings.* Ed. Meenakshi Mukherjee. Delhi: Pencraft International, 1999. 69–94.

Wong, Nicholas. "The English Novel in the Twentieth Century, 4: The Indian Novel in England." *Contemporary Review* 1 Apr (1996): 198–201.

Biography of Salman Rushdie

Joel Kuortti

In an interview with Brian Lynch of *The Georgia Straight*, Salman Rushdie comments on the autobiographical echoes in *Midnight's Children* as follows: "the [main] character in *Midnight's Children*, as a child, has a lot in common with me—he goes to my school and lives in my house. But the great difference is that he never leaves the country. And so as we get older, his life becomes very different to mine" (Lynch 2008). For Rushdie, such distancing commentary has been in order on many occasions, for not seldom have the protagonist, narrator, or events of his novels been linked with his own person or personal history. Most notably, this is true of Saleem Sinai of *Midnight's Children* and Malik Solanka of *Fury* (2001), but similar issues have surfaced with, for example, the narrator of *The Satanic Verses* (1988) and in more general terms with the course of events in *Haroun and the Sea of Stories* (1990).

It is, therefore, somewhat problematic to endeavor to outline the author's life in relation to a work that discusses one of his novels. I would like to suggest to the reader that a distance should be kept between the actual and fictional—even though Rushdie himself often plays with this very notion. The protagonist of Rushdie's story "The Avatar" declares: "I've heard a few ugly whispers which go as far as to throw mud on my personal good name, so I say, enough is enough, I mean silence is golden but truth is platinum, so here goes" (Rushdie, "Avatar" 111). So, here goes.

(Ahmed) Salman Rushdie was born, not on the stroke of midnight on August 14, 1947, but on June 19—some two months prior to Indian Independence—to Anis Ahmed Rushdie and Negis Rushdie (née Zohra Butt). In his memoir *Joseph Anton* (2012), Rushdie recalls a joke his father used to make about this event: "Salman was born and eight weeks later the British ran away" (55). Rushdie's personal 'tryst with destiny'—as Prime Minister Jawaharlal Nehru described the moment of Indian Independence—

started in Windsor Villa in the hills of Bombay (now Mumbai), and he attended the prestigious Cathedral School in the city.

Rushdie did not stay in India, as he indicates in the opening quotation. He left for England in January 1961 to be educated in the Rugby School in Warwickshire. After finishing the boarding school, he continued his studies at King's College in Cambridge. He specialized in history and graduated in 1968. After a short patch working for television in Karachi, Pakistan, Rushdie went back to London.

In the years to come, Rushdie tried his hand in several fields: acting, television work, advertising, publishing, copywriting, and community work. In the midst of this, he worked on several novels. Of these, *The Book of Pir* (1971), *Antagonist* (1975), and *Madam Rama* (1976) have not been published (Stadtler 36), but the one that he entered for the science fiction competition organized by Victor Gollancz, *Grimus* (1975), found its way to publicity—even though the critical reception was scarce and unappreciative.

The publication of *Midnight's Children* in February 1981, and the ensuing fame—and eventually fortune—guaranteed Rushdie a living so that he could engage himself in writing. The Booker Prize—as well as the subsequent extraordinary awards of the 25th anniversary Booker of Bookers (1993) and the 40th anniversary Best of the Booker (2008)—and other prizes Rushdie received for the novel marked it for posterity. While there had been attempts at turning *Midnight's Children* into film, the attempts had failed, despite Rushdie's intense interest in cinema and the abundant cinematic references and techniques he uses in his novels. In 2008, however, he met with the Indian-Canadian director Deepa Mehta, and the production began in 2010, after Rushdie had adapted the novel into a script. The film premiered in September 2012, and with it, one long process had reached a conclusion.

The publication of *Shame* (1983) was an eagerly-awaited occasion, although it was not met with the same enthusiasm as *Midnight's Children*. In France, however, it was awarded the best foreign book prize in 1984, the Prix du Meilleur Livre Étranger.

Rushdie's life was to change for good in 1989, after the publication of his third novel *The Satanic Verses* in September 1988. Before that, he had been invited to visit the Sandinistas in Nicaragua and wrote a travel book about his experiences, *The Jaguar Smile* (1987). *The Satanic Verses* was released to the market in the fall of 1988, and it got flattering, if sometimes confused reviews. It earned Rushdie, however, the Whitbread Novel Award. Soon, things began to get muddled. Muslims in Britain and India were infuriated about, above all, the representation of Prophet Muhammad in the novel. They marched against the book, it was publicly burnt in Bradford, and campaigns were launched to get the novel banned for blasphemy. It is subsequently banned in several countries: first in India, then in several other countries, from South Africa to Venezuela.

A more serious phase began on February 14, 1989, when Ayatollah Khomeini of Iran declared a *fatwa* on Rushdie—a religious decree by which he condemned Rushdie and his publishers to death. Rushdie went into hiding. Nobody could guess that the hiding would continue for almost a decade, until Iran lifted the threat on Rushdie's life in the fall of 1998. Rushdie discusses his time in hiding amply in *Joseph Anton*—named after the alias he adopted for himself during those years. It is a name based on his favorite writers, Anton Chekhov and Joseph Conrad.

Having to move from one safe house to another made working very hard. Rushdie managed, however, to write several works during the darkest years. The first was a children's book, *Haroun and the Sea of Stories* (1990). Allegedly, it is considered a children's book due to its brevity and narrative structure. Dedicated to his son Zafar, it tells a magical story of a boy searching for the source of stories. However, true to the Rushdiesque affinity for allegory, the story was interpreted as a fable about his plight. In 2010, Rushdie published a nominal sequel to *Haroun*, *Luka and the Fire of Life*, in which Haroun's younger brother Luka is searching for the fire of life. This time, the book was dedicated to Rushdie's younger son Milan.

Some other short works followed, including *Haroun*: *Imaginary Homelands* (1991), which collects Rushdie's essays and other non-fictional writing. *The Wizard of Oz* (1992) is a long essay on Victor Fleming's 1939 film by the same name, and *East, West* (1994) is a collection of short stories, some of which had been published previously. Only a couple of Rushdie's stories have not been included here, such as "The Avatar" (1981) and "The Golden Bough" (1983). Although Rushdie was busy campaigning for his liberty, his creativity did not cease totally.

The year 1995 saw the publication of Rushdie's first full novel since *The Satanic Verses*, *The Moor's Last Sigh*. It soon became a popular book among readers, and it also gained critical acclaim in the form of a Whitbread Novel Award (1995) and the European Union's Aristeion Literary Prize (1996). In this novel, Rushdie moves to new geographical locations—while remaining also in India. The continental European, particularly Spanish and Portuguese, connection with India and the shared Islamic history provided a fertile and spicy ground for creative expression. A similar setting, this time between Italy and India, can be found in the 2008 novel *The Enchantress of Florence*.

While closely embedded in Greek mythology and the myths of Orpheus and Eurydice, *The Ground Beneath Her Feet* (1999), then, is set in the world of music. Its fictional world is different from most of Rushdie's previous major novels—except for *Grimus*—as it takes place in a parallel universe instead of a fictionalized but actual one. In contrast, the publication of the next novel, *Fury* in 2001, coincided tragically with reality and the 9/11 terrorist attacks in the USA. Whatever the reasons may be, *Fury* got negative, even hostile reviews, and has remained one of Rushdie's least popular works. In the 2005 novel, *Shalimar the Clown*, Rushdie continued, among other things, with the theme of terrorism. The main character is India—the bastard daughter of the US ambassador to India—and the geographical setting is both in the United States and India, particularly the contested area of Kashmir.

With Elizabeth West, Rushdie edited the anthology *Mirrorwork: 50 Years of Indian Writing 1947–1997*, which was published in the UK as *The Vintage Book of Indian Writing*. The publication caused, once again, a furor—this time for Rushdie's comments in the Introduction on the relative superiority of Indian English writing in comparison with literatures written in other Indian languages (Rushdie 1997).

Rushdie had anthologized his non-fiction writings in 1991, and he continued this in *Step Across This Line* in 2002. Together, these two collections offer a wide spectrum on Rushdie's style and interests as a reviewer, columnist, commentator, and observer. An even more important and anticipated occasion was the publication of *Joseph Anton: A Memoir* in 2012. The publication of the memoir was followed by a huge interest in Rushdie's clandestine years and his experiences under heavy security.

Perhaps with eyes just as keen as those who read about Rushdie's predicament, readers delved into his personal relationships, especially the latest infatuation with the Indian model Padma Lakshmi, whom Rushdie designates as his "Millenarian Illusion." Apart from his literary endeavors, Rushdie's relationships have, indeed, been a staple diet of tabloid media for the past twenty-five years. His first marriage in 1975 with press officer, later Arts Council literature officer Clarissa Luard (1948–1999) ended in divorce in 1987. Their son Zafar was born in 1979. In 1988, Rushdie married the American novelist Marianne Wiggins, but their marriage was soon troubled by Rushdie's fatwa and forced hiding; they ended their relationship in divorce in 1993. During the years of hiding, Rushdie met literary editor Elizabeth West, and they married in 1997 and had a son Milan in 1999. Also, this marriage ended in divorce in 2004. Rushdie had moved to New York City in 2000, partly due to the hostility of the British media about the cost of his security. Another reason was his relationship with celebrity chef and model Padma Lakshmi. They married in 2004 and divorced in 2007. After that, Rushdie has been in the headlines over alleged relationships with several other women.

Despite many unsympathetic and bitter commentaries on Rushdie's life and loves, he has been recognized publicly with many prestigious commendations. Among the more distinguished honors, Rushdie has received one of the most exceptional ones: honorary professorship of the humanities at MIT in Cambridge, Massachusetts, for which Rushdie was nominated in 1993. The only other person to have been given the title is Winston Churchill, who received it in 1949. In 1999, Rushdie was nominated the French Commandeur de l'Ordre des Arts et des Lettres, and in 2008 he was elected as a Foreign Honorary Member at the American Academy of Arts and Letters. He served as President of PEN American Center from 2004 until 2006. Between the years 1998 and 2008, Rushdie received honorary doctorates from the Universities of Tromsø (Norway, 1998), Freien Universität Berlin (Germany, 1999), University of Liège (Belgium, 2000), L'Universite de Paris (France, 2003), Nova Southeastern University (Florida, 2006), and Chapman University (California, 2008).

After having served a term as Distinguished Writer in Residence at Emory University (Atlanta, GA, 2006–2011), Rushdie was nominated as Emory University's Distinguished Professor in 2011. In the same year, the Salman Rushdie Archive was opened at Emory. This has already proven to be a fruitful source of material (see e.g. Stadtler, Mishra), and further archival work is in progress. All this confirms that rather than a marginalized ghost of the past, Rushdie's avatar is hovering strongly in the world.

Works Cited

Hamilton, Ian. "The First Life of Salman Rushdie." *New Yorker* 25 Dec.–1 Jan. (1995–1996): 90–113.

Kuortti, Joel. *Place of the Sacred: The Rhetoric of the* Satanic Verses *Affair*. Frankfurt am Main: Peter Lang, 1997.

Lynch, Bryan. "Salman Rushdie Roams the Foreign Country of the Past." *The Georgia Straight* 11 Jun. (2008). Web. 3 Jan. 2014. < http://www. straight.com/life/salman-rushdie-roams-foreign-country-past >.

Mishra, Vijay. "Salman Rushdie, Aesthetics and Bollywood Popular Culture." *Thesis Eleven: Critical Theory and Historical Sociology* 119.1 (Dec. 2013): 112–128.

Rushdie, Salman. "The Avatar." *The Twilight Book: A New Collection of Ghost Stories*. Ed. James Hale. London: Victor Gollancz, 1981. 111–119.

_____. "Damme, This Is the Oriental Scene for You." *The Vintage Book of Indian Writing, 1947–1997*. Eds. Salman Rushdie and Elizabeth West. London: Vintage, 1997. ix–xxiii.

_____. "The Golden Bough." *Granta* 7: *Best of Young British Novelists* (1983): 247–251.

_____. *Joseph Anton: A Memoir*. London: Jonathan Cape, 2012.

Stadtler, Florian. *Fiction, Film, and Indian Popular Cinema: Salman Rushdie's Novels and the Cinematic Imagination*. London & New York: Routledge, 2013.

CRITICAL
CONTEXTS

Rushdie's Global Modernism

Significance of Genealogies

Genealogies are crucial to Salman Rushdie's *Midnight's Children*. The complicated family tree of narrator Saleem Sinai figures centrally in his retelling of the history of modern India. Indeed, Saleem portrays the story of India as inseparable from the story of his family. His grandfather Aadam Aziz was present at the event that catalyzed the independence movement, the 1919 Amritsar massacre; Saleem's descendents, he foretells in the novel's final paragraph, will continue to be present at key moments in the nation's history for the next 1001 generations. The family tree of the narrator is thus cast as an interpretive key to the history of India as a postcolonial nation state. India's first prime minister, Jawaharlal Nehru (1889–1964), is portrayed certifying the connection between nation and family, writing a letter celebrating the coincidence of Saleem's birth at the very moment of India's independence in 1947: "We shall be watching over your life with the closest attention; it will be, in a sense, the mirror of our own" (Rushdie, *Midnight's Children* 139).

The significance of genealogies is reinforced by Rushdie's own comments on his novel. In an essay written shortly after the publication of *Midnight's Children*, Rushdie articulates his own literary genealogy:

> But we are inescapably international writers at a time when the novel has never been a more international form [. . .] and it is perhaps one of the more pleasant freedoms of the literary migrant to be able to choose his parents. My own—selected half consciously, half not—include Gogol, Cervantes, Kafka, Melville, Machado de Assis; a polyglot family tree[.] (Rushdie, "Imaginary" 21).

The international genealogy Rushdie traces for himself as a writer is intriguing given that *Midnight's Children* purports to

Rushdie's Global Modernism   29 provide a specifically national narrative. Rather than conceiving of cosmopolitanism to be antithetical to nationalism, Rushdie's "mongrel" cosmopolitan genealogy is cast as the necessary precondition for writing the national narrative of modern India.

Midnight's Children *and Global Modernism*

The international genealogy Rushdie describes not only purports to guide interpretations of *Midnight's Children*; more sweepingly, Rushdie's genealogy also asserts that the significance of his novel needs to be understood in the context of a broader international phenomenon—what might be described as *global modernism*. The formal and stylistic characteristics of Anglo-American literary modernism of the early twentieth century—characteristics that literary scholars such as Rebecca Walkowitz have identified as including "wandering consciousness, paratactic syntax, recursive plotting, collage, and portmanteau language" (Walkowitz 2)—are appropriated by authors associated with the former colonial peripheries in the second half of the century. Indeed, Rushdie declares that his project is defined as much by literary modernism as by the history of India. In an interview, he declares: "I think *Ulysses* is the greatest novel of this century; it has a lot of stories in it, but its impulse is not narrative. I think one can't make that kind of naïve return to the world before Joyce" (Goonetilleke 4–5).

Rushdie's acknowledged debt to Joyce specifically, and to early twentieth-century literary modernism more generally, does not imply that he sought to imitate his predecessors in writing *Midnight's Children*. Rather, Rushdie redefines the parameters of modernism beyond the Eurocentric focus of canonical modernist figures, including T. S. Eliot (1921), Marcel Proust (2002), and Virginia Woolf (1924). Where T. S. Eliot drew his genealogy in explicitly Western terms in essays, such as "Tradition and the Individual Talent" (1921)—he evokes the notion of a "mind of Europe" as the repository of tradition—Rushdie draws inspirations globally, from the magic realism associated with Latin American authors such as Gabriel García Márquez and Jorge Luis Borges to Bollywood cinema.

Since its publication, *Midnight's Children* has assumed a central place in the genealogies of postmodernism and postcolonial theory. The novel's selective appropriations and deliberate mixing of cultural traditions has resonated with scholars of postmodernism, such as Linda Hutcheon (1988), who found in Rushdie's novel a prime example of historiographic metafiction. According to this idea, the novel critically reflects on the project of writing historical narratives, even as it elaborates an alternative to putatively institutionally-endorsed narratives of nationhood. Scholars of postcolonial theory, such as Homi Bhabha likewise found in *Midnight's Children* a narrative style that was subversive in its writing back to the imperial center. Indeed, Bhabha's definition of a world literature emerging in the postcolonial era seems to have Rushdie in mind:

> Where, once, the transmission of national traditions was the major theme of world literature, perhaps we can now suggest that transnational histories of migrants, the colonized, or political refugees—these border and frontier conditions—may be the terrains of world literature (Bhabha 12)

Rushdie's place within the canons of both postmodern and postcolonial literatures is striking, given the very different theoretical presuppositions of the two discourses. Postmodernism was understood as primarily an aesthetic phenomenon—perhaps a symptom of late capitalism, but a preoccupation of First World artists more interested in play than politics. Postcolonial theory, in contrast, emerged as an explicitly politicized discourse to explore the era of decolonization and efforts to respond to racist, Eurocentric histories. Yet Rushdie's novel invited explorations of the overlap between the postmodern and the postcolonial by Bhabha (1994), Hutcheon (1988), Anthony Appiah (1992), and others—with *Midnight's Children* figuring centrally in these discussions.

The Canonization of *Midnight's Children* and Its Implications

That *Midnight's Children* could be both postmodern and postcolonial in a way that no Anglophone novel previously succeeded was key to its success commercially and critically. Winning the 1981 Booker prize as well as the "Booker of Bookers" in 1993 and the "Best of the Booker" prizes in 2008, the novel acquired a canonical status rarely afforded a literary work, even rarer to a postcolonial work. It also played a key role in igniting global interest in English-language novels written by authors from the Indian subcontinent, including Amitav Ghosh, Rohinton Mistry, Arundhati Roy, and Vikram Seth. Its presence in literature classrooms across the Anglo-American academy and in scholarly books, articles, and dissertations has earned it a kind of special distinction, which M. Keith Booker sums up pithily as the "official Western masterpiece of the late Cold War years" (Booker 285).

The canonization of *Midnight's Children* testifies to the novel's success in representing political, social, and cultural tensions as elements of a flourishing nation-state rather than indicators of intractable social divisions. Rushdie's celebratory vision of fragmentation is articulated most recognizably in the 1982 essay "Imaginary Homelands," which becomes the titular essay in Rushdie's most famous collection of non-fiction and social criticism. In this essay, Rushdie declares that his novel was "born" the moment when he recognized that he could not recapture the vibrant diversity of Bombay within his memory or in the pages of a novel (Rushdie, "Imaginary" 9). His artistic "failure," however, is cast as the basis of the novel's value. Put another way, modernist fragmentation serves not to indicate social decline, but artistic creativity. The "broken mirror" of memory that, according to Rushdie, guides his writing frees the artist from being chained to describing the past, opening up possibilities for something new. Rushdie declares that "the shards of memory acquired greater status, greater resonance, because they were *remains*" (Rushdie, "Imaginary" 12; emphasis original). This artistic vision becomes the basis for claiming a vibrant, multicultural nation state defined not by a single homogeneous vision, but the summation of the visions of its diverse populations. Rushdie's vision, he declares, is "'my' India, a version and no more than one version of all the hundreds of millions of possible versions" (Rushdie, "Imaginary" 10). The fragmentary portrait of India in his novel, then, putatively celebrates the diverse views of the nation not directly described in its pages.

For Rushdie's critics, his focus on cultural diversity, migrancy, and hybridity has been read as an endorsement of an elitist cosmopolitanism, insensitive to the importance of nationalist struggles. For the literary scholar Timothy Brennan, who wrote the first and perhaps best book-length study of Rushdie's work, Rushdie demonstrates a "cosmopolitan sensibility" that acknowledges on the theoretical level the importance of nationalist movements to decolonization struggles (Brennan 166). Rushdie's failure, however, is his unwillingness to translate this theoretical knowledge into his fictional work, which consistently prefers to understand political struggle in abstract and too often parodic terms. According to this line of thinking, such a sensibility devalues the importance of fiction's capacity to mobilize readers to commit themselves to effecting political change.

The stylistic features of global modernism, then, are seen by Rushdie's critics as embracing Western ideals of aesthetic practice at the expense of conveying the uncomfortable realities of the political struggles that are putatively the subject of his work. For the Marxist critic Aijaz Ahmad, Rushdie extends the "literary imagination of High Modernism" in portraying the colonial world as "a supermarket of packaged and commodified cultures, ready to be consumed" (Ahmad 128). Here, the notion of cosmopolitanism as it emerges through modernist literary forms is seen to be entirely consistent with late capitalism, which is itself central to the history of colonialism and neocolonialism. Ahmad argues that such a sensibility dismisses notions of national belonging as unnecessary, parochial, and—worst of all—expressions of false consciousness. To believe in the importance of the nation is to be an ideological dupe.

From Rushdie's perspective, however, his modernism was not an elective decision, but a consequence of decolonization: "Writers are no longer sages, dispensing the wisdom of the centuries. And those of us who have been forced by cultural displacement to accept the provisional nature of all truths, all certainties, have perhaps had modernism forced upon us" (Rushdie, "Imaginary" 12). Put another way, modernist fragmentation becomes the literary mode appropriate to representing the social and cultural diversity of India and, putatively, an antidote to political moves to centralize state power and endorse a culturally homogeneous national identity.

The rhetorical move Rushdie makes to defend his work is itself a profoundly modernist one, made perhaps most famously in Virginia Woolf's "Mister Bennett and Mrs. Brown." Woolf declares that the defining characteristics of what would come to be known as literary modernism was the product of an historical rupture. The "season of failures and fragments" (Woolf 335) that define Woolf's generation of authors in contrast to their Edwardian predecessors is not a product of shifting literary taste so much as a response to broader social transformations—captured in Woolf's inimitable phrase, "in or about December, 1910, human character changed" (Woolf 320). Like Woolf before him, Rushdie establishes the conditions of his own literary production in contrast to a literary style that precedes him. The actual difference is far smaller than the rhetorical move: in Rushdie's account, John Fowles's *Daniel Martin* provides the strawman text endorsing the writer as guru. Fowles himself famously contrasts himself with the author-as-god figure in *The French Lieutenant's Woman*, writing a pastiche of the omniscient third person narrative associated with the Victorian novel.

Returning to the image of the "broken mirror" that Rushdie invokes in "Imaginary Homelands," the modernist move to establish historical ruptures as the basis for artistic innovation—the modernist present versus the premodern past—is modified. In this case, the historical rupture that is experienced through the individual's partial, fragmentary experience of the world is caused by the violence of European imperialism. That is to say, Rushdie's inability to recall the vibrancy of Bombay provides a lens to understand the broader disruptions caused by India's absorption within the British Empire. What constitutes modernist style emerges out of an experience of exile—not the metaphorical exile so often celebrated in literary modernism, but a literal one experienced by Rushdie and authors of his generation, who found themselves moving to the colonial center of England for education and opportunity denied them in their homelands. His personal biography, then, traces colonial history, and his artistic production becomes a response to the consequences of that history. A broken mirror thus signifies not only a critique of nineteenth-century realism and its pretensions to represent the totality of society within a single artistic lens but also a critique of colonial violence that shattered social and familial ties among those populations brought within European spheres of control.

Rushdie's global modernism, then, emerges out of a set of social conditions that necessitate a selective appropriation and revision of modernist precursors. Rushdie signals this in what initially begins as an homage to Marcel Proust. Arguing that his own preoccupation with memory in *Midnight's Children* initially was Proustian in inspiration, it subsequently changed over the course of writing the novel. Rushdie writes: "So my subject changed, was no longer a search for lost time, had become the way in which we remake the past to suit our present purposes, using memory as our tool" (Rushdie, "Imaginary" 24).

Midnight's Children and the Modernist Stylistics

The repurposing of modernist stylistics is apparent in the first sentence of *Midnight's Children*, which evokes the generic conventions of fairy tales in order to show their inadequacy to convey the subject matter. Saleem Sinai begins: "I was born in the city of Bombay once upon a time. No, that won't do, there's no getting away from the date: I was born in Doctor Narlikar's Nursing Home on August 15, 1947" (Rushdie, *Midnight's Children* 3). The sly irony of casting his personal life story as a failed fairy tale—"once upon a time"— reinforces the allegorical connections between personal events and the history of postcolonial India, as Saleem goes on to confess that he was born precisely at the moment of India's independence.[1]

The historical specificities of postcolonial India are cast as governing the form of the novel, correcting the flights of fancy taken by its narrator. The modernist device of self-consciously breaking generic conventions enables Rushdie to convey the impossibility of his narrator divorcing himself from history through the abstraction of fairytale. This enables the novel to make its central conceit—that it provides a form of historical knowledge that cannot be reproduced through more traditional means of writing history. Readers are given, in other words, a unique grasp of the history of India, which the novel asserts through the linkage of the personal and national, Saleem and India: "I had been mysteriously handcuffed to history, my destinies indissolubly chained to those of my country" (Rushdie, *Midnight's Children* 3).

The argument that *Midnight's Children* provided a distinctive form of historical knowledge through its modernist stylistics emphasizes the conjunction in Rushdie's mind between aesthetic and political values. For Rushdie, India as a viable postcolonial nation emerges analogously to the novel: through highlighting the moments when its diversity belies any construction of its unity. Rushdie writes: "After all, in all of the thousands of years of Indian history, there never was such a creature as a united India" (Rushdie, "Imaginary" 27). Or, as he will declare in a 1984 essay reflecting on the assassination of Indira Gandhi: "For a nation of seven hundred millions to make any kind of sense, it must base itself firmly on the concept of multiplicity, of plurality and tolerance, of devolution and decentralization wherever possible. There can be no one way—religious, cultural, or linguistic—of being an Indian; let difference reign" (Rushdie, "Assassination" 44). The preoccupation with fragmentation, multiple points of view, and self-conscious representation of the unreliability of any representation makes modernism uniquely suited to highlighting cultural difference as the basis of national identity.

Defending nationalism through modernist stylistics is a curious move on Rushdie's part, given that modernism as an artistic movement has come to be associated with the defense of cosmopolitanism—the world citizen, not the national citizen. The tension between nationalism and cosmopolitanism that scholars, such as Neil ten Kortenaar, have identified as crucial to understanding the significance of *Midnight's Children* is present here. What becomes apparent is that the tension between these two potentially "irreconcilable cultural frameworks," to use ten Kortenaar's phrase, is held together through modernist style (ten Kortenaar 256).

Narrative Technique

The most significant technique Rushdie employs for stitching together such irreconcilable cultural frameworks comes through the narrative device of Saleem's co-creator and sometime lover, Padma. Padma's critiques of Saleem's digressions, errors, and unreliability provide the means for the novel to highlight how its narrative diverges from a premodern, realist style. Indeed, the modernist break with literary realism's omniscient and objective view of the world provides the literary analog for Rushdie's break with the politics of Indira Gandhi. After insisting that he has told Padma the truth, "Memory's truth" (Rushdie, *Midnight's Children* 242), Saleem goes on to reassure her that her doubts about his narrative are not only appropriate for the literary exegesis of unreliable narrators but also the very point of postcolonial literary fictions, which encourage readers to redeploy the suspicions he has cultivated about his own narrative to those narratives circulated by the nation's political leaders. Saleem declares: "Padma: if you're a little uncertain of my reliability, well, a little uncertainty is no bad thing. Cocksure men do terrible deeds. Women, too" (Rushdie, *Midnight's Children* 243).

In other words, the so-called "hermeneutics of suspicion" that philosophers, such as Paul Ricoeur, identify in various forms of literary modernism cultivated in readers are cast as crucial to "reading" political debates as well. In this case, the expansion of the pronoun to include the feminine serves to foreshadow the emergence of the Widow, who is patterned after Indira Gandhi. It will be Indira Gandhi—and her spokesperson, the Widow's Hand—who will endorse the linear, realist style from which *Midnight's Children* so explicitly distinguishes itself. Alluding to the Congress Party's political slogan, "*Indira is India and India is Indira*" (Rushdie, *Midnight's Children* 491), *Midnight's Children* establishes a claim that realism necessarily distorts the reality it purports to represent by creating a falsely unified and coherent view. In other words, the move to equate India and Indira necessarily disenfranchises cultural, religious, and ethnic groups across the country.

The novel emphasizes the partiality and unreliability of its narrator, in order to certify its own truthful claims regarding the political failures of India. A narrative that seeks to "succeed" where Saleem fails in representing India is, by definition, politically suspect—an effort to impose a sectarian vision upon a heterogeneous nation. The novel emphasizes this point through its representation of the 1975–1977 State of Emergency initiated by Prime Minister Indira Gandhi (1917–1984). Saleem declares that the hidden purpose of the State of Emergency was to eliminate all potential forms of opposition to Gandhi's rule. According to the conceit of the narrative, Saleem and his fellow one thousand Children of Midnight were the nation's central symbol of hope for independence: a "mirror" of the nation itself, and each child was born with a special power.

Evoking the sterilization programs headed up by Indira's son Sanjiv, Rushdie portrays the Widow hunting down all of these children and sterilizing them in an effort to centralize power and ensure that there would be no legitimate alternatives to her rule. As the Widow's Hand explains, the people of India "worship our Lady like a God. Indians are only capable of worshiping one God" (Rushdie, *Midnight's Children* 503). When Saleem argues that Hinduism has millions of gods, in addition to the deities of other religions practiced in India, the Widow's Hand dismisses this response as a misunderstanding: while other deities can exist, all power must be centralized to one unquestioned authority.

The series of anxious glosses on *Midnight's Children* provided by Rushdie in response to its reception points to the tension produced by his conflicting genealogies: as a cosmopolitan writer educated in Great Britain, writing in English, utilizing a highly complex style associated with literary modernism; as an author whose ability to write about India depends heavily on his status as an "authentic" Indian. This is nowhere more evident than in Rushdie's sometimes tenuous claims to have been influenced by oral traditions of India. In several articles written after the novel's publication, he defends his knowledge of the "real" history of India and claims that the mistakes and historical errors of the novel's protagonist were deliberately inserted by the author. As the literary scholar Sara Suleri recognized in Rushdie's subsequent novel, *Shame* (1984), *Midnight's Children* preserves its multiple genealogies by casting itself as written for two audiences simultaneously: an Indian migrant writing to other Indians, and a stateless cosmopolitan writing to Anglo-Americans. Of *Shame*, Suleri writes: "Its reinvention of history was thus shamefully fraught with the fear that finally, postcolonial narrative can only replicate the will to power that impelled colonial historical texts" (Suleri 176). The additional fear is that any narrative of nation can only replicate the political propaganda that Rushdie would wish to repudiate.

The risk highlighted by Suleri haunts modernist projects, such as Rushdie's, whose aspirations to global relevance stand in tension with their ability to speak to specific historical situations with which readers may have limited familiarity. If the novel fails to provide sufficient knowledge for readers to engage with the historical specificities of modern India, the novel collapses into simplistic allegories of a kind that Rushdie has been highly resistant to endorsing (Goonetilleke 18). Allegory certainly provides a means for readers with relatively limited knowledge of India's history to engage with the novel, yet the risks of trivializing or generalizing are significant. Rushdie's own anxiety regarding his narrative is related to its potential to homogenize the diversity that he purports to celebrate.

Literature and Politics

Rushdie ultimately attempts to address this concern by arguing that the political force literature wields comes less from its capacity to reclaim lost histories than from its imaginative potential to reframe existing historical accounts. Rushdie's argument that literary modernism is particularly suited to countering state propaganda is made through reference to two of the most famous political dissident novelists of the twentieth century, the American Richard Wright and the Czech Milan Kundera:

> I must say first of all that description is itself a political act. The black American writer Richard Wright once wrote that black and white

Americans were engaged in a war over the nature of reality. [. . .] And particularly at times when the State takes reality into its own hands, and sets about distorting it, altering the past to fit its present needs, then the making of the alternative realities of art, including the novel of memory, becomes politicized. "The struggle of man against power," Milan Kundera has written, "is the struggle of memory against forgetting." Writers and politicians are natural rivals. Both groups try to make the world in their own images; they fight for the same territory. And the novel is one way of denying the official, politicians' version of truth (Rushdie, "Imaginary" 14).

The use of modernist stylistics to portray modern India as teeming, inescapably heterogeneous provides Rushdie the means to argue that representations of India as a coherent, Hindu nation state are inaccurate and repressive.

The politicization of memory in *Midnight's Children* becomes most explicitly stated in its conclusion. Having been disillusioned, disappointed, and now sterilized, Saleem spends his days working in a pickle factory and his nights writing and reciting his memoir to Padma. The two activities are seen as intertwined: Saleem describes the chapters of his memoir through the metaphor of pickling. His narrative preserves the past—not simply as a set of factual and counterfactual details, but also as a collection of affective experiences of the past. His readers, Saleem asserts, will know his vision of the past on the level of feeling. And while official state versions of history may circulate for the moment, his narrative remains available: "Thirty jars stand up on a shelf, waiting to be unleashed upon the amnesiac nation" (Rushdie, *Midnight's Children* 530).

Indeed, Saleem's assurance that he keeps an additional empty jar to be filled by the future is cast as a fundamental and ineradicable sign of hope in a novel, in which previous signs have all disappointed. Whereas the previous descriptions of heroic leaders and moments of democratic opportunity have all been crushed, the novel argues that its form, rather than its content, represents the basis for hope. The jar, not its contents, reminds readers that the future remains open.

The argument that literary narrative, particularly in its modernist forms, engages readers on the level of feeling underlies Rushdie's claim that literary narratives are not only an alternative to official state narratives, but also their corrective. That is to say, there are not simply multiple narratives circulating, all of which are equally distorting the past. This has historically been one of the key claims of literary modernism in its various forms: that its distortions are precisely what make them more realistic, more truthful representations of reality. Modernist stylistics thus has a kind of self-corrective in its focus on fragmentary narrative. By acknowledging, through its own representations of the past, the inevitable distortions of any narrative, *Midnight's Children* argues that its narrative thereby reveals the unacknowledged distortions of Indira Gandhi and her supporters.

Late in the novel, Saleem acknowledges the first lie of his narrative: that his rival and fellow Child of Midnight, Shiva, was not actually killed, as he had claimed in the previous chapter. What begins as an acknowledgment of fallibility rapidly becomes an assertion regarding limitations of state propaganda: "I fell victim to the temptation of every autobiographer, to the illusion that since the past exists only in one's memories and the words which strive vainly to encapsulate them, it is possible to create past events simply by saying they occurred" (Rushdie, *Midnight's Children* 510). The implication in this moment of self-conscious acknowledgment of distortion, of course, is that other moments in the story are, in fact, true. What Saleem earlier called "memory's truth," then, emerges from acknowledging moments of distortion, and the inability of such distortions to change fundamentally the past.

The Continuing Relevance of *Midnight's Children*

The novel strains to claim more political force than simple redescription, suggesting instead that the past leaves traces whether or not they are remembered. And for those politicians intent on forgetting, such traces provide the basis for ongoing political resistance. In drawing the attention of readers to such traces, *Midnight's Children* claims a kind of historical determinism that is otherwise contrary to its claims for the contingency of history, and its capacity to be represented otherwise than in its current forms. In suggesting that every Widow forgets something, the novel asserts the limits of state power and the inevitable failure of Prime Minister Indira Gandhi's efforts. That the novel was composed after her stunning electoral defeat in 1977 gave Rushdie the benefit of hindsight to portray his narrator articulating his prophecy with such certitude.

Has the significance of *Midnight's Children* diminished in the past ten years? Scholarly interest in postmodernism has significantly waned and has been replaced by attention to the rise of global neoliberalism—an issue on which Rushdie's novel has a relatively little to say. Postcolonial studies has also shifted focus, away from the conversations between the colonial center and its peripheries— an issue that has been central to Rushdie's writing throughout his career. Nonetheless, *Midnight's Children* stands as a signal literary achievement of the second half of the twentieth century. In an era in which fiction is often cast as middlebrow entertainment or the purview of comprador intellectuals, Rushdie has argued that his work is symptomatic of a broader global trend, in which literary production is inseparable from broader historical shifts: "In almost every country and in almost every literature there has been, ever so often, an outburst of this large-scale fantasized, satiric, anti-epic tradition, whether it was Rabelais or Gogol or Boccaccio" (Goonetilleke 17). That such an assertion continues to have significant credibility among scholars testifies to the power of his work to make it so.

Note

1. For further exploration of how Rushdie uses genre, see John J. Su, "Epic of Failure: Disappointment as Utopian Fantasy in Salman Rushdie's *Midnight's Children*."

Works Cited

Ahmad, Aijaz. *In Theory: Classes, Nations, Literatures*. London: Verso, 1992.

Appiah, Kwame Anthony. *In My Father's House: Africa in the Philosophy of Culture*. New York: Oxford UP, 1992.

Bhabha, Homi K. *The Location of Culture*. London: Routledge, 1994.

Booker, M. Keith. "Midnight's Children, History, and Complexity: Reading Rushdie after the Cold War." *Critical Essays on Salman Rushdie*. Ed. M. Keith Booker. New York: G. K. Hall & Co., 1999. 283–314.

Brennan, Timothy. *Salman Rushdie and the Third World: Myths of the Nation*. New York: St. Martin's Press, 1989.

Eliot, T. S. "Tradition and the Individual Talent." 1919/1920. In Eliot, *The Sacred Wood: Essays on Poetry and Criticism*. New York: Alfred A. Knopf, 1921. 42–53.

Goonetilleke, D. C. R. A. *Salman Rushdie*. 2nd ed. New York: Palgrave Macmillan, 2010.

Hutcheon, Linda. *A Poetics of Postmodernism: History, Theory, Fiction*. New York: Routledge, 1988.

Proust, Marcel. *In Search of Lost Time*. Transl. Lydia Davis, et al. 7 vols. 1913–1927. London: Allen Lane, 2002.

Rushdie, Salman. "Imaginary Homelands." 1982. In Rushdie, *Imaginary Homelands: Essays and Criticism, 1981–1991*. London: Granta, 1991. 9–21.

————. "The Assassination of Indira Gandhi." 1984. In Rushdie, *Imaginary Homelands: Essays and Criticism, 1981–1991*. London: Granta, 1991. 41–46.

————. *Midnight's Children*. 1981. New York: Penguin, 1991.

Su, John J. "Epic of Failure: Disappointment as Utopian Fantasy in Salman Rushdie's *Midnight's Children*." *Twentieth-Century Literature* 47.4 (2001): 545–568.

Suleri, Sara. *The Rhetoric of English India*. Chicago: U of Chicago P, 1992.

ten Kortenaar, Neil. *Self, Nation, Text in Salman Rushdie's* Midnight's Children. Montréal: McGill-Queen's UP, 2004.

Walkowitz, Rebecca. *Cosmopolitan Style: Modernism beyond the Nation*. New York: Columbia UP, 2006.

Woolf, Virginia. "Mister Bennett and Mrs. Brown." 1924. *Collected Essays*. Ed. Leonard Woolf. Vol. 1. London: Hogarth, 1966. 319–337.

Under Scrutiny: *Midnight's Children* and Its Critics_____

Joel Kuortti

Salman Rushdie's Reception

When I was compiling *The Salman Rushdie Bibliography* in the late 1990s, criticism of Salman Rushdie's works was already a soundly established field of study and was growing steadily (Kuortti 1997). The first systematic bibliography of Rushdie's works had been compiled some years back by M. D. Fletcher for the *Journal of Indian Writing in English* (Fletcher 1991). An updated version of this was included in *Reading Rushdie: Perspectives on the Fiction of Salman Rushdie*, edited by M. D. Fletcher (361–398). As successive bibliographies, one can mention V. Indira Sambamurthy (2001) and Kuortti (2003). At the moment, there is no up-to-date critical Rushdie bibliography, so the best source for the latest criticism can be found in recent books and articles on Rushdie, which (may) contain bibliographical details. My discussion here of the critical material on Rushdie, and *Midnight's Children* in particular, is obviously selective.

Fletcher helpfully annotated the material and categorized it by the novels, but there was also a separate section for criticism discussing both *Midnight's Children* and *Shame*. Another exception in this—in Fletcher's intention—comprehensive bibliography concerns the *Satanic Verses* Affair (often called 'the Rushdie Affair') that began on February 14, 1989. Fletcher comments that he had "not attempted inclusive coverage of the Affair" (361). This exclusion is understandable, for the critical (and less critical) commentary on Rushdie and his works spread out into all forms of media throughout the globe in an unprecedented way, and the number of possible titles in English alone is several thousand.

The Affair is a clear watershed in Rushdie criticism, as it has (sometimes quite anachronistically) influenced the later readings of Rushdie's earlier works. In reading critical pieces on Rushdie, it is

_____

thercfore important to bear this on mind and to consider whether a given text is influenced by the hindsight of the Affair. This does not mean, however, that the critique prior to the Affair is somehow automatically more authentic or critical, but that later criticism needs to be evaluated differently.

In my analysis, the critical reactions to Rushdie's work can be categorized so far into three distinct, approximately decade-long stages. The first stage begins with *Grimus* (1975) and continues up to the publication of *The Satanic Verses* (1988). During this time, Rushdie also wrote *Midnight's Children* (1981), *Shame* (1983) and *The Jaguar Smile* (1987). The second, most intensive stage of criticism starts with the *Satanic Verses* Affair in 1989 (with early repercussions already in late 1988), and it lasts until *The Moor's Last Sigh* (1995). This period also includes four other works: *Haroun and the Sea of Stories* (1990), *Imaginary Homelands: Essays and Criticism, 1981–1991* (1991), *The Wizard Of Oz* (1992), and the short story collection *East, West* (1994). The third, still ongoing stage can be said to begin with Iran officially lifting the death threat on Rushdie in September 1998. This stage emerges with *The Ground Beneath Her Feet* (1999) and continues through *Fury* (2001), *Step Across This Line: Collected Nonfiction 1992–2002* (2002), *Shalimar the Clown* (2005), *The Enchantress of Florence* (2008), *Luka and the Fire of Life* (2010), and *Joseph Anton: A Memoir* (2012). The main directions that the reactions have taken, then, can be divided, broadly, into three categories: 1) the various literary analyses, 2) the discussions of the controversial issues, and 3) the considerations of the political elements in Rushdie's works.

There is a wealth of general introductions to Rushdie, often titled *Salman Rushdie* (at times with a subtitle). The first of these is by James Harrison (1992), and the others include works by Catharine Cundy (1996), D. C. R. A. Goonetilleke (1998), Damian Grant (1999), Andrew Blake (2001), Andrew Teverson (2007), and Stephen Morton (2008). The numerous monographs focusing on Rushdie's works include, first of all, *Uma Parameswaran's The Perforated Sheet: Essays on Salman Rushdie's Art* (1988), which is actually a collection of her articles. Since then, there has been a steady flow of monographs published on Rushdie,[1] as well as edited anthologies.[2] There is no proper biography of Rushdie yet, although Rushdie's 2012 memoir *Joseph Anton* chronicles his life in some detail, and in 1995, Ian Hamilton published a significant biographical article. Some of Rushdie's numerous interviews have been collected in two important volumes,[3] and they contain, among other things, biographical material.

Midnight's Children in Criticism

There is very little critical literature on Rushdie before the publication of the groundbreaking *Midnight's Children. Grimus*, which had come out six years earlier, did not stir much interest,[4] but after *Midnight's Children*, criticism began to flourish and made Rushdie a staple diet within the fields of Indian, postcolonial, diasporic, and Commonwealth literature. The wide-ranging literary interest continued up until the publication of *The Satanic Verses* in 1988, after which the focus shifted to views for and against Rushdie himself, rather than about his works. Rushdie had become a slogan for different, often contradictory types of discourse: defense of freedom, Islamic apostasy, diasporic citizenship, cosmopolitan writing, and Indian English literature—so much so that many sources that use his name, even in the field of literature, do not actually discuss his works. More or less a decade later, then, critical attention focused again on the novels, but now it was often more sensitive of the contextual problems kindled by Rushdie's provocative writings. Rushdie's unique history within the domain of criticism makes the assessment of his reception both complex and exciting.

In February 1981, the world welcomed *Midnight's Children* with instant praise, and even the critical section was appreciative. Despite its textual complexity and structural multi-layeredness, the novel became a key popular novel to understand India. People of all walks of life, from literary critics to academics and laypersons to journalists, wanted to find out what contemporary India was "truly" like. This prompted Rushdie himself to think whether *Midnight's Children* was "the best introduction to India" (Rushdie, "Doing the Dangerous Thing" 220); he found the idea at the same time embarrassing, pleasing, and amusing.

Meenakshi Mukherjee defines *Midnight's Children* as "a landmark novel," "a catalyst" for the significant transformations taking place in India and within Indian English literature in the 1980s, and, furthermore, "easily [...] one of the contenders for [the] position" of a seminal book for late twentieth century (Mukherjee 10–12). Already with *Grimus*, the critics focused on Rushdie's themes and sources, elements of Menippean satire and postmodernism, as well as language and satire—themes that have been present in criticism ever since. With *Midnight's Children*, a new crucial theme emerged, when it was identified as an allegory of the Indian nation (ten Kortenaar). The phrase "Midnight's Children" in the novel's title came to stand for both post-independence India as a whole and the numerous Indian writers who surfaced in the aftermath of its global success as an international bestseller and the winner of both the 1981 Booker and James Tait Black Memorial Prizes. Later on, it received further recognition as it was awarded the Booker of Bookers Prize in 1993 and the Best of Bookers in 2008 (Huggan).

The novel did not receive its critical position immediately, however. There were any number of book reviews and short analyses in the media around the globe, but proper literary critical attention came after some consideration—the book was, after all, linguistically challenging, structurally complicated, and simply 446 intense pages long. Some of the first critics took a comparativist look at Rushdie, connecting his work with other emerging Asian writers' novels such as Lloyd *Fernando's Scorpion Orchid* (1976) from Malaysia and Russell Soaba's *Wampis* (1977) from Papua New Guinea (Shepherd). In her provocative study of Rushdie within Indian English writing, Feroza Jussawalla considered *Midnight's Children* too parodic in comparison to such eminent Indian writers as Mulk Raj Anand and R. K. Narayan. In her view, the interpretive community was needed to provide an ethically balanced reading for intercultural texts (Jussawalla 119).

Among the early critics were Shyamala Narayan and Dieter Riemenschneider, and they discussed *Midnight's Children*, quite naturally like many other critics, with other works within the Indian English literary tradition. Its problematic position as a diasporic text in relation to works written in India prompted a lot of debate, which has continued ever since, not least due to Rushdie's own self-conscious usage and often controversial commentary on the importance of the English language, guaranteeing that the issue would remain in critical awareness (Rushdie, "The Empire Writes Back" 8; Rushdie, *Mirrorwork*; Bhaya Nair, "What Did Rushdie Mean"; Shankar, "Midnight's Orphans" 65; Srivastava, "Languages of the Nation"; Gane, "Postcolonial Literature").

The influential issue of the history, development, and socio-cultural status of Indian English writing emerged as one of the key elements in the critical study of Indian writing in general. One term that rose to the fore from the novel was *chutnification*. Mundanely, it refers to the process of making pickles, which is a process so central for the novel's narrative. Allegorically, it became a catchphrase that signified both the new type of Indian English language—adopted and utilized in *Midnight's Children*—as well as the idea of cultural hybridity prevalent in postcolonial criticism.[5]

Other critics have located Rushdie within other literary histories: magic realism, postmodernism, metafiction, satire, fantasy, postcolonial literature, Commonwealth literature, and so on. Rushdie has been compared with writers as varied as Gabriel García Marquéz, Günter Grass, Rudy Wiebe, Chinua Achebe, and Derek Walcott.[6] This international literary legacy provided grounds for discussing issues like cosmopolitanism, nationalism, and history—despite the fact that the book itself was very Indian and very Bombayite.

Even with its immense success, *Midnight's Children* really only attracted more extensive critical attention after the publication of *Shame*, when it was possible to consider Rushdie's works as an *oeuvre*, a totality with specific characteristics, themes, and techniques.[7] This has continued with the publication of each new book, and a wealth of comparative criticism is now available. There are specific volumes discussing it,[8] and in David Smale's 2003 book, there is a discussion of selected criticism of *Midnight's Children*

---

and *The Satanic Verses* from a thematic point of view. All in all, *Midnight's Children* remains the most popular and the most studied of Rushdie's novels.

Developments after *Midnight's Children*

With *Shame*, certain topics and features emerged and intensified in Rushdie's writing and the commentary on it. Gender issues became a critical interest in the representation of women,[9] and this has continued to be a focus of discussion of his other writing.[10] Another strand in the criticism of *Shame* is political allegory. If *Midnight's Children* was read as an allegory of the history of a nation, in *Shame* the current political situation in Pakistan was turned into a fictional form.[11]

When *The Satanic Verses* was launched in September, the first reviews were positive. However, there were soon protests against it in Britain and in India, and the book was banned in October. The conflict spread rapidly, with other countries banning it, and finally, it escalated to the scandalous *fatwa* declared by the late Iranian Ayatollah Khomeini in February 1989. For a long time, this extra-literary context dominated the discussion of the Rushdie debate.[12] Due to the overriding presence of the affair, purely literary analyses of the novel were relatively few and far apart for a decade. Since then, analyses, especially comparative ones, have been published steadily, and among the thematic concerns—apart from the political, religious, intercultural, social and other conflictual issues—have been migrancy, violence, cinema, hybridity, postmodernism, language, and translation.[13]

In 1996, Rushdie published his first major novel since *The Satanic Verses*. *The Moor's Last Sigh*, which involved such themes as postcolonialism and aesthetics, hybridity and diaspora, palimpsest, cinema, and the mechanisms of religious fundamentalism.[14] Other aspects of rewriting history have also been the focus of several critical essays.[15]

The most recent stage in Rushdie criticism treats the novels he has written since he came out of hiding in 1998: *The Ground Beneath Her Feet* (1999), *Fury* (2001), *Shalimar the Clown* (2005), and *The Enchantress of Florence* (2008). It is, in many ways, a combination of the earlier phases: there is the literary interest, and then there is the controversial side. Often, these are integrated into analyses, but sometimes they appear separately. Although a growing number of articles have already been published on each of the four books, it is yet premature to assess this last phase in any great detail as the material is still proliferating. In the following, however, a preliminary outline of the developments on Rushdie's latest four major novels is offered. For the last two books, this is predictably the most limited.

Only with the publication of *The Ground Beneath Her Feet* (1999) did the balance of literary critical attention to Rushdie turn in favor of literary and aesthetic concerns, with a critical anthology to mark this emphasis.[16] Thematically, interest has been on popular music, photography, travel, the urban space, trauma theory, myths, and globalization. In the critique of *Fury* (2001), the thematic field was extended to include terrorism, cosmopolitanism, postethnicity, and technocapitalism. With *Shalimar the Clown*, terrorism remained in focus, and other topics have been Kashmir, psychology, and history. With *The Enchantress of Florence*, storytelling re-entered as a theme in criticism,[17] together with the themes of love and problems of intercultural communication. Finally, *Joseph Anton* has marked—along with the obvious biographical issues—a strong interest in Rushdie's non-fiction, judging from the presentations in recent international conferences; no publications have emerged from these as to yet. This seems to be one of the emphatic current directions in criticism, especially with the establishment of the Salman Rushdie Archive at Emory University in 2010.

Prospects for New Analyses

In the above, I have tried to encompass the major avenues into the criticism on Rushdie's *Midnight's Children*. As with the work of any other living author, this is a somewhat thankless endeavor, since the number of titles is expanding by the day. The author's oeuvre is in constant flux, since the publication of yet another work might override the emphases, categories, themes, and lines of development that have previously been predominant in criticism. I have here tried to do justice to the multiplicity of popular and academic discussions of the novel. Due to the critical diversity, any possible canonization of Rushdie criticism is still pending, even though existing anthologies of criticism are undoubtedly paving a way for this. However, it is my contention that there is room for many more views than have so far been expressed. I hope my outline can function as an inspiration, open up prospects for new relevant critical analyses, and offer tools for understanding, explicating, and probing *Midnight's Children* and other similar works.

Notes

1. Brennan in 1989, Petersson in 1996, Kuortti in 1998, Dutheil in 1999, Sanga in 2000, Hassumani in 2002, Deszcz in 2004, Jani in 2010, and Frank in 2011
2. e.g. Taneja & Dhawan in 1992, Fletcher in 1994, Mukherjee in 1998, Booker in 1999, Bloom in 2003, Rajeshwar & Kuortti in 2003, Ray & Kundu in 2006, Gurnah in 2007, and Bharat in 2009
3. See Reder in 2000 and Chauhan in 2001
4. see, however, Johansen, 1985 and 2007; Rahimieh, 1988; Cundy, 1992; Syed, 1994; Massé, 1995; Petersson, 2003
5. See Sharma 1982, Crane 1992, Banerjee 2002
6. Bader 1984, Howells 1985, Sangari 1985
7. Mahanta 1984, Murti 1985, Brigg 1987
8. Mukherjee 1999, Schürer 2004, ten Kortenaar & Louie 2005, Mitra 2006, Dey 2008, Procter 2009
9. Grewal 1988, Ahmad 1991, Moss 1992, Parameswaran 1996
10. Verma 1991, Natarajan 1994, Kamra 1996, Kuortti 2001
11. Islam 1988
12. Cohn-Sherbok 1990, Kuortti *Place* 1997
13. e.g. Seminck 1993, Gane 2002, Cavanaugh 2004
14. Schultheis 2001, Gabriel 2003, Salgado 2007, Stadtler 2007, Trousdale 2004, Ahmad 2005
15. Cantor 2003, Narain 2006
16. Linguanti & Tchernichova, *The Great Work of Making Real*
17. Deresiewicz, "Salman Rushdie's Imaginative New"

Works Cited

Ahmad, Dohra. "'This Fundo Stuff is Really Something New': Fundamentalism and Hybridity in *The Moor's Last Sigh.*" *The Yale Journal of Criticism* 18.1 (Spr. 2005): 1–20.

Bader, Rudolf. "Indian Tin Drum." *International Fiction Review* 11.2 (1984): 75–83.

Banerjee, Mita. *The Chutneyfication of History: Salman Rushdie, Michael Ondaatje, Bharati Mukherjee and the Postcolonial Debate.* Heidelberg: Universitätsverlag Winter, 2002. 95. American Studies, A Monograph Ser.

Bharat, Meenakshi. *Rushdie the Novelist: From* Grimus *to* The Enchantress of Florence. New Delhi: Pencraft International, 2009.

Bhaya Nair, Rukmini. "What Did Rushdie Mean and Why?" *The Hindu* 17 Aug. (1997): 33.

Blake, Andrew. *Salman Rushdie: A Beginner's Guide.* London: Hodder & Stoughton, 2001.

Bloom, Harold. *Salman Rushdie: Bloom's Modern Critical Views.* New York: Infobase Publishing, 2003.

Booker, M. Keith. *Critical Essays on Salman Rushdie.* New York: G. K. Hall, 1999.

Brennan, Timothy. *Salman Rushdie and the Third World: Myths of the Nation.* London: Macmillan & New York: St Martin's Press, 1989.

Brigg, Peter. "Salman Rushdie's Novels: The Disorder in Fantastic Order." *WLWE* 27:1 (1987): 119–130.

Cantor, Paul A. "Tales of the Alhambra: Rushdie's Use of Spanish History in *The Moor's Last Sigh.*" *Bloom's Modern Critical Views: Salman Rushdie.* Ed. Harold Bloom. Philadelphia: Chelsea House, 2003. 121–144.

Chauhan, Pradyumna S. *Salman Rushdie Interviews: A Sourcebook of His Ideas.* Westport: Greenwood, 2001.

Crane, Ralph J. "The Chutnification of History." *Inventing India: A History of India in English-Language Fiction.* Ed. Ralph J. Crane. Basingstoke & London: Macmillan, 1992. 170–189, 200.

Cundy, Catherine. "'Rehearsing Voices': Salman Rushdie's *Grimus.*" *The Journal of Commonwealth Literature* 27.1 (*1992*): 128–138.

Cundy, Catherine. *Salman Rushdie*. Manchester: Manchester UP, 1996. Contemporary World Writers Ser.

Deresiewicz, William. "Salman Rushdie's Imaginative New '*The Enchantress of Florence*'." *The Nation* 15 Sep. (2008). Web. 21 Dec. 2013. < http://www.thenation.com/article/salman-rushdies-imaginative-new-enchantress-florence>

Deszcz, Justyna. *Rushdie in Wonderland: Fairytaleness in Salman Rushdie's Fiction*. Frankfurt: Peter Lang, 2004. European University Studies: Series 14, Anglo-Saxon Language and Literature, 405.

Dey, Pradip Kumar. *Salman Rushdie's* Midnight's Children. New Delhi: Atlantic, 2008.

Eaglestone, Robert and Martin McQuillan. *Salman Rushdie: Contemporary Critical Perspectives*. London: Bloomsbury, 2013.

Fletcher, M. D., ed. *Reading Rushdie: Perspectives on the Fiction of Salman Rushdie*. Amsterdam & Atlanta: Rodopi, 1994. Cross/Cultures, 16.

Fletcher, M. D. "Salman Rushdie: An Annotated Bibliography of English Language Articles about His Fiction." *Journal of Indian Writing in English* 19 (1991): 15–23.

_____. "Salman Rushdie: An Annotated Bibliography of English Language Articles about His Fiction." 1991. *Reading Rushdie: Perspectives on the Fiction of Salman Rushdie*. Ed. M. D. Fletcher. Cross/Cultures, 16. Amsterdam & Atlanta: Rodopi, 1994. 361–396.

Frank, Søren. *Salman Rushdie: A Deleuzian Reading*. Copenhagen: Museum Tusculanum Press, 2011.

Gane, Gillian. "Postcolonial Literature and the Magic Radio: The Language of Rushdie's *Midnight's Children.*" *Poetics Today* 27.3 (Fall 2006): 569–596.

Goonetilleke, D. C. R. A. *Salman Rushdie*. 1998. London: Macmillan, 2010.

Grant, Damian. *Salman Rushdie*. Plymouth: Northcote House & the British Council, 1999.

Gurnah, Abdulrazak. *The Cambridge Companion to Salman Rushdie*. Cambridge: Cambridge UP, 2007.

Hamilton Ian. "The First Life of Salman Rushdie." *The New Yorker* 71.42 (25 Dec.–1 Jan. 1995): 90–113.

Harrison, James. *Salman Rushdie*. New York: Twayne, 1992.

Hassumani, Sabrina. *Salman Rushdie: A Postmodern Reading of His Major Works*. Madison: Fairleigh Dickinson UP, 2002.

Hennard Dutheil de la Rochère, Martine. *Origin and Originality in Rushdie's Fiction*. Bern: Peter Lang, 1999.

Howells, Coral Ann. "Rudy Wiebe's *The Temptations of Big Bear* and Salman Rushdie's *Midnight's Children*." *The Literary Criterion* 20.1 (1985): 191–203.

Huggan, Graham. "The Postcolonial Exotic: Salman Rushdie and the Booker of Bookers." *Transition: An International Review* 64 (1994): 22–29.

Islam, Shamsul. "Rushdie and Political Commitment: A Study of *Midnight's Children* and *Shame*." *Literature and Commitment: A Commonwealth Perspective*. Proceedings of the Third Commonwealth-in-Canada Conference, October 1985. Ed. Govind Narain Sharma. Toronto: TSAR, 1988. 125–131.

Jani, Pranav. *Decentering Rushdie: Cosmopolitanism and the Indian Novel in English*. Columbus: Ohio State UP, 2010.

Johansen, Ib. "The Flight of the Enchanter: Reflections on Salman Rushdie's *Grimus*." *Kunapipi* 7.1 (1985): 20–32.

Johansen, Ib. "Tricksters and the Common Herd in Salman Rushdie's *Grimus*." *The Cambridge Companion to Salman Rushdie*. Ed. Abdulrazak Gurnah. Cambridge: Cambridge UP, 2007. 77–90.

Jussawalla Feroza F. *Family Quarrels: Towards a Criticism of Indian Writing in English*. New York: Peter Lang, 1985. American University Studies Series IV: English Language and Literature, 17.

Kuortti, Joel. "A Bibliography of the Rushdie Criticism." *Salman Rushdie: New Critical Insights*, Ed. Rajeshwar Mittapalli & Joel Kuortti. Vol. 2. New Delhi: Atlantic, 2003. 177–217.

_____. *Fictions to Live In: Narration as an Argument for Fiction in Salman Rushdie's Novels*. Frankfurt: Peter Lang, 1998.

_____. *The Salman Rushdie Bibliography: A Bibliography of Salman Rushdie's Work and Rushdie Criticism*. Frankfurt: Peter Lang, 1997.

Linguanti, Elsa and Viktoria Tchernichova. *The Great Work of Making Real: Salman Rushdie's* The Ground Beneath Her Feet. Pisa: Edizioni ETS, 2003.

Mahanta, Aparna. "Allegories of the Indian Experience: The Novels of Salman Rushdie." *Economic and Political Weekly* 19.6 (1984): 244–247.

Massé, Sophie. "Transfictional Identities in Salman Rushdie's *Grimus*." *Etudes Britanniques Contemporaines* 8 (1995): 89–95.

Mitra, Reena, ed. *Salman Rushdie's* Midnight's Children. New Delhi: Atlantic, 2006.

Morton, Stephen. *Salman Rushdie: Fictions of Postcolonial Modernity*. Houndmills: Palgrave Macmillan, 2008.

Mukherjee, Meenakshi. Introduction. *Rushdie's* Midnight's Children: *A Book of Readings*. Ed. Meenakshi Mukherjee. Delhi: Pencraft, 1998. 9–27.

Mukherjee, Meenakshi. *Rushdie's* Midnight's Children: *A Book of Readings*. Delhi: Pencraft, 1998.

Murti, K. V. S. "Secular Fantasy: Salman Rushdie's Fiction." *Journal of Indian Writing in English* 13.2 (1985): 41–47.

Narain, Mona. "Re-imagined Histories: Rewriting the Early Modern in Rushdie's *The Moor's Last Sigh*." *Journal for Early Modern Cultural Studies* 6.2 (2006): 55–58.

Narayan, Shyamala A. "*Midnight's Children*." *Literary Criterion* 18:3 (*1983*): 23–32.

Natarajan, Nalini. "Woman, Nation, and Narration in *Midnight's Children*." *Scattered Hegemonies: Postmodernity and Transnational Feminist Practices*. Eds. Inderpal Grewal & Caren Kaplan. Minneapolis: U Minnesota P, 1994. 76–89.

Parameswaran, Uma. "'Handcuffed to History': Salman Rushdie's Art." *Ariel* 14:2 (1983): 34–45.

_____. *The Perforated Sheet: Essays on Salman Rushdie's Art*. New Delhi: Affiliated East-West Press, 1988. 1–11.

_____. *Salman Rushdie's Early Fiction*. Jaipur: Rawat, 2007.

Petersson, Margareta. "*Grimus* and the Alchemical Tradition." *Salman Rushdie: New Critical Insights*. Ed. Rajeshwar Mittapali & Joel Kuortti. Vol. 1. New Delhi: Atlantic, 2003. 1–29.

Petersson, Margareta. *Unending Metamorphoses: Myth, Satire, and Religion in Salman Rushdie's Novels*. Lund: Lund UP, 1996.

Procter, James. *Salman Rushdie's* Midnight's Children*: A Routledge Guide.* London: Routledge, 2009.

Rahimieh, Nasrin. *"Grimus:* Salman Rushdie's First Experiment with Post-Modern Narrative." *Literature and Perspective.* Proceedings of the Third Commonwealth-in-Canada Conference, October 1985. Ed. Govind Narain Sharma. Toronto: TSAR, 1988. 116–124.

Rajeshwar, Mittapalli and Joel Kuortti. *Salman Rushdie: New Critical Insights.* New Delhi: Atlantic, 2003.

Ray, Mohit Kumar & Rama Kundu, ed. *Salman Rushdie: Critical Essays.* Vols. 1–2. New Delhi: Atlantic, 2006.

Reder, Michael, ed. *Conversations with Salman Rushdie.* Jackson: UP of Mississippi, 2000.

Riemenschneider, Dieter. "History and the Individual in Anita Desai's *Clear Light of Day* and Salman Rushdie's *Midnight's Children*" in *World Literature Written in English* 23.1 (1984): 196–207.

_____. "History and the Individual in Salman Rushdie's *Midnight's Children* and Anita Desai's *Clear Light of Day." Kunapipi* 6.2 (1984): 53–66.

_____. *The New Indian Novel in English: A Study of the 1980s.* Ed. Viney Kirpal. New Delhi: Allied, 1990. 187–200.

Rushdie, Salman. "'Doing the Dangerous Thing': An Interview with Salman Rushdie." Interview with T. Vijay Kumar, Hyderabad 10 Mar. 1983. *Rushdie's* Midnight's Children*: A Book of Readings.* Ed. Meenakshi Mukherjee. New Delhi: Pencraft, 1999. 212–227.

_____. "The Empire Writes Back with a Vengeance." *The Times* 3 Jul. (1982): 8.

_____. Introduction to *Mirrorwork: 50 Years of Indian writing, 1947–1997.* Eds. Salman Rushdie and Elizabeth West. New York: Henry Holt, 1997. vii–xx.

Sambamurthy, V. Indira. "Salman Rushdie." *An Annotated Bibliography of Indian English Fiction.* New Delhi: Atlantic, 2001. 1225–1310. 3 vols.

Sanga, Jaina C. *Salman Rushdie's Postcolonial Metaphors: Migration, Translation, Hybridity, Blasphemy, and Globalization.* Westport: Greenwood, 2001. Contributions to the Study of World Literature, 109.

Sangari, Kumkum. "Marquez and the Politics of the Possible." *Journal of Arts and Ideas* 10–11 (Jan.–Jun. 1985): 37–58.

_____. "The Politics of the Possible, or the Perils of Reclassification." *The Politics of the Possible: Essays on Gender, History, Narratives, Colonial English*. Sangari. New Delhi: Tulika, 1999 & London: Anthem, 2002, 1–28.

Schürer, Norbert. *Salman Rushdie's* Midnight's Children*: A Reader's Guide*. New York & London: Continuum, 2004.

Shankar, Subramanian. "Midnight's Orphans, or A Postcolonialism Worth Its Name." *Cultural Critique* 56 (2004): 64–95.

Sharma, D. R. "Chutnification of India." *New Quest* 33 (May–Jun. 1982): 169–171.

Shepherd, Ron. "Growing Up: A Central Metaphor in Some Recent Novels." *The Writer's Sense of the Contemporary: Papers in Southeast Asian and Australian Literature*. Nedlands: Centre for Studies in Australian Literature, University of Western Australia, 1982. 51–55.

Smale, David, ed. *Salman Rushdie:* Midnight's Children / The Satanic Verses*: A Reader's Guide to Essential Criticism*. Houndmills: Palgrave Macmillan, 2003.

Srivastava, Neelam. "Languages of the Nation in Salman Rushdie's *Midnight's Children* and Vikram Seth's *A Suitable Boy*." *Ariel* 36.1–2 (2005): 207–232.

Syed, Mujeebuddin. "Warped Mythologies: Salman Rushdie's *Grimus*." *Ariel* 25:4 (1994): 135–152.

Taneja, G. R. & R. K. Dhawan, eds. *The Novels of Salman Rushdie*. New Delhi: Indian Society for Commonwealth Studies, 1992.

ten Kortenaar, Neil. "*Midnight's Children* and the Allegory of History." *Ariel* 26.2 (Apr 1995): 41–62.

ten Kortenaar, Neil & Kam Louie. *Self, Nation, Text in Salman Rushdie's* Midnight's Children. Montreal, Kingston & London: McGill-Queen's UP, 2005.

Teverson, Andrew. *Salman Rushdie*. Manchester: Manchester UP, 2007. Contemporary World Writers Ser.

Trousdale, Rachel. "'City of Mongrel Joy': Bombay and the Shiv Sena in *Midnight's Children* and *The Moor's Last Sigh*." *The Journal of Commonwealth Literature* 39.2 (2004): 95–110.

'America, the Great Attractor, whispered in my ears': From Bombay to New York; Mapping Geopolitical Shifts in Rushdie's Fiction_____

Marianne Corrigan

Midnight's Children and Commodification

This chapter seeks to map geopolitical shifts in Salman Rushdie's fiction through a comparative exploration of *Midnight's Children, The Ground Beneath Her Feet*, and *Fury*. Argued here is that, from the point of *The Ground Beneath Her Feet* onwards, Rushdie's thematic focus shifts from the legacies of British colonialism in India and Pakistan to concerns with globalization and American-propagated neo-liberalism at the turn of the twenty-first century. *The Ground Beneath Her Feet* marks the emergence of a broader geo-political and cultural focus in Rushdie's fiction, with his later body of work registering the cultural and social consequences of an increased de-regularization in global economic markets in the late twentieth century. The focus of *The Ground Beneath Her Feet* and *Fury* is on discourses of global consumer culture, American cultural imperialism, and capitalist economics, as opposed to the cultural and political processes of decolonization in India explored in *Midnight's Children*. Through a comparative analysis of *Midnight's Children* and these two later novels, this essay argues that a dialogue can be drawn between economic, political, and anthropological theorizations of globalization in the late-twentieth and early twenty-first century and the aesthetic and thematic properties of Rushdie's later fiction.

Midnight's Children is widely regarded as one of the pinnacle novels of the latter half of the twentieth century. Winner of the Booker Prize, winner of the Booker of Bookers prize, winner of the English Speaking Union literary award and the James Tait prize, critics have acclaimed its importance. In her introduction to the novel, the novelist Anita Desai described Rushdie's narrative as "the voice of a new age: strong, original and demanding of attention"

(Desai vii). The eminent scholar of Orientalism, Edward Said, praised its achievement in expressing the "liberating imagination of independence itself, with all of its anomalies and contradictions working themselves out" (Said 260), and the literary scholar Michael Gorra applauded its articulation of postcolonial identity and stratification of English as an Indian language:

> No one else has done so much to make English into an Indian language; no one else has so fully used that language to probe the nature of national identity or to define a model for the postcolonial self. No other writer in English has so energetically and joyously peopled the immigrants' London or the great city of Bombay; and no one since Dickens has offered as engaging a gallery of self-dramatizing rogues and charlatans and madmen (Gorra 147).

Yet such levels of commercial success have been viewed by some critics as problematic, particularly given that postcolonial novels are typically concerned with registering a resistance to the machinations of global capitalism. The postcolonial critic Graham Huggan, whilst acknowledging *Midnight's Children*'s "verbal richness and stylistic pyrotechnics", argues that Gorra's stance "testifies to the inflationary rhetoric," which characterized the critical reception of *Midnight's Children* (Huggan 69). The critical discourse surrounding *Midnight's Children* and certainly the attention on Rushdie in more recent years has frequently centered on the dichotomy of the text's geopolitical subject of India, Indian-ness, and Indian independence, and the predominantly Western site of its reception and consumption. For critics like Huggan, a text like *Midnight's Children* merely highlights the extent to which the anti-imperial, emancipatory discourses of postcolonialism are invariably entwined with consumer capitalism:

> [postcolonialism] implies a politics of value that stands in obvious opposition to global processes of commodification. Yet a cursory glance at the state of postcolonial studies at Western universities, or at the worldwide marketing of prominent postcolonial writers like Salman Rushdie, is enough to suggest that these two apparently conflicting regimes of value are mutually entangled. It is not just that

postcolonialism and postcoloniality are at odds with one another, or that the former's emancipatory agenda clashes with the latter's; the point that needs to be stressed here is that postcolonialism is *bound up with* postcoloniality—that in the overwhelmingly commercial context of late twentieth-century commodity culture, postcolonialism and its rhetoric of resistance have themselves become consumer products (Huggan 7).

Huggan's argument highlights how the production and circulation of texts, such as *Midnight's Children*, in accordance with the market conditions of global capitalism results in the commodification of the discourses of postcolonialism itself. According to Huggan, the global marketing and distribution of *Midnight's Children* represents the "exoticizing" or re-packaging of post-independence India, for consumption by a largely Western reader-audience. Rushdie occupies a similar position to writers, such as Arundhati Roy and Jamaica Kincaid, in that critics like Huggan have problematized his work as a result of a perceived conflict between the postcolonial nation it seeks to narrate, and the geopolitical situation of its reader audience. The scope of his novels ranges from the United States to South Asian territories, such as India, Pakistan, and the contested Kashmir, to European countries, such as Italy, England, and Spain; yet the majority of Rushdie's writing is published, circulated, and consumed by readers in northern Europe and the United States.

The issues surrounding the commodification of a postcolonial text, such as *Midnight's Children* and, in particular, questions relating to the sites of representation and reception of the postcolonial novel, are explored by the postcolonial cultural critic Sarah Brouillette in her text *Postcolonial Writers in the Global Literary Marketplace*. Brouillette argues that "the postcolonial author has emerged as a profoundly complicit and compromised figure whose authority rests, however uncomfortably, in the nature of his connection to the specificity of a given political location" (Brouillette 3). Brouillette's argument is especially relevant when mapping geopolitical shifts in Rushdie's fiction. Whereas *Midnight's Children* is certainly identifiable as a postcolonial novel, which explores India's emergence from British colonial rule, from *The Ground Beneath Her Feet* onwards, Rushdie's fiction is more identifiable as international in it geographic, cultural, and political scope, centering on discourses of globalization, consumer culture, terrorism, and migration. However, as Brouillette argues, this means that Rushdie emerges as a compromised figure. The profound success of *Midnight's Children* inevitably marked him as something of a posterboy for the postcolonial novel, meaning that his authority is frequently read as resting in his connection to India. Yet *Fury* and *The Ground Beneath Her Feet* move away from explicit concerns with narrating the postcolonial Indian subcontinent and towards consumer culture in America, which, in turn, invites a re-consideration of how we think about Rushdie in terms of his identity as a writer. Stephen Morton, scholar of postcolonial Anglophone literatures, describes the "worldliness" (Morton 16) of Rushdie's fiction, and I have previously argued that Rushdie's interest in thematizing globalization and cultural connectivity have helped to define him as an international writer in the twenty-first century (Corrigan 35).

Globalization

An increasing integration of domestic economies into the world capitalist system in the late twentieth century has resulted in amplified global connectivity on a political, social, and cultural level. In *Transnational Connections*, the social anthropologist Ulf Hannerz's various lines of enquiry into the social and cultural dimensions to globalization stem from his principal argument that "distances, and boundaries, are not what they used to be" (Hannerz 3). Boundary-crossing is a prominent theme in *Midnight's Children*, and it is explored both in terms of Saleem's hybrid identity and the novel's formalistic and narrative properties. The literary scholar Pradip Kumar Dey argues that "the narrative technique blurs the chronological boundaries" (Dey 128), resulting in a de-stabilization of received notions of time and space. Rushdie employs magic realism in the novel to explore Saleem's hybrid identity as a postcolonial subject, suspended between two perceived binary points of opposition: a colonial subject in British imperial India, and a postcolonial subject in post-independence India. In short,

---

Saleem occupies the space in-between. Wendy B. Faris, a specialist in comparative literature, argues that magic realism is an effective means of narrating the postcolonial subject, given that "the text suspended between the two discursive systems [of realism and fantasy] corresponds to the postcolonial subject suspended between two or more cultural systems, and so it is an appropriate mode in which to represent that situation" (Faris 135).

However, we can register a considerable shift in the formalistic and narrative properties of Rushdie's fiction when contrasting *Midnight's Children* with *The Ground Beneath Her Feet* and *Fury*. Magic realism gives way to a more realist form of first-person narrative in *The Ground Beneath Her Feet*, with the narrator, Rai Merchant, providing snapshots of the world he encounters through a narrative form that corresponds to his profession as a photographer. Rai's photography parallels Saleem's storytelling in *Midnight's Children*. Both characters obsessively foreground their desire to document their subjectivity through forms of narrative, namely the story and the image. Both are modes through which the past may be recalled and relived, but each also represents a tension between the empirical event itself and the reproduction of the event in the form of narrative or image. The postcolonial scholar Cristina Sandru highlights the ways in which Rushdie thematizes photography in order to draw attention to the persistent dialogue between human memory and signifying technologies, such as photographic equipment, in order to interrogate questions of truth, validity and meaning:

> central to Rushdie's use of visual technologies in his fiction is, on the one hand, a preoccupation with memory and the role played by artefacts (whether objects, photographs, films or other types of visual representation) in preserving and relaying a meaningful past, and on the other, the potential for distortion, falsification, and commodification inherent in the very act of producing these representations (Sandru 142).

In the late twentieth and early twenty-first century, the intersection of globalization and technology has resulted in a transformation of the ways in which subjectivity is recorded, re-configured, and re-presented through forms of digital media. Technologies, such as the camera, the webcam, and the Internet, which produce second-order representations of the living subject, enable the digital re-staging of the body in cybernetic spaces, such as Facebook, Twitter, Blogs, and websites, which can be accessed by a global audience. The result is a discourse of spectacle, whereby the image, as signifier, effects a blurring of the boundaries between the subject and its simulacrum. Through Rai's role as photographer in *The Ground Beneath Her Feet*, Rushdie questions how second-order significations of self and identity, such as the photograph or film, relate to the discourses of celebrity and spectacle within a global cultural economy.

Fury's formalistic properties also correspond to its thematic explorations. Unlike *Midnight's Children*, the narrative contains no magic realism; instead, the story of *Fury*'s protagonist, Malik Solanka, is recounted in the third person, adding to the novel's sense of realism. Consumer culture in America is aestheticized in the novel through passages lexically dense with references to consumer capitalism, as in the opening paragraph:

> Stores, dealerships, galleries struggled to satisfy the skyrocketing demand for ever more recherché produce: limited-edition olive oils, three-hundred-dollar corkscrews, customised Humvees, the latest anti-virus software, escort services featuring contortionists and twins, video installations, outsider art, featherlight shawls made from the chin-fluff of extinct mountain goats (Rushdie, *Fury* 3).

The surface stylistics of the prose draws attention to the bombardment of images the average citizen living in New York at the turn of the twenty-first century might experience. The seemingly relentless invitations from global firms keen to convince the subject to consume increasingly non-vital goods are aestheticized through a text crammed with references to popular culture and absurd commodities, such as the shawls made from the chin fluff of extinct goats. When reading *Fury* comparatively alongside *Midnight's Children*, it is clear that the latter is concerned with examining British imperialism, whereas

Fury seeks to interrogate discourses of neo-liberalism and consumer culture in twenty-first century America.

Migration and Travel

In *The Ground Beneath Her Feet* and *Fury*, the increasing sense of global interconnectedness resulting from globalization at the turn of the twentieth century is aestheticized through the juxtaposition of seemingly diverse cultural material. Such a stylistic device can be read as a textual manifestation of the "organization of culture," which Hannerz identifies as a significant point of critical focus when exploring theories of globalization and transnational connections. Through nuanced surface stylistics, Rushdie's later fiction draws attention to its own intertextuality, which itself mirrors the wider tropes of migrancy and movement thematized through narratives of global movement.

The Satanic Verses asks "how does newness come into the world?" (Rushdie 8), a question, which is broadly at the heart of much of Rushdie's fictional examinations of postcolonial migrant subjectivity. We can read this argument in dialogue with Hannerz's assertion that there exists a "desire to cultivate new understandings of how the world hangs together, of transnational connections, in the organization of meanings and actions—and move beyond mere astonishment over new mixtures and combinations" (Hannerz 4). Writing in 1996, Hannerz is referring here to a shift he perceived in the field of anthropological scholarship in the lead up to the turn of the twenty-first century. In part, Hannerz's remarks refer to his assessment of the self-reflexivity of anthropology as a discipline that is frequently being "'rethought,' 'reinvented,' 'recaptured'" (Hannerz 4). More importantly, however, we can read a dialogue between what Hannerz registers as an anthropological enquiry into transnational connections and new mixtures and combinations of culture, and the aesthetic and thematic concerns of Rushdie's later novels.

Fury and *The Ground Beneath Her Feet* share a common ground through their protagonists. Both novels feature major characters who have migrated from former colonial nations to the metropolitan centers of America's major cities: Malik in *Fury* and Rai and Vina Aspara in *The Ground Beneath Her Feet*. This stands in opposition to *Midnight's Children*'s Saleem, who is searching for his sense of self in a newly independent nation, India. Rai, Vina, and Malik all experience social and cultural displacement through their experiences of travel and migration.

The postcolonial researcher Anshuman A. Mondal argues that amongst the major themes of the two novels are "the ontological questions concerning being and the fragmentation of identity; and, pre-eminently, the effects of migration" (Mondal 170). Mondal's argument can be read in conjunction with Hannerz's theories on the transnational when considering the prominent theme of migrancy in *Fury* and *The Ground Beneath Her Feet*. Rai, Vina and Malik face ontological questions regarding their subjectivity through their displacement and relocation to America. The novels thus represent an enquiry into how we can cultivate new understandings of how the world connects and of the ways in which meanings, actions, and culture are organized and registered.

In *The Ground Beneath Her Feet*, Rai frequently expresses his desire to leave Bombay and re-locate to America:

> I remember the thrill of the whispered word on my young lips— America. America, the open-sesame. America, which got rid of the British long before we did. Let Sir Darius Xerxes Cama dream his colonialist dreams of England. My dream-ocean led to America, my private, my unfound land (Rushdie, *Ground Beneath Her Feet* 59).

His values and aspirations are shaped by a culture infiltrated by glamorous images of American society. Sociologists Bernd Hamm and Russell Smandych argue that Western popular culture poses as an alluring metropolitan alternative to life in a smaller locality, particularly that of a developing nation:

> Neo-liberal political and economic strategies pave the way for, and are accompanied by, the influx of Western media, of monopolistic Western conceptions of human rights and good governance, of Western popular culture and tourism […] Junk food or pop music,

fashion clothing or soap-operas, Hollywood movies or stock exchange pattern, this image says: Life is easy, why do you stick to your old traditions? Why don't you accept the promises of capitalism? Why do you stay with your folks in that garbage village? (Hamm and Smandych 27).

Clearly, in *The Ground Beneath Her Feet,* both Rai and Vina do indeed accept the promises of capitalism and relocate to America, where Vina's iconicity and status as a global star sees her image commodified in various cultural forms for international consumption.

Rushdie begins his exploration of the cultural dimension to globalization by examining the connective properties of music and its potential as a de-territorializing and re-territorializing instrument. In *Enlightenment Orpheus: The Power of Music in Other Worlds*, the interdisciplinary music researcher Vanessa Agnew highlights an important aspect of the Orphic myth, which is particularly significant when examining Rushdie's intertextual exploration of the tale in *The Ground Beneath Her Feet*: "We remember Orpheus as the heartbroken lover inventing music and poetry but forget his first love, travel" (Agnew 11). It is important to register, however, that for Rushdie, travel is not simply the process of geographic relocation, and, for example, *The Ground Beneath Her Feet* examines how culture travels, circulates, and connects as a result of the economic changes brought about by globalization.

As part of Rushdie's examination of globalization, his writing explores the complex dichotomy between progress and stasis. This emerges in *Midnight's Children* through the juxtaposition of the characters Tai and Dr. Aadam Aziz. Aziz is presented as a hybrid subject who has travelled, whereas Tai is described as rooted in one spot. As Aziz begins to diagnose Tai's ailments, the ferryman eyes his doctor's bag: "to the ferryman, the bag represents Abroad; it is the alien thing, the invader, progress" (Rushdie, *Midnight's Children* 22). Tai resents this amalgamation of different cultural influences, and, as a result, is portrayed as a 'simplistic' character, lacking in political consciousness.

Rushdie's characters are often problematic in that they are portrayed as adhering to one of two systems of thought: either they are of the 'roots' inclination (i.e. their sense of self is fixed and rooted in the place of their birth), or they are identifiable as a 'routes' character (they embrace travel, migrancy, and displacement and have a desire to re-locate). Such discourse can be read as problematic in that it is consistently critical of any character who desires to remain in a given locality, particularly if it is his or her birthplace. Such characters are portrayed as backward or ignorant for refusing to succumb to the inevitable desire to travel: "Freedom to reject is the only freedom. Freedom to uphold is dangerous. Life is elsewhere. Cross frontiers. Fly away" (Rushdie 146). According to Rushdie, one should be in a continual state of motion or journey, as to remain in a fixed location is to stagnate. A feeling of 'belonging' in a given locality is at best an ancient myth and, at worst, an ideological form of brainwashing to control the population:

> What if all of it —home, kinship, the whole enchilada—is just the biggest, most truly global, and centuries-oldest piece of brainwashing? Suppose that it's only when you dare to let go that your real life begins? When you're whirling free of the mother ship, when you cut your ropes, slip your chain, step off the map, go absent without leave, scram, vamoose, whatever: suppose that it's then, and only then, that you're actually free to act! (Rushdie, *Ground Beneath Her Feet* 177).

For Rushdie, social opportunity arises from travel and migration. Modernity consists not only of the circulation of information, goods services, but also of people; the human condition is to somehow drift and displace through the shifting irregularities of contemporary social structures.

The Ground Beneath Her Feet and *Fury* nonetheless ask the important question of why individuals re-locate; what are the economic, social, and in turn, psychological reasons that motivate a person to move from one location towards another. In *The Ground Beneath her Feet*, it is Vina and Rai's frustration with the economic conditions in Bombay and the desire for social mobility offered by a metropolitan centre that has seen the advances of modernity, which fuel their desire to relocate. In *Fury*, Malik is an economic migrant driven by a deep personal rage and disenchantment with his personal relationships which propels him to move to America. Both novels explore the protagonists' disenchantment with the promises of capitalism and the complex sense of self-confliction that arises from the processes of migration in the late twentieth century political economy.

American Consumerism

Fury examines Malik Solanka's disenchantment with American consumerist society at the turn of the twenty-first century. Globalization is examined through the presentation of a rabid consumerist culture that is obsessed with the concept of selfhood. Whereas *Midnight's Children* examines concepts of self and identity within the space of a newly formed postcolonial nation state, *Fury* looks at the ways in which globalization and technological cultures have enabled an acquisitive sense of materialism in contemporary American society. Mondal notes *Fury*'s close thematic relationship with *The Ground Beneath Her Feet* as a result of each text's examination of the dialogue between globalization, consumer capitalism, and discourses of spectacle and celebrity that emerge through networks of global, digital media. Mondal asserts that each novel is concerned with a sustained critique of the relationship between global capitalism and consumer culture, yet "at the same time these novels oscillate towards an aestheticism which consistently undermines this critique" (Mondal 170). As previously discussed, the superlative stylistics of *Fury*'s prose present a complex dichotomy, which can be read as both complicit and in critique of consumer capitalism.

By profession, Malik is a doll-maker. His creations gain enormous commercial acclaim. His most celebrated creation is *Little Brain*, a doll who ignites something of a consumerist frenzy within the new society Malik finds himself within. Such veneration on a grand, commercial scale soon begins to signify all that Malik apparently detests in contemporary American society. Through his artistic creations, Malik has seemingly involuntarily furthered the expansion of an acquisitive culture which, in reality, disgusts him. We can read Malik's plight in light of Karl Marx and Friedrich

Engels' assertion that "the need of a constantly expanding market for its products chases the bourgeoisie over the whole surface of the globe. It must nestle everywhere, settle everywhere, establish connexions everywhere" (Marx and Engels 83).

Here, Marx and Engels identify what is a crucial argument to this thesis: that of global connectivity and the significance of migrant labor in capitalist expansion. What we understand as globalization at the turn of the twenty-first century is the result of a complex history of intensified capitalist economic development over the long twentieth century, as predicted by Marx and Engels. Marx and Engels go on to argue that the Bourgeoisie "compels all nations, on pain of extinction, to adopt the bourgeois mode of production" to ensure the mass implementation of "what it calls civilization [...] i.e., to become bourgeois themselves. In one word, it creates a world after its own image" (Marx and Engels 84). They present an effective description of neoliberalist capitalist expansionism. Anthropologists Jean Comaroff and John L. Comaroff extend Marx's critique by urging us to recall that consumption "was the hallmark disease of the eighteenth and nineteenth centuries" and yet, at the close of the nineteenth century, "it is the factor, the principle, held to determine definitions of value, the construction of identities, and even the shape of the global 'ecumene'" (Comaroff and Comaroff 3–4).

My reading of globalization in *The Ground Beneath Her Feet* and *Fury* draws directly on Comaroff and Comaroff's argument that consumption has become the significant factor that shapes society, value, and identity in late-twentieth and early twenty-first century western society. The present stage of capitalism's seemingly endless treadmill of material production, circulation, and consumption fuels an acquisitive culture in today's contemporary global climate. Consumerism is undoubtedly assisted by the greater ease with which economic markets trade and manufacturing industries produce and subsequently transport goods through increased channels of connectivity and interdependence brought about by globalization. *Fury* and *The Ground Beneath Her Feet* thematize these theoretical ideas by highlighting the ways in which postcolonial migrants assume positions in society through their ability to contribute to this cycle of production and consumption.

Yet *The Ground Beneath Her Feet* attempts to record a resistance to American cultural imperialism by re-writing the history of rock and roll music through the optic of an Indian recording artist and the Indian photographer who registers her image. Vina is an internationally acclaimed singer, and she dominates the world stage as an Asian woman. However, the novel fails to escape the machinations of consumer capitalism: the global brand is evident everywhere and indicates a dominance of mass-produced American culture, which manifests through the global channels of internationally-marketed consumerist capitalism. As Morton argues:

> Rai's attempt to posit the Indian rock 'n' roll music of Ormus Cama's fictional band VTO as an alternative to the *cultural* dominance of the West in the twentieth and twenty-first centuries does not in itself address the global political and economic dominance of the United States, or the way in which contemporary South Asian music has been packaged as World Music or Asian cool: an exotic commodity for Western consumer society (Morton 107).

We return again to Huggan's theories relating to the re-packaging of the postcolonial product for consumption by a wider western audience. Malik's plight is more complex. The products he produces—dolls and virtual gaming environments—are not explicitly postcolonial products exoticized for consumption by an American consumer economy. Instead, he emerges as a compromised author of his creations. Brouillette registers a certain element of complicity in Malik's entanglement with the processes of global media marketing and the consumer capitalism, in which he partakes. Indeed, she argues that "his life has been, and continues to be, defined by a serious entanglement in consumer culture and the media that markets it" (Brouillette 92). Thus Brouillette highlights a link between what we can read as a problematic evaluation of Rushdie as a postcolonial writer, and his relocation to the metropolitan territory of New York.

In a departure from *Midnight's Children*, where the role of the narrator or creator of narrative is one of a celebrated postcolonial freedom, *The Ground Beneath Her Feet* and *Fury* are particularly concerned with exploring how the role of the artist, or producer of cultural texts, becomes bound up in this discourse of spectacle through his or her inevitable participation in the global processes of production and consumption, which market cultural products.

Disenchantment with the Processes of Commodification

From the above analysis, it is clear that postcolonial ideologies relating to acts of resistance and the deconstruction of imperial hegemony that are explored in Midnight's Children are extended towards a more global, international consideration of culture and politics at the turn of the twenty-first century. *The Ground Beneath Her Feet* and *Fury* explore the influence of a global, capitalist economy on postcolonial cultures. Whereas *Midnight's Children* is interested in probing the complexities of a hybridized, postcolonial identity, these two later novels extend this enquiry into selfhood by examining the issues facing migrants who relocate from former colonial nation states to metropolitan centres for differing reasons.

The promises of capitalism are juxtaposed with the protagonists' disenchantment with the processes of commodification to which commercial texts, such as art, music, or literature are subject in order to generate items which have economic, as well as artistic, value. A comparative analysis of these three novels marks Rushdie as transitioning from a celebrated postcolonial writer, to a more problematic, compromised figure, emerging in the twenty-first century as what we might define as an 'international' writer, concerned with exploring the broader concerns of globalization and consumer capitalism within an increasingly networked global ecumene.

Formalistic approaches to narration clearly transition from a magical realist approach to a more realist form of narrative, which centers on the ways in which digital technologies, such as photography and gaming have emerged as prominent methods of recording the human condition, as opposed to the explorations of traditional Indian forms of oratory examined in *Midnight's Children*. What emerges, however, is consistent: Rushdie's work continues to ask questions regarding the role of the postcolonial subject in an increasingly interconnected global ecumene.

Works Cited

Agnew, Vanessa. *Enlightenment Orpheus: The Power of Music in Other Worlds*. Oxford: Oxford UP, 2008.

Brouillette, Sarah. *Postcolonial Writers in the Global Literary Marketplace*. Hampshire and New York: Palgrave Macmillan, 2007.

Comaroff, Jean & John L. Comaroff. *Millennial Capitalism and the Culture of Neoliberalism: Millennial quartet*. Durham: Duke UP, 2001.

Corrigan, Marianne. "Rushdie as an International Writer." *Salman Rushdie: Contemporary Critical Perspectives*. Eds. Robert Eaglestone and Martin McQuillan. London: Bloomsbury, 2013. 34–44.

Desai, Anita. Introduction. *Midnight's Children*. By Salman Rushdie. New York: Knopf, 1981. vii–xxi.

Dey, Pradip Kumar. *Salman Rushdie's Midnight's Children*. New Delhi: Atlantic, 2008.

Faris, Wendy B. *Ordinary Enchantments: Magical Realism and the Remystification of Narrative*. Nashville: Vanderbilt UP, 2004.

Gorra, Michael Edward. *After Empire: Scott, Naipaul and Rushdie*. Chicago: U of Chicago P, 1997.

Hamm, Bernd and Russell Smandych, *Cultural Imperialism: Essays on the Political Economy of Cultural Domination*. Toronto: U of Toronto P, 2005.

Huggan, Graham. *The Postcolonial Exotic: Marketing the Margins*. London and New York: Routledge, 2001.

Hannerz, Ulf. *Transnational Connections: Culture, People, Places*. London: Routledge, 1996.

Marx, Karl and Friedrich Engels. *The Communist Manifesto*. 1848. Trans. Samuel Moore. Harmondsworth: Penguin, 1967.

Mondal, Anshuman A. "*The Ground Beneath Her Feet* and *Fury:* The Reinvention of Location." *The Cambridge Companion to Salman Rushdie*. Ed. Abdulrazak Gurnah. Cambridge: Cambridge UP, 2007. 169–183.

Morton, Stephen. *Salman Rushdie*. Hampshire and New York: Palgrave Macmillan, 2008.

Rushdie, Salman. *Fury*. London: Vintage, 2001.

_____. *The Ground Beneath Her Feet*. London: Vintage, 1999.

_____. *Midnight's Children*. 1981. London: Knopf, 1995.

_____. *The Satanic Verses*. London: Viking, 1988.

Said, Edward W. *Culture & Imperialism*. London: Vintage, 1993.

Sandru, Cristina. "Visual Technologies in Rushdie's Fiction." *Salman Rushdie and Visual Culture: Celebrating Impurity, Disrupting Borders*. Ed. Ana Cristina Mendes. New York and London: Routledge, 2012. 139–157.

From Salman Rushdie to Arundhati Roy: Issues of Continuity in Indian Fiction in English____

Anuradha Marwah

A Celebrated Landmark Publication

The publication of Salman Rushdie's *Midnight's Children* in 1981 has been widely considered as a landmark event. Along with the acclaim brought by the Booker Prize, it became the debut of Indian fiction in English on the world stage. For the first time, the entire English-speaking world celebrated a novel about India written in deliberate Indian English by a writer with an Indian name. The postcolonial sections especially marked it as a triumph of David over Goliath because, by winning one of the biggest literary awards, Rushdie seemed to pose a challenge to the Eurocentric literary establishment. This sentiment was echoed when Bill Ashcroft, Gareth Griffiths, and Helen Tiffin used the title of Rushdie's essay "The Empire Writes Back with a Vengeance" (1982) as the title for their theoretical work, *The Empire Writes Back: Theory and Practice in Postcolonial Literature* (1989). Their book is one of the earliest and most significant expositions of literatures being written in former colonies. It may be concluded that when it was published, *Midnight's Children* was widely received as a paradigmatic postcolonial text with an emancipative agenda. However, today, we find an ironic reversal of that reputation in significant quarters, like Left-oriented criticism.

Pranav Jani's book-length critical study of the Indian novel in English *Decentering Rushdie: Cosmopolitanism and the Indian Novel in English* (2012), for instance, makes a persuasive case for the need to de-center Rushdie in order to appreciate the variety and nuances of other Indian postcolonial writings. In his book, Jani critiques *Midnight's Children* as the key text that facilitated the collapse of postcolonial theory into postmodernism and compromised its subversive agenda (Jani 19). Jani's thesis is the full theoretical elaboration of various charges leveled against Rushdie through the

---

nineties by various Left-inclined critics. For instance, Aijaz Ahmad, in an influential essay, had lashed out at Rushdie's postmodern claim of "belonging nowhere because he belongs everywhere" and condemned his marking out the area of imagination as a kind of "supermarket of packaged and commodified cultures, ready to be consumed" (Ahmad 127–128). Timothy Brennan, too, criticized Rushdie for facilitating the commodification of cosmopolitanism and conversion of third-world politics itself into a source of aesthetic play (Brennan). Various India-based nativist critics, whose points of view I summarize later, similarly alleged that the diasporic Rushdie set himself up as a native informant without adequate knowledge of regional Indian languages or commitment and loyalty to the mother-country.

This chapter discusses the schizophrenic status of *Midnight's Children* as an emancipative text and a "dishonest" text with reference to the symbolic value of Rushdie as a celebrity-intellectual. It also contrasts Rushdie's career with that of Arundhati Roy's, who may be regarded as the second international writer-celebrity that India has produced and whose novel *The God of Small Things* Jani valorizes in his study. In this essay's view, literary texts by writer-celebrities pose problems of interpretation that have a great deal to do with changing political situations and the authors' orientation and acceptability.

Rushdie in India

In India, *Midnight's Children* was welcomed warmly in the beginning. It was an instant bestseller. In 1984, a commentator noted, with regard to the popularity of *Midnight's Children*: "Publishers claim that the novel has sold four thousand copies in hardcover, and forty-five thousand in paperback (in addition to the pirated editions); these sales figures are unprecedented for an Indian-English novelist" (Narayan 79). As the relative smallness of this "unprecedented" sales figure indicates, it is clear that the constituency for Indian fiction in English in India of the eighties was the minuscule English speaking elite. It needs to be added that Rushdie's novel may have already broadened this constituency beyond the comprador.

Some sections of Indian society were still mentally colonized to the extent that they considered anything Indian to be second-class and proved somewhat resistant to Rushdie's flamboyantly 'bastardized' sensibilities. David Davidar, who is credited with revolutionizing fiction publishing in India as the Chief Editor at Penguin India in the late eighties and nineties, shares an anecdote to establish that there was discomfort with Rushdie's Indian English in the beginning and that writing *Midnight's Children* was a kind of literary activism on his part. In Bombay after his triumphant Booker in 1983, Rushdie was accosted by a young woman who worked for *The Times of India*:

'Mr Rushdie', she said loudly, 'I bought your novel ages ago but haven't finished it.' Rushdie was only half-listening but her next sentence commanded his full attention. 'It's written in such a strange way with all these Indian words and all. I couldn't get past page 23' (Davidar 97).

However, most Indian English speakers were enthused by the freedom from the Queen's English that *Midnight's Children*'s success signaled. It seemed to release the floodgates of creativity for a lot of younger writers. The impact of the creative and commercial legacy of *Midnight's Children* slowly and surely became palpable. Indian fiction in English, which was at best a trickle in the seventies, became like a fast-flowing river within fifteen years of its publication.

The publishing scene was also changing for the better and Rushdie's status as the first global Indian novelist definitely played a role in it. With the setting up of Penguin Books India (1987) and Ravi Dayal Publisher (1989), and along with older publishers like Rupa and Co., Roli and others, a lot of Indian English fiction began to see the light of day. In the late eighties, and spilling over to the nineties, the Indian writer in English, cast in Rushdie's mould, became a familiar figure in the Indian metropolis. Rushdie's influence may be read in the career and works of I. Allan Sealy, Amitav Ghosh, Shashi Tharoor, Mukul Kesavan, Vikram Chandra, Vikram Seth, and Nina Sibal, all of whom explore the individual's relationship with the nation. Rushdie has been credited with spearheading the big national allegory in Indian writing in English.

However, the Children of *Midnight's Children*—as the writers who had followed in Rushdie's wake were being called—although numerically more than the earlier generation of Indian writers—still belonged to a very small social and intellectual clique. In fact, all except one writer named above had graduated from the small and select St. Stephen's College of Delhi University (Vikram Chandra studied in an American University). Many Indian critics targeted the affluent backgrounds of these 'Stephanians' (Gandhi), and their lack of knowledge about rural and provincial hinterlands of the country: it was alleged that the Indian postcolonial literature being produced to great acclaim was hopelessly elitist and excluded the majority of the country from its concerns.

It did not help that in 1997, Rushdie declared himself the mentor of the new literature and proclaimed in print—via an essay in *The New Yorker* that went on to become the introduction to the anthology he edited with Elizabeth West—that Indian literature in English was "stronger and more important" than what has been written in all other Indian languages since India's independence in 1947 (Rushdie, *Vintage Book of Indian Writing* 50). Predictably, this ill-informed and arrogant view brought forth an avalanche of criticism from Indian critics and writers and paved the way for his ultimate rejection by the Indian intelligentsia.

However, all Indian critics were not united in dismissing Rushdie. Compiling a book of readings on *Midnight's Children* the Indian critic Meenakshi Mukherjee balances the praise and blame of two decades in her introduction: "But even the critics in India who were not particularly impressed by Rushdie's novel and who disputed its claim to be categorized as 'Indian' cannot now deny that its influence on younger writers confers on *Midnight's Children* a retrospective importance" (Mukherjee 11). In one of the essays anthologized by Mukherjee, the literary scholar Josna Rege underlines the significance of *Midnight's Children* for the Indian novel in English and explains that Rushdie's reputation underwent a change in India from the eighties, when he first published and was received enthusiastically, to the late nineties, when, in a bid to reclaim centrality and due to his "own feelings of rejection and displacement from India," he laid a claim to India by asserting that the new writing in English has a preeminent place in the country. Rege cites several domestic and international reasons for India's rejection of Rushdie, the most important among them being the rise of sub-nationalisms in India and elsewhere that enervated the nation state and the 1989 Irani *fatwa* (Rege 188). Rege reminds us that *Midnight's Children* needs to be seen in an ideological context before Prime Minister Indira Gandhi's assassination by her Sikh bodyguards in 1984; the challenge posed to the nation-state by the intensified globalization of the 1990s; and contemporary intellectual critique of nationalism and political fragmentation of the large, universalizing nation-state (Rege 185). Mukherjee succinctly summarizes Rege's assessment of Rushdie's ideological position while he was writing *Midnight's Children*:

> [Reg]e also sees a basic ambivalence at the heart of the novel, because like his creation Saleem, Rushdie is formed by the ideals of Nehru and Congress when the country was new and full of hope. As a left-leaning student of history he recognizes intellectually the limitations of the idea of the nation he has inherited, and he critiques it; but he has an emotional investment in this ideal of a secular and plural India and fears its disintegration (Mukherjee 26).

This is very far from the postmodern vagrancy and lack of rootedness that have been attributed to Rushdie by Brennan, Ahmad, and Jani.

It is undeniable that *Midnight's Children* is a significant book and also true that there is little Rushdie could have done differently to save himself from the bizarre death sentence that was pronounced on him by the Ayatollah. The *fatwa* perforce metamorphosed Rushdie, the outspoken critic of British racism and the literary champion of postcolonial subversions, into a fugitive from Islamic fundamentalism and an asylum seeker with the white, erstwhile colonial power. It also served to harden the Orientalist distinction between "Western liberalism" and "Eastern (Islamic) intolerance" in various Western discourses and also, perhaps, in Rushdie's mind.

When the death threat was lifted in 1998, Rushdie's relief and delight to be free in an anonymous Western metropolis began to find expression even in his political commentary. Coinciding with and subsequent to his shift to New York in 2000, as postcolonial critic Ruvani Ranasinha points out, Rushdie (like Christopher Hitchens and some other Western intellectuals) went on to make several controversial statements in support of the "authority of the United States as the best current guarantor of 'freedom' against 'tyranny, bigotry, intolerance, fanaticism'" (Ranasinha 55). She notes that this is "a striking shift in his politics" and "contrasts sharply with his critique of American imperialism in his non-fictional work *The Jaguar Smile* based on a three-week stay in Nicaragua in 1986" (Ranasinha 55).

With Rushdie's alleged support for the Iraq war and various controversial articles that suggest a tacit understanding on his part of the Right-wing Islamophobia in the United States, it has become increasingly difficult for a Left-inclined reader to accept *Midnight's Children* as a text that empowers the margins. Although Rushdie has denied the conservative shift in his world view and tried to justify his statements, it seems incomprehensible that the author, who wrote *Midnight's Children* as a self-consciously anti-colonial novel, should accept knighthood from the British queen in 2007, or that after making such a strong case for Nehruvian secularism and identifying Hindu fundamentalism as the major threat to the Indian nation, he should be unable to recognize the reactionary import of his pro-American statements. The tendency among some critics is to identify a continuum of conservatism and view his earlier work through the lens of the present.

1997 and the Dethroning of Rushdie

However, it has to be remembered that reputations of writers are primarily constructed in a field where the media plays a pre-eminent and sometimes decisive role and commercial interests are paramount. In the last two decades, the global market has started to intrude to an unprecedented degree in the making and remaking of literary reputations.

In 1997, Rushdie's reputation as the first global Indian writer faced a major challenge from another writer, Arundhati Roy, whose debut novel *The God of Small Things* had garnered phenomenal publicity even before being published. Starting out as the biggest thing to happen to Indian fiction in English after Rushdie, Roy was soon being celebrated as the first authentic Indian writer to win the Booker. It has been argued that Roy played the market consummately and in fact defeated Rushdie at his own game. However, their careers follow very different or even diametrically opposite trajectories. Whereas Rushdie moved from a Left-oriented position to becoming an apologist for American imperialism, Roy, with her activist writings, has been one of the most vociferous critics of American foreign policy and emerged as a celebrated icon of the Left. Their political position-taking runs parallel with their literary reputations and, to my mind, the complete concurrence of literary criticism with the authors' current media profiles raises some issues regarding our practice of reading literary texts.

In the beginning, Roy was predictably posited as a legitimate successor to Rushdie. The marketing campaign for *The God of Small Things* began with Rushdie's blessings and Roy, photographed "squeezed between Vikram Chandra and Anita Desai, laughing playfully as Salman Rushdie rests a supportive hand on her shoulder," was clearly, "the chosen one, crown princess to the throne of Indian fiction" (Squires 143). This is a reference to the famous photograph, taken in London, of eleven Indian writers in *The New Yorker* double issue on Indian fiction of June 1997.

However, too soon, the new product, *The God of Small Things*, began to be challenged by the established reputation of Rushdie as the grandfather of Indian fiction. To begin with, some reviewers and admirers of Rushdie felt that Roy's debut just did not match up to the older writer's achievements. Squires notes: "Rushdie's role in Roy's fairytale threatened to transmogrify from godfather into ogre" (Squires 143). In Squires's submission, Roy did something extremely savvy by mounting a surprise attack on the potential ogre. She scored a point over Rushdie by stressing the fact that, unlike him, she lives in India. Squires quotes from Jason Cowley (17), "an emphatic Roy supporter":

> She (Roy) says: 'When I was in America I went on a couple of TV shows with Rushdie. And he said (she borrows the voice of an officious schoolmaster) 'The trouble with Arundhati is that she insists that India is an ordinary place.' Well, I ask, 'Why the hell not?' It is my ordinary life. The difference between me and Rushdie begins there' (Squires 144-145).

The point of Roy being a more authentic Indian as she lives here was picked up by many admirers. In the words of Shobha De, a novelist herself: "It is the first time a true Indian, a home-grown product who has not lived or worked in the West or looks to it for inspiration, has won" (Cooper 1). Reviewing *The God of Small Things*, the feminist critic Ruth Vanita wrote:

> When I read the first sentence, 'May in Ayemenem is a hot, brooding month', I thought this was going to be yet another exotic postcolonial novel about the land of heat and dust, incense and spices. But *The God of Small Things* rapidly reveals its disinterest in trying to encapsulate India, and its complete immersion in one community's, one family's universe (Vanita 32).

The disparaging references to Rushdie's diasporic status and the national allegory he had patented are unmistakable in these extracts. However, a question needs to be asked at this point: Was there indeed such a difference between Rushdie and the writers who came after him and Roy's contexts for the latter to be designated the more authentic Indian? Or was it as in Squires's gentle criticism, "the ungenerous critic might hint that she [Roy] is point-scoring by claiming that she lives nearer the pickle factory" (Squires 145)?

From the media reports and interviews of the time, it would seem that *The God of Small Things* was sui generis. The media projected Roy's unconventional lifestyle as a hippie turned actress turned aerobics instructor turned writer to establish that the novel was a phenomenon, a perfect literary gem whose creation was by more than human agency. In several interviews, Roy, too, spoke of not being very educated and thereby different from other well-known Indian writers in English. Padmini Mongia, who has studied extensively the marketing of Indian literature, is frankly impatient with the blatant misinformation campaign that was launched to establish Roy as a naive practitioner of fiction: "Repeatedly stressing claims of an unknown writer making it big, the media largely ignored the fact that Roy was by no means an unknown, and in her connections and allegiances was very well connected to a powerful elite in New Delhi and in the UK" (Mongia 109).

Her fairly high-profile journalistic writings—prior to the publication of the novel—are glossed over in media anxiety to build her up as a daughter of the soil. It is clear that to emphasize the home-grown quality of her writing was predicated upon her being an unschooled genius, and a willful suppression of facts was required. Roy, by refusing to acknowledge any influences on her work and by repeatedly claiming that she never rewrote a single sentence of her book, fuelled the myth.

It has been persuasively argued that Roy's novel situates her as a practitioner of postmodern, postcolonial fiction, much in the fashion of Rushdie and other children of *Midnight's Children. The God of Small Things* is a self-consciously literary text that attempts to interrogate the 'big' national allegory by prioritizing the small in its very title. Roy's language is experimental and as much a literary construction as that of Rushdie. Besides, the text also evokes and challenges colonialist constructions of India in its theme. Several literary critics have discussed *The God of Small Things* as part of the tradition of contemporary—Rushdiesque—Indian fiction in English. It would be difficult to situate it in any other way except by marking it out as "unique" among contemporary Indian English novels as Jani does with reference to what he deems as its national rootedness. In his submission, *The God of Small Things* is closer in spirit to the works of the earlier generation of Indian women writers like Nayantara Sahgal and Anita Desai (Jani 194). However, he too concedes that *The God of Small Things* is similar to post-national novels like *Midnight's Children* in being "magic realist" and in "its representation of Indian spaces as sites of suffering, despair, and loss" (Jani 195).

After *The God of Small Things*, Roy went on to write a series of political essays and is today a significant public intellectual. In Jani's summation: "Fiercely critical of Western nations for corporate globalization and imperialist wars—but also of postcolonial states for their complicity in the neo-liberal project—Roy has developed a unique perspective and emerged as one of the most prominent public intellectuals of the international Left in the first decade of the twenty-first century" (Jani 192). Jani's analysis of *The God of Small Things* is intended to situate it in the ideological context of Roy's activist writings.

However, *The God of Small Things* may be so situated only if the making and marketing of Roy in 1997 is overlooked in the analysis of the novel. As suggested above, the mode of production of the novel is contrary to the activist spirit that is being attributed to it retrospectively. Published in 1997 to coincide with the worldwide celebration of fifty years of India's independence, *The God of Small Things* occupied the same platform as Rushdie and West's anthology *The Vintage Book of Indian Writing* and was one of the objects tastefully displayed to sell the newly liberalized nation to the globe. *The God of Small Things* occupied that platform because, due to its imagery and writing style, it could be read as imaging an India at least as exotic as that of Rushdie's *Midnight's Children.*

Explaining the strategy by which Indian writers have succeeded in the West in his book *The Post Colonial Exotic: Marketing the Margins*, Graham Huggan observes: "The success of writers like Rushdie and, more recently, Arundhati Roy owes to the skill with which they manipulate commercially viable metropolitan codes" (Huggan 81). Huggan explains the "strategic exoticism" of these writers by showing how their works critique, but simultaneously also reconfirm, "an exoticising imperial gaze" (Huggan 81). Huggan, Mongia, and several other critics discuss Roy as responding to the demands of the global market by writing a lush and sexy novel that deploys well-established Orientalist tropes of the Indian beauty myth and India as a primal tourist destination.

In fact, the irony is that a case can be made to establish how the market was more instrumental in the making of the author's reputation in Roy's case than in Rushdie's. Studying the two moments in the history of the Booker Prize, Sandra Ponzanesi argues that, whereas Rushdie managed to reach star allure due to his flamboyant personality and cross-cultural elite upbringing by playing the game of the culture industry, he did so only *after* winning the Booker. In Roy's case, the marketing offensive started much earlier, even before the book was published. Ponzanesi puts the reasons for the unprecedented hype around Roy down to the changes in the publishing industry:

> The thumping economic advance conferred on Roy had not only to do with the fact that a new star on the occasion of India's fiftieth anniversary of independence (Rushdie was by then a bit worn out as an Indian icon) had to be created, but also with the fact that publishing houses by then had entered into an interconnected system. They now had to operate in terms of the modalities of multinationals, which at the end of the day meant succeeding in the task of bidding high enough to hook an author before another company did (Ponzanesi 9).

Thus, *The God of Small Things* and Roy acquired a formidable international reputation for literary subversion and activism in the same way that Rushdie did with the publication of *Midnight's Children*.

In both cases, the market played an important role. Where Rushdie continued to deploy fiction in the same manner—and encountered a major hurdle to his life and purpose as a writer by way of the *fatwa*, Roy turned away from fiction to intervene directly in social and political processes via her political essays. The two writers occupy distinctly different political and literary spaces today. Their key texts thus pose a major challenge to the reader who seeks to find in literature a social orientation and political message. How indeed should we read *Midnight's Children* and *The God of Small Things* today?

Reading *Midnight's Children* Today

From the above, it may seem this essay is going to prioritize the text over the context and make a case for reading *Midnight's Children* as an emancipative text on the basis of its form, style, or use of language. The essay is, in fact, going to emphasize that context is most important, and a text has to be read in terms of what it does in its historical context. This—and this point is crucial—might necessitate the separation of what we know about the author today from what the author stood for when the work was first published.

The Marxist critic Terry Eagleton emphasizes that the literary text should be read as the "product of the "complex historical articulations" of various structures. He proposes (Eagleton 62–70) the following comprehensive schema for interpretation of literary texts:

(i) General mode of production
(ii) Literary mode of production
(iii) General ideology
(iv) Authorial ideology
(v) Aesthetic ideology
(vi) Text

If we were to use this schema to understand *Midnight's Children*, we might indeed reach a conclusion that is at variance with Rushdie's contemporary political position. This essay has already touched upon the history of the Indian novel in English and the liberative change that *Midnight's Children* has been credited with bringing in it. It remains to be added that *Midnight's Children* was also an important liberative political novel in the subcontinent.

The Emergency imposed by India's then Prime Minister Indira Gandhi from June 26, 1975 to March 21, 1977 was independent India's bleakest period as far as freedom of expression is concerned. Many dissenting writers and intellectuals were imprisoned and persecuted in this period. Rushdie's outspoken criticism of the machinations of the "Widow" therefore expressed the anger and disappointment of many progressive Indians against the state of Indian politics. Indira Gandhi's authoritarianism was further exacerbated by her shifting away from the affirmative Nehruvian practice of prioritizing the interests of Indian minorities like Muslims and Dalits. Many political commentators have pointed out that, after the Emergency, appeasing Hindu sensibilities to win votes became the practice of the Congress party. As a progressive Indian Muslim, Rushdie identifies and critiques this trend astutely in *Midnight's Children.*

Marxist theorists have been the earliest to point out that "meaning" of a literary text is inextricably tied up with its mode of production. Eagleton, for instance, observes: "Every literary text intimates by its very conventions the way it is to be consumed, encodes within itself its own ideology of how, by whom and for whom it was produced" (Eagleton 62). Thus, the time and circumstances of the publication of a text—its market—is of utmost importance. Many critics—including Left-oriented critics like Jani—do not deal systematically with market-processes in their analysis of literary texts. It is not surprising because, as indicated by the above-described battle for the throne of Indian fiction in English, it is obvious that the market also deals in half-truths and sometimes in outright lies. It is difficult to reconcile its cynicism and lack of scruples with the creative impulses of literature. However, most writers and especially writer-celebrities have to negotiate the media and the market extensively. Both Rushdie and Roy have not only written bestsellers, but they are also endlessly provocative and keep themselves in the news. Their sales-conscious spirit would have to be juxtaposed continuously with the activist achievements of their texts to analyze their political value.

The above is also meant to suggest that *Midnight's Children* should not to be read uncritically. Jani's argument regarding Rushdie's elitism and failure to represent the subaltern—especially the subaltern woman—are substantive and need to be grappled with; so do Ahmad and Brennan's discomfort with the commodification of Indian fiction that Rushdie (accidentally) facilitated. However, these issues would need to be qualified by the ideology, in which the writer was operating and also the ideology, in which global Indian fiction in English and a lot of bestselling literary fiction continues to operate.

It is also important to keep in mind that Rushdie's literary career was rudely interrupted by a very real death-threat. That his contemporary author-avatar should be starkly different from the earlier one may be regrettable, but then may have very little to do with the text of his previous life discussed here.

Works Cited

Ahmad, Aijaz. "Salman Rushdie's *Shame*: Postmodern Migrancy and the Representation of Women." *In Theory: Classes, Nations, Literatures*. Aijaz Ahmad. London: Verso, 1992. 123–158.

Ashcroft, Bill, Gareth Griffiths, and Helen Tiffin. *The Empire Writes Back: Theory and Practice in Postcolonial Literature*. London: Routledge, 1989.

Brennan, Timothy. *At Home in the World: Cosmopolitanism Now*. Cambridge, MA: Harvard UP, 1997.

Cooper, Jason. "For India, No Small Thing: Native Daughter Arundhati Roy Wins Coveted Booker Prize." *Washington Post* 20 Oct. (1997).

Davidar, David. "Stars of India's Newest Literature." *The Book Industry in India: Context, Challenge and Strategy*. Ed Sukumar Das. New Delhi: The Federation of Publishers' and Booksellers' Associations in India, 2004. 97–103.

Eagleton, Terry. "Ideology, Fiction, Narrative." *Social Text* 2 (1979): 62–80.

Gandhi, Leela . "Indo-Anglian Fiction: Writing India, Elite Aesthetics, and the Rise of the 'Stephanian' Novel. *Australian Humanities Review* Nov.–Jan. (1997–1998). *AHR*. Web. 20 Dec. 2013.

Huggan, Graham. *The Postcolonial Exotic: Marketing the Margins*. London: Routledge, 2001.

Jani, Pranav. *Decentering Rushdie: Cosmopolitanism and the Indian Novel in English*. New Delhi: Orient Blackswan, 2012.

Mongia Padmini. "The Making and Marketing of Arundhati Roy." *Arundhati Roy's* The God of Small Things. Ed. Alex Tickell. London: Routledge, 2007. 103–109.

Mukherjee, Meenakshi. "Introduction." *Rushdie's* Midnight's Children: *A Book of Readings*. Ed. Meenakshi Mukherjee. New Delhi: Pencraft International, 1999. 9–27.

Narayan, Shyamala. "1983 Bibliography." *Journal of Commonwealth Literature* 19.2. (1984): 79–82.

Ponzanesi, Sandra. "Boutique Postcolonialism: Literary Awards, Cultural Value and the Canon." *Fiction and Literary Prizes in Great Britain.* Ed. Holger Klein and Wolfgang Görtschacher. Vienna: Praesens Verlag, 2006. 107–134.

Ranasinha, Ruvani. "The *Fatwa* and its Aftermath." *The Cambridge Companion to Salman Rushdie.* Ed. Abdulrazak Gurnah. Cambridge: Cambridge UP, 2007. 45–59.

Rushdie, Salman. "The Empire Writes Back with a Vengeance." *The Times* 3 July (1982): 8.

_____. "Life and Letters: Damme, This Is the Oriental Scene for You!" *The New Yorker* 23–30 June (1997): 50–61.

Rushdie, Salman and Elizabeth West. *Vintage Book of Indian Writing 1947–1997.* New York: Vintage, 1997.

Rege, Josna. "Victim into Protagonist: *Midnight's Children* and the Post-Rushdie National Narratives of the Eighties." *Rushdie's Midnight's Children: A Book of Readings.* Ed. Meenakshi Mukherjee. Delhi: Pencraft International, 1999. 182–211.

Squires, Claire. *Marketing Literature: The Making of Contemporary Writing in Britain.* London: Palgrave Macmillan, 2009.

Vanita, Ruth. "No Small Achievement: *The God of Small Things* by Arundhati Roy." *Manushi* 103 (Nov–Dec 1997): 32–33.

CRITICAL
READINGS

Nasal Connections: The Possibility of Ethical Deconstruction in *Midnight's Children*_____

Tuomas Huttunen

During the past 32 years, *Midnight's Children* has become the target of a multitude of studies through varying approaches. In this millennium, it has been treated, among other things, as a carnivalesque subversion of national collectivity (Bennett 177–194), a magical realist, postcolonial text (Upstone 260–284), a transnational narrative, and much more. Recently, it has also been treated as a cosmopolitan, postnational novel. Contemporary cosmopolitanism is characterized by cultural rootlessness, corresponding to "cultural identity rooted in individual experience rather than geographical location" (Jackson 109). It signifies a state of being that transcends nationally conceived borders by producing more flexible and varied forms of cultural identity. The cultural identity of each cosmopolitan person would thereby be unique, not affected by national rhetorics or geography. Ideally, this kind of identity free of geographical or national affiliations could then represent a quest for the narration of common humanity. According to Jon Binnie et al., the ethical nature of cosmopolitanism is evident in that it implies "a philosophy of world citizenship which simultaneously transcends the boundaries of the nation-state and descends to the scale of individual rights and responsibilities" (Binnie et al. 13). This is, of course, partly true concerning the narrator-protagonist of *Midnight's Children*, Saleem Sinai, who shuttles between India and Pakistan, is very much immersed in his individual ethics while writing his memoirs.

However, this more recent version of cosmopolitanism does not quite fit *Midnight's Children* as a whole because its protagonist and narrator is, before all, a nationalist. Despite Partition, religious and communal riots, Indo-Pakistani wars, and, finally, the Emergency, he never lets go of the original dream of Mahatma Gandhi and Jawaharlal Nehru for a Western-type, democratic and secular Indian nation. Further, his identity is not exactly flexible. It may be varied (he metaphorically holds within himself the whole of Indian people), but it is cracking apart "into specks of voiceless dust" (Rushdie 463; further references preceded by *MC*) alongside his body. It may be that *Midnight's Children* previously has been labeled cosmopolitan largely because its author, Salman Rushdie, can be considered a cosmopolitan. Rushdie the writer also often enters critiques that are ostensibly written about his novel, which can be deemed methodologically susceptible. Although the novel does share some of the more contemporary cosmopolitan concerns, such as the endeavor to construct a narrative of individual ethical responsibility, let's presume that it is predominantly nationalist and postmodernist in its concerns. It is, basically, a deconstruction of the national rhetoric through an ethical approach to language, truth, and reality. Postcoloniality in it is present rather as a temporal aspect than a strongly thematized struggle with the British heritage.

In his insightful work on cosmopolitanism in the Indian novel in English, Pranav Jani, a specialist in postcolonial literatures, makes a basic division of these novels into nationalist texts, which see the nation as an emancipatory force and call for solidarity and ethical commitment to the nationalist project, and to post-national novels. In nationalist novels, "agency (for characters and for the readers) emerges out of the ability to identify the processes of hegemony and dominance, and then to manipulate subject positions effectively in order to forge spaces for change" (Jani 8). In post-national novels, history and the adjacent power constructions are deemed so "overwhelming and transcendent that only the solitary, migrant, protagonist/storyteller/writer can have agency" (Jani 8). In Jani's view, the general change from nationalist to postnational novels coincides with the Emergency of 1975–1977, when the last remnants of the nationalist ideology delineated by Nehru and Gandhi were shattered. Despite its publication after the Emergency, *Midnight's Children* is in many ways a very nationalist novel. Saleem's longing for the original concept of a democratic, secular, and pluralistic state that Nehru and Gandhi represented is evident throughout the novel, although the narrative does relate the shattering of these ideals. Through his telepathic abilities, Saleem even establishes a conference, Midnight's Children's Conference (MCC), very similar to the Indian National Congress (INC) founded by Nehru and Gandhi. Saleems's birth is, of course, a metaphor for the birth of the nation. His person then goes through and reflects what happens to the nation during the thirty years after its birth.

This chapter looks at the ways in which the novel's narration deconstructs the official, established version of Indian national history. At the same time, the potentially ethical nature of this process comes under scrutiny. This essay will also try to find out how the adjacent question of agency is fulfilled in the novel. It is common knowledge that those within the hegemonic discourse have agency and power, but whether there can be such a thing as ethical agency in a narrative remains in doubt.

Literalization of Metaphors and the Relativity of Truth

Midnight's Children is renowned for narrator Saleem's extensive use of metaphors and his relation of magic-realist events. There are many magic realist features in the novel (think about the unbelievable talents of the children of midnight). Concerning metaphors, however, it seems that by describing events metaphorically, Saleem is actually making them literal. By this means he is deconstructing the heavily metaphorical national rhetoric from his single subject position, thereby making an ethical interruption into this hegemonic discourse. The idea of Saleem's literalization of national metaphors by introducing his own was originally put forward by Neil ten Kortenaar who writes that "Saleem's self-conscious thematization has the effect of heightening the events of national history and rendering them fantastic. Paradoxically, it does so, not by making the literal figurative but the reverse, by making literal the common metaphor implicit in national history of the nation as a person" (ten Kortenaar 32–33). In this way, Saleem's metaphors become literal, truthful metaphors of those advocated by the national rhetoric. The novel's magic becomes the literalization of the metaphorical (ten Kortenaar 63).

One of the tokens of the larger metaphor for the nation as a person is, as ten Kortenaar phares it, birth and the subsequent growth: "Historians speak of growth and maturity, as if the nation were a human child; of direction and progress and dangers, as if the nation were on a journey; of trauma and memory, desire and fear, as if the nation had a psychology" (ten Kortenaar 42). The same rhetoric presents Nehru as the father of the nation. Saleem's literalization of the metaphorical is not, however, restricted to national matters only. One of the more hilarious, although only partly nationally determined, examples of this is the scene where Ahmed Sinai's assets are frozen. He climbs up from his office shouting: "Amina! Come here wife! The bastards have shoved my balls in an ice-bucket!" (*MC* 135). Amina leads Ahmed to their bedroom to calm her husband down, but when caressing him she exclaims: "'Oh my goodness, Janum, I thought you were just talking dirty but it's true! So cold, Allah, so coooold, like little round cubes of ice!'" (*MC* 136). Here, the metaphor of freezing the family assets is made literal and concrete.

On a larger scale, the particular version of official Indian history that Saleem is literalizing and thereby deconstructing is Stanley Wolpert's *A New History of India* (1977). The whole of the novel is characterized by sudden insertions from this work. In these instances, the narratorial voice changes, as Saleem paraphrases sections from Wolpert's book, which, of course, is written in the matter-of-fact language appropriate for a serious historian. Sometimes, these sections are preceded or followed by Saleem's own versions of the same events, but in other instances, they function as a general background to what is happening in Saleem's personal life. A more extensive study on the correlations between *Midnight's Children* and Wolpert's history of India has been conducted by David Lipscomb, who lists the insertion on pages 205–206 of the novel as a typical example of Wolpert's text intruding on Saleem's own voice (Lipscomb 170–171). The sequence, which has to do with the simultaneous occurrence of Saleem's tenth birthday and the failure of the second Five Year Plan, is paraphrased from Wolpert's history and inserted into the narrative in parentheses. The only significant difference from Wolpert's text seems to be that Saleem retains his position as the first-person participant narrator, a quality that Wolpert naturally could not adopt in his history. This is, of course, an instance of typically postmodernist historiographic metafiction à la Linda Hutcheon, but it is illuminating to observe where Saleem's targets for literalization come from.

As far as narrative technique is concerned, the novel is clearly an offspring of the 'linguistic turn' brought about by the post-structuralist philosophers during the 1970s: it conceives the reality as constructed by various linguistic arrangements. The literal, real, reality becomes meaningless and truth comes to lie in words. The "point is not that there is no truth, but that there is no literal level of truth. The literal is always already a fiction. But the truth lies in fiction" (tcn Kortenaar 40). Similarly, as Saleem observes: "Reality can have metaphorical content; that does not make it less real" (*MC* 200). Truth, reality, and memory are all connected as linguistic constructions, in other words, as narratives: "'I told you the truth,' I say yet again, 'Memory's truth, because memory has its own special kind. It selects, eliminates, alters, exaggerates, minimizes, glorifies, and vilifies also; but in the end it creates its own reality, its heterogeneous but usually coherent version of events'" (*MC* 211). Furthermore, everyone needs to believe in his or her own structure and own narrative version of the past.

Thus, for Saleem, there are numerous narrative (linguistic) truths that are equally valid, but there is no one ultimate literal truth that can be reached through narration. As shown above, there are several references to the relativity of truth as well as the relationship between truth and reality in the novel. Among them is the following on the relationship between illusion and reality:

> Reality is a question of perspective; the further you get from the past, the more concrete and plausible it seems—but as you approach the present, it inevitably seems more and more incredible. Suppose yourself in a larger cinema, sitting at first in the back row, and gradually moving up, row by row, until your nose is almost pressed against the screen. Gradually the stars' faces dissolve into dancing grain; tiny details assume grotesque proportions; the illusion dissolves—or rather, it becomes clear that the illusion itself *is* reality... (*MC* 165–166, emphasis and ellipsis original).

Later, Saleem "waxes rhetorical" on the question of truth and reality and begins to explain the metaphysics of the universe to Padma by telling her that:

> Hindus accept [...] that the world is a kind of dream; that Brahma dreamed, is dreaming the universe; that we only see dimly through that dream-web, which is Maya. Maya [...] may be defined as all that is illusory; as trickery, artifice, and deceit. Apparitions, phantasms, mirages, sleight-of-hand, the seeming form of things: all these are parts of Maya (*MC* 211).

Here, Saleem is naturally speaking of his own trickery with language, which corresponds to Maya. The real reality, which is Brahma's dream, is concealed by Maya's web (corresponding to language), which only shows us alternating forms and apparitions. This is, of course, tantamount to the poststructuralist ontology: that language is all we have—it is all we see; it is Maya's web. *Midnight's Children* is a postmodern novel in the sense that at least it applies the poststructuralist philosophies of language that lie behind the postmodern condition. This is something that its metafictionally conditioned narrator is well aware of: "If I say that certain things took place that you, lost in Brahma's dream, find hard to believe, then which of us is right?" (*MC* 211).

In preparation for the coming nation, Gandhi chose religion as the source of interconnection between Indians, but compiled his "own eclectic and pluralistic morality" out of various religious traditions (Khilnani 154). Gandhi believed that a nation without history is a happy nation—he distrusted the typical Western nationalist history: nationalists wanted "to construct a reliable future out of a selected past" (Khilnani 164). To this he preferred the legends and stories of popular religious traditions: a heterogeneous religious morality that was to act as glue between people (Khilnani 164). This is reminiscent of the trick that Saleem is using against Padma in the section about Maya. He is trying to convince her that what he is writing is true, is at least one truth, and he does this by invoking a common religious myth about the creation of the universe and setting it beside his attempts at creating his. Heterogeneous religious morality is, of course, also something that Saleem would like the MCC to develop later.

Nasal Ethics—Connections Beyond Language

Despite the prevailing relativity of truth, there is one reference to a kind of unattainable, ultimate truth, which is emphasized in the original text by the use of italics: "'What's real and what's true aren't necessarily the same.' *True*, for me, was from my earliest days something hidden inside the stories Mary Pereira told me [...]. *True* was a thing concealed just over the horizon towards which the fisherman's finger pointed in the picture on my wall, while the young Raleigh listened to his tales" (*MC* 79). This penultimate truth, then, is somewhere within stories and pictures, but it cannot be achieved through language: it is just beyond our reach. It is, in other words, transcendent. This brings us close to ethics, and meta-ethics, and what came to be called the 'ethical turn' in the literary studies of the late 1990s.

In 1998, philosophers C. A. J. Coady and Seumas Miller expressed the developments in the field of ethics in relationship to literary studies as follows:

> One of the striking features of contemporary literary theory, and indeed cultural studies more generally, is what might be termed its socio-politicisation of the ethical. Literary texts, traditionally viewed as repositories of moral and aesthetic insight or challenge, tend now to be seen as predominantly ideological constructions, or sites of power struggles between social powers of various kinds (Coady and Miller 201).

Ethics came to be seen as a counterforce to language, especially hegemonic discourses, and, in the novel, as an ethically aware genre. As the literary theorist, Andrew Gibson, expresses it, the novel "presents us with individuality and diversity alike without any attempt to reduce either to the terms of a singular scheme of totality" (Gibson 8), totality here corresponding to the established national history. In Saleem's narration, socially incommensurable entities turn into expressions of the ethics of pluralism. This happens by intertwining individual people from vastly different backgrounds with the characteristics of the surrounding society, thereby creating heterogeneous wholes.

The most notable, heterogeneous whole in the novel is, of course, Saleem's head. Just seconds before his nose starts to 'function' in the bathroom in his mother's unwitting presence, he had a "mind filled with thoughts which have no shape, tormented by ideas which refuse to settle into words" (*MC* 161). And then this voice begins to sing in a deafening and terrifying many-tongued noise inside his head (*MC* 162). Saleem becomes a kind of radio transmitter. At first, he can only hear voices, "a headful of gabbling tongues, like an untuned radio" (*MC* 163). Shortly afterwards, he learns to control the voices, to select individual voices, and eventually can turn the whole apparatus off inside his head. He is, at this stage, essentially a radio. Conveniently, at the same time these voices, which are "profane, and as multitudinous, as dust" (*MC* 168), occur inside Saleem's head, there are language marches demanding the partition of the state of Bombay along linguistic boundaries (*MC* 167).

Ethics in the novel is represented and symbolized through Saleem's nose. It is the nose that allows him to enter other peoples' dreams, to develop a form of telepathy, and to smell things that could not be expressed through words, such as emotions and sentiments, and even more comprehensive aspects of people, like their morals and ethics. The nose enables him to establish connections that are not linguistic, but ethical. He is, after a considerable amount of rehearsing, finally able to develop his nasal skills to the extreme and has an epiphany: "I understood that my work must, if it was to have any value, acquire a moral dimension; that the only important divisions were the infinitely subtle gradations of good and evil smells. Having realized the crucial nature of morality, having sniffed out that smells could be sacred or profane, I invited [...] the science of *nasal ethics*" (318, emphasis added). He even discerns "the olfactory incompatibility of Islam and socialism" (318).

There is, then, a discernible tension in the narrative between post-structuralist tenets on textuality and ethical tendencies. The novel exhibits a confusing conglomeration of the linguistic strategies of both universal humanism and postmodernism. There is a postmodern recognition of the treachery of words, but at the same time, there are also references to ethical humanist ideals. The implication here is that this tension is a product of the simultaneous application of approaches very close to ethics, on the one hand, and deconstruction on the other. Saleem is deconstructing the official, established, narrative of Indian history (here, Wolpert's version), by setting himself as the agent, or participant, in many nationally important events. In the following examination of this merger, the general outlines follow those put forward by Adam Newton in his *Narrative Ethics*:

> Ethical answerability here is not a flattened prescription for action; it is not a moral recipe book. Nor is deconstruction an indifference to answerability; it is at its best a scrupulous hesitation, an extreme care occasioned by the treachery of words and the danger of easy answers (Newton 37).

Deconstruction and Ethics

Indisputably, the foremost philosopher in the meta-ethical domain of the 2000s has been Emmanuel Levinas, who criticized the ontological assumptions of Western philosophy. Levinas holds that the other is appropriated by the self, because the self is the producer of meaning to the world. The alterity, or ultimate otherness, of the Other is beyond the cognitive abilities of the self and can therefore never be fully reached by consciousness. In simple words, the Other exists beyond the notion that everything can be expressed comprehensively and fully through linguistic representation (Levinas). Consequently, the Other, as well as that which is ethical, cannot ultimately be described discursively, but they are transcendental. The self can only 'know' things by projecting on them through language what it already contains in itself. Knowledge, then, involves the linguistic appropriation of the object of knowing. This, of course, is precisely what Saleem is doing with his narrative rearrangement of the past. His constant worries about getting everything right, and whether he is to be trusted as a narrator in the first place, let us know that he is aware of this ethical problem involved in the political power inherent in all language use.

According to Levinas, communication has two dimensions, which he refers to as *Saying* and the *Said* (Levinas 34–51). The Said represents the surface level, where we use language to communicate themes, ideas, and observations to one another. When Saleem begins to use his ability to hear a multitude of voices in his head (his telepathy, as he expresses it), he is the level of language and linguistic communication: "In the beginning, when I was content to be an audience—before I began to *act*—there was a language problem. The voices babbled in everything from Malayalam to Naga dialects, from the purity of Lucknow Urdu to the Southern slurrings of Tamil. I understood only a fraction of the things being said within the walls of my skull" (*MC* 168, emphasis in the original).

Saying, however, is the ethical dimension where the genuine encounter with the other ideally takes place. Saying is pre-discursive, and although it leaves a trace in the Said, it has its own significance that cannot be represented within the Said: "Saying states and thematizes the Said, but signifies it to the other, a neighbor, with a signification that has to be distinguished from that borne by words in the Said" (Levinas 46). Saying, then, cannot be contained within the Said, which is the dimension of linguistic 'knowing' and narrative. In the words of the philosopher Simon Critchley, Saying represents "the non-thematizable ethical residue of language that escapes comprehension, interrupts philosophy, and is the very enactment of the ethical movement from the Same to the other" (Critchley 7). This is the level, to which Saleem gradually proceeds: "Only later, when I began to probe, did I learn that below the surface transmissions—the front-of-mind stuff which is what I'd originally been picking up—language faded away, and was replaced by universally intelligible thought-forms which far transcended words ..." (*MC* 168, ellipsis in the original). This is how Saleem moves from the surface transmissions in language (the Said) into the magical ethical utopia, where everybody understands each other equally and without words (the Saying).

This idea of a non-linguistic, pre-discursive trace within linguistic discourse resonates strongly with historian Gyan Prakash's idea of subalterity and its presence within the dominant discourse. We can here compare the dominant discourse (official, established, national history) to Levinas's Said, and the way the subaltern—here, Saleem—is present within this discourse to the ethical Saying. In Prakash's view, subalterity functions and affects inside the dominant discourse. It exists within "the system of dominance, but only as an intimation, as a trace of that which eludes the dominant discourse" (Prakash 288). Prakash further claims that "the subaltern poses counterhegemonic possibilities not as inviolable otherness from the outside but from within the functioning of power, forcing contradictions and dislocations in the dominant discourse and providing sources of an imminent critique" (Prakash 288). As Ubaraj Katawal, who is touching on the same issue, has it, "the subalterns speak ineluctably and simultaneously with the elites, rather than being contained by them" (Katawal 87).

It is quite clear that Saleem does not belong to the subaltern classes of India. He is instead part of the upper classes. He does, however, have the role of the subaltern in relationship to national historiography, and he continuously takes advantage of that role by staging himself as the inconspicuous agent in many events, some of them nationally important. His role is, however, somewhat duplicitous. At times, at the moments of his every-now-and-then-surfacing self-aggrandizement, he claims himself guilty of these incidents and even boasts of the fact. At other times, he complains of being handcuffed to history without a will of his own. He claims not to have meant any of the deeds he has done, but was forced to commit them by his inseparable connection to history. Nevertheless, he seems to leave a trace—a subaltern intimation, to use Prakash's phrase—of these events in the narrative of the novel.

The Question of Agency and Ethical Deconstruction

In fiction, the contrasting views on language and the mystical experiences transcending discourse can be approached more easily than in philosophical argumentation. However, hovering around the interface between linguistic and meta-ethical communication creates the problem of agency. It is quite obvious that those in the possession of, or fluent in, the prevailing discourse do have agency and power, but what about those who are outside this system, like, for instance, Saleem, who is subaltern to national history. "From Ayah to Widow, I've been the sort of person *to whom things have been done*; but Saleem Sinai, perennial victim, persists in seeing himself as protagonist" (*MC* 237, emphasis in the original). Later, he asks: "how, in what terms, may the career of a single individual be said to impinge on the fate of a nation?" (*MC* 238).

Saleem claims to have a relationship to history both literally and metaphorically as well as actively and passively. Of these four instances, or modes of connection, he forms hyphenated pairs: Active-literal (when he provided the language marchers with their battle cry), passive-metaphorical (the state trying to gain land from the sea and Saleem's "explosive efforts at growth"), passive-literal (things that had a direct effect on him, like the freezing of his father's assets or the explosion at Walkeshwar Reservoir) and active-metaphorical, "occasions on which things done by or to me were mirrored in the macrocosm of public affairs, and my private existence was shown to be symbolically at one with history" (*MC* 238). This refers to the simultaneous separation of Saleem from his fingertip and the bloody process of rearranging the state of Bombay.

One of the more obvious, active-metaphorical modes of connection Saleem has with national history is his alleged presence in the bloodless coup involving President Mirza and General Ayub Khan. General Zulfikar, who is the executioner of the coup, is explaining his strategy to others involved, and Saleem illustrates the movements of the military forces by moving pepper pots on the table. Hence pepper pots make history (*MC* 290). In this instance, Saleem contradicts his earlier view of himself as a passive object of the actions of others (*MC* 237) and assumes agency over grand designs on the platform of public affairs: "What began, active-metaphorically, with pepper pots, ended then; not only did I overthrow a government—I also consigned a president to exile" (*MC* 291). This is clearly a moment of self-aggrandizement, but it can also be conceived as representing the subaltern ethical trace that functions and affects inside the dominant discourse. To quote Prakash again, Saleem acts inside "the system of dominance, but only as an intimation, as a trace of that which eludes the dominant discourse" (*MC* 288). There seems, then, to exist at least a trace of singular and personal agency on the ethical side.

On a more collectively ethical level, Saleem uses his telepathic abilities to call together the MMC, which constitutes a motley crowd of people from all castes, classes, religions, languages, communities, etc. As Michael Gorra observes, the conference is, in many ways, reminiscent of "another sort of narrative, [that] of the India that the Mahatma Gandhi and Nehru conceived as a democratic, secular, and pluralist state, a dream that found its political voice in the Indian National Congress" (Gorra 113). This is what Saleem wants his conference to mirror. When his arch-rival, Shiva, wants to discuss the matter of who is to become the boss of the group, Saleem answers: "That wasn't exactly my idea for the conference; I had in mind something more like a, you know, sort of loose federation of equals, all points of view given free expression ... (*MC* 220, ellipses in the original).

Unfortunately, the conference fails due to internal disagreements concerning the variety of its partakers and their quotidian childhood affiliations. Mundane linguistic and religious issues tear it apart, and afterwards, The Widow (Indira Gandhi) hunts the children down during the emergency. Nonetheless, the conference was an ethical endeavor. It featured people from extremely heterogeneous backgrounds, who were, it originally seemed, capable of communicating beyond the power-politics of language. Saleem mourns that they never gained the active-literal level of mode of connection to India, which had been born on the same hour as they. At the same time, of course, INC was also losing its influence, although it did continue to exist. The MCC fails to form into a collective ethical agent, which could have balanced the dominant political discourse on the scene of public affairs. This, presumably, would have been the purpose that Saleem so desperately wanted to find for the group (*MC* 228).

Nose, Language, and Reality

As a whole, the novel can be conceived as an ethical deconstruction of the established history of India. Saleem conducts this by literalizing the metaphors inherent in national history writing. There is also the transcendent conference, symbolizing the birth of official India and the historical INC. In the narrative, the conference (collective) and Saleem (personal) represent blind spots, traces and intimations within the official historiography, which is given as a commentary in the form of references to Wolpert's history of India.

There are nasal, extra-linguistic ways of cognition, but ethical agency remains only as an insignificant trace on the personal level, while collective attempts at it are in vain. It turns out that, in the end, Saleem has no other option but to resort to language for self-realization and for the construction of truths and realities. His truth, or truths, differ considerably from those of established history, but, ultimately, official and personal histories are equals in epistemological and ontological sense. Both are narration, capable of claiming truths and producing realities.

Works Cited

Adamson, Jane, Richard Freadman, and David Parker. *Renegotiating Ethics in Literature, Philosophy, and Theory*. Cambridge, U.K.: Cambridge UP, 1998.

Bennett, Robert. "National Allegory or Carnivalesque Heteroglossia? *Midnight's Children's* Narration of Indian National Identity." *Bucknell Review: A Scholarly Journal of Letters, Arts and Sciences (BuR)* 43.2 (2000): 177–194.

Binnie, Jon, Julian Holloway, Steve Millington, and Craig Young, eds. *Cosmopolitan Urbanism*. London: Routledge, 2006.

Coady, C. A. J. and Seumas Miller. "Literature, Power and the Recovery of Philosophical Ethics." *Renegotiating Ethics in Literature, Philosophy, and Theory*. Eds. Jane Adamson, Richard Freadman and David Parker. Cambridge, U.K.: Cambridge UP, 1998. 201–210.

Critchley, Simon. *The Ethics of Deconstruction*. Edinburgh: Edinburgh UP, 1999.

Gibson, Andrew. *Postmodernity, Ethics, and the Novel*. London: Routledge, 1999.

Gorra, Michael Edward. *After Empire: Scott, Naipaul, Rushdie*. Chicago: U of Chicago, 1997.

Hutcheon, Linda. *A Poetics of Postmodernism: History, Theory, Fiction*. New York: Routledge, 1988.

Jackson, Elizabeth. "Transcending the Politics of 'Where You're From': Postcolonial Nationality and Cosmopolitanism in Jhumpa Lahiri's *Interpreter of Maladies*." *ARIEL* 43.1 (2012): 109–125.

Jani, Pranav. *Decentering Rushdie: Cosmopolitanism and the Indian Novel in English*. Columbus: Ohio State UP, 2010.

Katawal, Ubaraj. "In *Midnight's Children*, the Subaltern Speaks!" *Interdisciplinary Literary Studies* 15.1 (2013): 86–102.

Khilnani, Sunil. *The Idea of India*. London: Penguin, 1998.

Leivinas, Emmanuel. *Totality and Infinity: An Essay on Exteriority*. 1961. Pittsburgh: Duquesne UP, 1969.

Leivinas, Emmanuel. *Otherwise than Being, Or, Beyond Essence*. 1974. Pittsburgh, PA: Duquesne UP, 1998.

Lipscomb, David. "Caught in a Strange Middle Ground: Contesting History in Salman Rushdie's *Midnight's Children*." *Diaspora: A Journal of Transnational Studies* 1.2 (1991): 163–189.

Newton, Adam. *Narrative Ethics*. Cambridge: Harward UP, 1995.

Prakash, Gyan. "The Impossibility of Subaltern History." *Nepantla: Views from South* 1.2 (2000): 287–294.

Rushdie, Salman. *Midnight's Children*. 1981. London: Pan Books, 1982.

ten Kortenaar, Neil. *Self, Nation, Text in Salman Rushdie's* Midnight's Children. Montreial: McGill-Queen's UP, 2004.

Trousdale, Rachel. *Nabokov, Rushdie, and the Transnational Imagination: Novels of Exile and Alternate Worlds*. New York: Palgrave Macmillan, 2010.

Upstone, Sara. "Domesticity in Magical-Realist Postcolonial Fiction Reversals of Representation in Salman Rushdie's *Midnight's Children*." *Frontiers: A Journal of Women Studies* 28.1 (2007): 260–284.

Wolpert, Stanley A. *A New History of India*. New York: Oxford UP, 1977.

Faithful versus Free: Padma and Saleem as Competing Translators_____

Jenni Ramone

Translation and Narrative Needs

This chapter explores the relationship between Padma and Saleem Sinai in Salman Rushdie's *Midnight's Children* and the pressures that each of their narrative needs exerts upon the story of India's independence and that of protagonist Saleem. While Padma as narratee insists on clear, factual, chronologically organized information, Saleem only offers digression, fragmentation, and imprecision. Both, though, seek to register a version of India's independence that makes more sense to their experiences than the dominant version. In this way, both Padma and Saleem can be understood as translators of the story of Indian independence and of its analogue in Saleem Sinai's narrative of development. Their translation styles are very different and arguably comparable with the archetypal translation principles of faithful (Padma) versus free (Saleem) translation.

Faithful versus Free Translation

It is necessary first to clarify exactly how *Midnight's Children* and the narrative voice within it can be read through the framework of translation. The linguist Roman Jakobson suggests that there are three categories of contemporary translation: 'intralingual' translation, a rewording of signs in one language with signs from the same language; 'interlingual' translation, or the interpretation of signs in one language with signs from another language (translation 'proper'); and 'intersemiotic' translation, or the transfer ('transmutation') of signs in one language to non-verbal sign systems (from language into art or music) (Jakobson 139). 'Intralingual translation' enables stories to be retold for new audiences or purposes, from an alternative perspective, or in a new historical moment. In this way, Saleem's narration of his life story and its bond with the narrative of India's independence can be analyzed as a type of translation. Saleem's narrative rethinks (or rewords) the dominant story of Indian independence by offering an unconventional response to those events, driven by the common postcolonial impulse to retell. This retelling involves reconstituting Indian independence figuratively as a family story and conveying how Saleem's body becomes a site for its physical and geographical manifestations. These include the Partition of India and the creation of Pakistan, the remnants of colonial influence as felt in the house where Saleem lives and in his school, and the drawing up of boundaries dependent on language groups within states.

Despite its clear relationship with India's recent history, Saleem's narrative is not straightforward. It is complex and unreliable, but more importantly, it is mediated by Padma. Padma is Saleem's lover, of sorts—Saleem is, at the time when his narration takes place, impotent, and Padma is engaged in attempting to find a cure for his predicament so that they can be married. Padma is also Saleem's narratee, the figure to whom the story is directed and for whom it is shaped. Yet, Padma does not fit the pattern of Saleem's ideal reader or listener; instead, she complains loudly when the story repeatedly fails to meet her needs because of its inconsistencies, its unexpected revelations, and its digressions. They both seek a story that can explain why Saleem finds himself "crumbling" (Rushdie 9; further references preceded by *MC*) away, impotent (*MC* 38), and disintegrating into "(approximately) 630 million particles of anonymous, and necessarily oblivious dust" (*MC* 37). While Padma expects to find an answer that accords with received wisdom about recent history and that can help to secure a happy ending involving their marriage, Saleem's story points to the impossibility of fixed or certain histories or identities.

Both Padma and Saleem need to translate the story of India's independence because the existing history leaves them with questions and irreconcilable inconsistencies: despite the promise of Independence, there is no peace or hope after the withdrawal of colonial power and instead Saleem's father declares "this country is finished. Bankrupt. Funtoosh" (*MC* 301) before moving the family to Pakistan. Padma repeatedly insists on a faithful rendering of the story: demanding clarity and factual detail, she becomes irritated whenever the narration "becomes self-conscious" as a result of Saleem's interruptions and interpretations of the events (*MC* 65). For Saleem, it proves impossible to convey anything other than a free interpretation of those events. He conveys detailed and specific knowledge of his grandfather's thoughts and feelings, which would not be accessible to him even via his telepathic gift. His telepathy is one of the tentative strands that hold the narrative together; the other is his exceptional sense of smell, which earns him a job as the army's top sniffer 'dog' following an accident that erases his memory and aspects of his humanity. By the end of the text, Saleem himself begins to question both his telepathy and his amnesia: "Sometimes, [...] Saleem appears to have known too little; at other times, too much [...]. I am obliged to offer no more than this stubborn sentence: It happened that way because that's how it happened" (*MC* 460–461). Saleem's stubbornness could also be understood as his adherence to principles of free (rather than faithful) translation.

I use the terms 'faithful' and 'free' in direct reference to the fundamental question that has preoccupied translation studies since its beginnings and continues to influence translation theory and popular responses to translations. In his influential textbook *Introducing Translation Studies*, Jeremy Munday notes that, until recent decades, translation theory was dominated by the debate over literal, free, and faithful translation. This began with the distinction first made between "word-for-word" (literal) and "sense-for-sense" (free) translation, where literal translation was exactly what it appears to be: the replacement of each individual word of the source text with its equivalent in the target language (Munday 19–20). Munday explains that the debate turned from one of 'literal' versus 'free' to 'faithful' versus 'free' when, towards the end of the seventeenth century, fidelity "came to be identified with faithfulness to the meaning rather than the words of the author" (Munday 25). One of the earliest instigators of the faithful versus free debate was Perrot d'Ablancourt (1606–1664), a French translator of Greek and Roman classical texts who was, for his time, outspoken and experimental.

D'Ablancourt wrote about his translation practices in introductions to his translated works, admitting: "there are many passages I have translated word for word, [...] there are also passages in which I have considered what ought to be said, or what I could say, rather than what he [the original author] actually said" (d'Ablancourt cited in Lefevere 9). The notion that a translator can decide what 'ought' to be said and can assume the right to insert in the text what they themselves 'could say' based on their experiences, knowledge, or ideological position, perhaps, is both audacious and empowering, depending on the translation context.

'Free' translation has a fundamentally different meaning in colonial and postcolonial contexts. The postcolonial writer writes back to the Empire by translating freely and undermining the structures, which had brutalized the colonized subject's culture and identity, thus reclaiming power and a voice. However, when colonial translators started to translate texts into English and French for Western consumption, their tendency to undertake 'free' translation was based on the notions that European metaphors and moral codes were superior to those found in the texts that they were translating. For example, Edward Fitzgerald, translator of the *Rubaiyat of Omar Khayyam*, discards 'Persian' metaphor in favor of description based on his own European sensibility. Fitzgerald rejects the comparison of Moses' white hand to a whiteness "leprous as Snow", in the Persian, replacing it with whiteness "as our May-blossom in Spring perhaps" (Fitzgerald). This disregards the fact that 'our' (British) May-blossom would be entirely alien as an image to the Persian poet Khayyam. The debate persists: Cecilia Wadensjö has observed that even today, many translators respond to questions of translatability by using oppositions like 'faithful' versus 'free', 'literal' versus 'figurative', or 'equivalent' versus 'non-equivalent" (Wadensjö 28).

Translating Indian Independence

Midnight's Children is a narrative of independence. Although Saleem is famously born on the stroke of midnight at the moment of Indian independence, August 15, 1947, the narrative explores a greater historical arc, a significant amount of which is outside the narrator's direct experience. Saleem narrates events beginning in 1915, when his grandfather Aadam Aziz returns to Kashmir as a newly qualified doctor, and ending close to Saleem's thirty-first birthday, which would be in 1978, with Padma's insistence on a Kashmiri wedding. Between these dates are a number of significant events in the postcolonial history of India, including: Mahatma Gandhi's assassination in 1948; territorial wars with China in 1962, with Pakistan over Kashmir in 1965, and again with Pakistan in 1971, leading to the second Partition of South Asia and the creation of Bangladesh from the former East wing of Pakistan; and then in 1975, the State of Emergency declared by Indira Gandhi, which led to the enforced sterilization program lasting two years. All of these events are conveyed in Saleem's narrative, and as a result, the text is often read as a literary history. Indeed, Rushdie has described how early responses to the text showed readers' insistence on positioning the novel as a history or guide book, noting that Saleem narration was judged as inadequate for the "reference book or encyclopedia" that they were seeking (Rushdie 25). Saleem says that he is 'handcuffed to history', but not straightforwardly—rather, he is "*mysteriously* handcuffed to history" (*MC* 9, emphasis added), and it is his questioning stance that means his translation of those historical events, upon which he is so dependent, is idiosyncratic, fragmentary, and uncertain. It is this uncertainty that creates an opposition between himself and Padma.

Like her name, which refers to the Dung Goddess and connects her to the spheres of both the spiritual and the earthly, Padma's designation as a faithful translator is based on her seemingly contradictory demands for proof and reliance upon faith. In an attempt to cure Saleem of his impotence, Padma procures a potion from a holy man, expecting it to produce a straightforward cure: "I am a simple woman, if holy men tell me, how should I argue?" (*MC* 193), she explains. In this way, she demonstrates the same contradictory space as those early, faithful translators whose scientific translation methods were undertaken in order to uphold the certainty of God's words, something that depended entirely on faith.

Faithful translators attempt to represent the original text without alteration. Petrus Danielus Huetius, a seventeenth-century French bishop and translator, was a proponent of faithful translation, and we might use one of his essays on what he deems appropriate translation to explore some of the features of faithful translation. Huetius writes:

> We do not like translations that eat up the author's fat or put more fat on him, nor do we like translations that clear up obscure passages, correct mistakes, or sort out bad syntax. We would rather have a translation that shows us the whole author, closely copied in our native style, and one that makes it possible for us to either praise his virtues, [...] or scoff at his vices (Huetius 88).

The objective of translation is, for Huetius, to represent the original clearly and directly. This becomes almost a scientific exercise and therefore, as Huetius continues, the translator should "not allow his mind [or, imagination] to interfere" (Huetius 90). This is a method that accords with Padma's favored manner of representing a story. Padma insists on logic: "What nonsense," she responds to Saleem's figurative reflection upon a mildewing photograph that he claims has run out of words: "How can a picture talk? Stop now; you must be too tired to think" (*MC* 45). Padma requires accuracy in representation; when Saleem jokes about her name, she asserts that it is perfectly respectable: "What do you know, city boy? [...] In my village there is no shame in being named for the Dung Goddess. Write at once that you are wrong, completely" (*MC* 32). For Padma, like Huetius, there is a fixed, correct way of doing things, and a wrong way. The correct way involves, too, an idea of the proper time to tell stories: "Begin" (*MC* 106), she commands, at the precise moment of "Mountbatten's ticktock" which, "English-made, [...] beats with relentless accuracy" (*MC* 106). Saleem's digressive narrative indicates wilful resistance to the markers of colonial order, and his style also frustrates Padma's need for chronology: it is her presence that forces the narrative trajectory "back into the world of linear narrative, the universe of what-happened-next" (*MC* 38).

Padma's role is that of faithful, logical narratee, a position that she defends with her muscularity, and it is in direct opposition to Saleem's fragmentariness. While Saleem is "crumbling" (*MC* 9) and "falling apart" (*MC* 37), having been 'buffeted by too much history' (*MC* 37), Padma remains "strong" (*MC* 24). It is her very physicality, her strength and muscularity, which stands out when she is first introduced to the reader; Padma is described as robust: "plump", "thick of waist, somewhat hairy of forearm" (*MC* 24). It is in these terms that she is always described: when Saleem recalls their first meeting, he states that Padma "planted herself" in front of him, and again here it was her arms, "akimbo" and covered in "perspiration" (*MC* 456), to which he draws attention. Saleem reveals just how vital Padma's strong physical presence is to his ability to narrate, when he indulges in a lengthy scrutiny of Padma's muscles and their reactions to his story: her 'calf-muscles' which 'show no strain'; her "thigh-muscles, rippling through sari-folds"; her "biceps and triceps," from which "there is no escape" (*MC* 270). When the story is inflected with too much of Saleem's interfering mind and not enough of logic, Padma is on hand to ask for clarification: "What? [...] What's this now?" (*MC* 269). When the digressions and hesitations overpower the linearity, Padma commands: "Why you're waiting? Begin" (*MC* 347). Lacking confidence in his story because of the increasing risk of unreliability with every passing day, Saleem uses Padma's muscles as a guide: "The dance of her musculature helps to keep me on the rails; because in autobiography, as in all literature, what actually happened is less important than what the author can manage to persuade his audience to believe" (*MC* 270–271).

Saleem permits "errors," "overstatements," and "jarring alterations" (*MC* 270) to enter his story. The original 'text' is the dominant narrative of India's independence. *Midnight's Children* insists that one dominant story is inadequate to represent the 1,001 children who were born at that moment (the original number of midnight's children), or the "(approximately) 630 million" (*MC* 37) Indians alive at the moment of Saleem's narration, also the figure that Saleem fixes on as the number of fragments his disintegrating body will create. Resisting the idea of a singular history, Saleem translates his story freely and achieves what Edwin Gentzler has described as translation's potential: 'Instead of translations fixing the same meaning, translations can also allow further room for play, extend boundaries, and open up new avenues for further difference" (Gentzler 160–161). After all, as George Steiner has claimed, translation is "an attempt to reinvent the shape of meaning" (Steiner 246). Reinventing the shape of meaning, by means of reinventing the shape of narrative, is Saleem's goal. This can be seen in the way specific historical events are represented, and Rushdie's play between faithful and free translation is discernible in the historical detail that emerges between Saleem's fragments and Padma's logic.

Perhaps the most significant of these historical details is the emergence of Bangladesh, which is represented in the chapter titled "The Buddha," the peaceable nature of such a title belying the military focus of the episode. Saleem had, at this point, become the "Buddha," an animalistic version of his former self, who performed the role of army sniffer dog and had lost most of his memory, leaving him in a subhuman condition. Bangladesh, formerly the east wing of Pakistan, was formed as a result of a war between the Pakistani army and Bengali nationalists, whose political leader was Sheikh Mujib-ur-Rahman (known as Mujib). Mujib had campaigned for Bengali rights and representation, as—although Bengalis were the majority of the population in Pakistan—they suffered ethnic and state discrimination. Mujib was arrested by the Pakistani army, whom he opposed, and who suspected him of conspiring with India. Saleem reveals that he was the sniffer 'dog' who located Mujib and thus accelerated the border tension leading to the second partitioning of South Asia. Saleem struggles to narrate this section, relying heavily on distractions from within both the story-time (the time at which the events happened) and the text-time (the time at which those events are narrated), to use Gerard Genette's terms. Saleem's naïve young soldier-handlers litter story-time with the language of filmic bravado: "Up and at 'em [...]! Ka-bang! Ka-dang! Ka-pow!" (*MC* 355). A second soundtrack to the events is provided by Jamila Singer—"Amar Sonar Bangla" ("Our Golden Bengal") is playing from an unlikely "unseen gramophone" (*MC* 355). Exactly where this gramophone could be located on a requisitioned civilian bus en route to a military camp is left unexplained. While this impossible music is evidence of Saleem's free translation, his rendering of events in a non-factual way, it is, at the same time, a statement about why it is necessary to tell a story that is discordant: 'Our Golden Bengal' is sung in Bengali, a language that Saleem and the soldiers do not speak. Because of this, they are "protected against the insidious subversion of the lyric" (*MC* 355) which supports Mujid's pro-Bengali agenda. By interrupting his translation of the event with a pro-Bengali song, Saleem inserts a second, oppositional history that is incompatible with his actions as part of an opposing military machine.

From the text-time, it is, of course, Padma who provides the distraction; Saleem relies upon her to hear his story, saying: "Yes, Padma: when Mujib was arrested, it was I who sniffed him out" (*MC* 355). At the same time, Padma's emotional response halts the story: "Padma is almost beside herself with anguish. 'But mister, you didn't, can't have, how would you do such a thing…?'" (*MC* 356). Here Padma's emotional need to grasp on to the dominant narrative is uncovered as false: as Padma wails "No, not true," Saleem insists that "the same denials have been made about most of what befell that night" (*MC* 356) and the translator's freedom is revealed as necessary, not just to subvert but to uncover necessary truths, to write against the grain, a fundamental postcolonial strategy.

Padma's 'muscularity' is a marker of her faithful translation style; she represents legitimacy, physicality, testability, and a sense of connectedness with dominant narratives of the nation. As a result, she is endowed with a potent bodily presence. However, this idea is complicated by her working class (even subaltern) status and her disconnection from world events, which would dissociate her from those dominant narratives even as she seeks to uphold them. She is once again placed in contrast with Saleem who actually inhabits a powerful position and is thoroughly involved in national affairs— even if he is prone to exaggeration and self-aggrandizement, it is worth remembering that he comes from a wealthy family and that, when in Pakistan, he overhears and has some involvement in a military coup: General Zulfikar (Saleem's uncle, and a general in the Pakistani army) describes troop movements while Saleem "moved pepperpots symbolically" on the table and thus "we made the revolution" (*MC* 290). Later, Saleem—in the guise of a sniffer-dog—is part of the military unit directly responsible for events leading to the partitioning of Pakistan. Saleem's involvement in the history of his nation throughout his childhood and early adulthood is marked by his unwillingness to succumb to singular, straightforward, dominant narratives, and in this way, *Midnight's Children* is the story of an individual's personal development and an exploration of how far he can locate a place for himself in society. To an extent, *Midnight's Children* can be read as a *Bildungsroman*, but it cannot be read straightforwardly as an example of the genre because of Saleem's free and unreliable narrative—or translation—style.

The Postcolonial *Bildungsroman*

The *Bildungsroman* is usually defined as a novel of education or of personal development. The novel usually explores the development of an individual protagonist from childhood to adulthood, at which point of maturity the protagonist has rejected whatever failings in personality or situation had prevented himself (usually, in traditional examples of the genre) or herself from operating sympathetically and successfully in society. Perhaps the best known example of the genre is Charles Dickens' *Great Expectations*; at the novel's close, protagonist Pip has learned, and come to terms with, the identity of his benefactor, the person whose generosity had allowed him to leave his rural village as the ward of a blacksmith and to live like a gentleman in London. This knowledge forces Pip to question his lifestyle, which involves debt and socializing, and allows him to move on from his youthful infatuation with Estella in order to take a job overseas which, the text suggests, is a method of making a contribution to society. Jane Austen's *Emma* is another often-cited example. As a young woman, Emma has limited opportunities to find a place in society: little more than marriage is offered to her, but still, she learns that outspokenness, frivolity, and whimsical matchmaking schemes must be rejected by the mature woman and eventually settles down and marries. *Midnight's Children* is a narrative of education and development about one individual's lifetime and the ways in which he is shaped by society, and in this way, it could be considered an example of the *Bildungsroman* genre.

Like Pip and Emma, the young Saleem is naïve and makes mistakes: for instance, when his telepathic gift is first triggered, he announces to his parents that "Archangels have started to talk to me" (*MC* 164). After his claim is rejected violently, Saleem quickly realizes that his initial, childish supposition is wrong: "understanding that the voices in my head far outnumbered the ranks of angels, I decided, not without relief, that I had not after all been chosen to preside over the end of the world. [...] Telepathy, then" (*MC* 168). And once he starts to use his telepathy, he assumes—again, naïvely—that he is able to make moral judgments about others and then act on those judgments. Saleem takes it upon himself to sabotage the extra-marital affair of Lila Sabarmati and Homi Catrack, resulting in their deaths at the hand of Lila's husband, and leading to his mother abandoning her affair with estranged first husband, Nadir Khan. However, his revenge plot has "a number of unlooked-for developments" (*MC* 265), and these episodes resemble steps taken on a journey towards adulthood, indicating that *Midnight's Children* conforms, to a certain extent, to the *Bildungsroman* genre.

In his discussion of the postcolonial *Bildungsroman*, José Santiago Fernández Vázquez draws attention to key features of the genre, one of which in particular can be applied fruitfully to Saleem. Vázquez notes that "the protagonist of the Bildungsroman usually exhibits a special sensitivity, which sets him apart from his peers and family" (Vázquez 86). Saleem's special sensitivities are multiple and extreme: his telepathy is, of course, the most remarkable of these, and this immediately forces Saleem to place emotional barriers between himself and his family. In an act of public repentance for claiming to have spoken to angels, Saleem pretends he has made up the story and "scrubbed teeth tongue roofofmouth gums with a toothbrush covered in the sharp foul lather of Coal Tar Soap" (*MC* 169). Although he wins back his family's affection, he does so by keeping secrets from them. And later, on discovering that he and his midnight's children rival Shiva were swapped at birth, Saleem

---

is forced to separate himself from his peers again, closing down the Midnight's Children's Conference communications that he convenes in his head nightly, in order to protect his secrets once more.

However, there are aspects of the text, which do not conform to the *Bildungsroman*. Although Saleem describes his childhood and conveys his naïve emotions and ideas, he does so as an experienced, rather than an experiencing, narrator: the story is not a chronological one, following Saleem's personal development, but a hastily conveyed reflection on his life from a point that, he believes, is near the end. And his unreliability as a narrator is not always due to his lack of experience or knowledge, but often stems from his excess of experience and knowledge and his intention to distort that knowledge. The introduction of Saleem's (or, Shiva's) son Aadam at the end of the text creates a cyclical rather than a linear structure and introduces another naïve figure right at the story's end rather than fixing on a resolution. Similarly, the introduction of Durga the dhoban at this final stage, with "a dozen new stories" (*MC* 445) to tell every day, resists a resolution.

The (Im)possibility of Postcolonial *Bildungsroman*

Midnight's Children is not unique in its dependence upon the structures and patterns of the *Bildungsroman*. Vázquez has argued that postcolonial writers have embraced the *Bildungsroman* for a number of reasons, which might include, he suggests, a desire to represent nostalgic versions of home from a position of exile, and the narrative potential for writers who set their stories in the early years following independence "in order to draw parallels between the experience of the new nations and their young characters" (Vázquez 86). Vázquez goes on to suggest that, from a political perspective, the emphasis of the *Bildungsroman* on questions of identity, pedagogy, and power is relevant to questions of postcolonial subjectivity. Similarly, postcolonial writers use the *Bildungsroman* "to incorporate the master codes of imperialism into the text, in order to sabotage them more effectively" (Vázquez 86).

Bapsi Sidhwa's *Cracking India* (1991) is another narrative of South Asian Partition and independence and explores communalist hostility from the perspective of a young protagonist, this time in Pakistan. And the genre continues to be used to explore contemporary South Asian postcolonial and neo-colonial contexts. Indra Sinha's *Animal's People* (2007) has been called a "toxically transfigured" *Bildungsroman* (Carrigan 168), "toxically transfigured" because the society that Animal chooses to remain in, fight for, and shape himself to fit, is transfigured by the toxic gas leak that has given him his shape and his name, in the context of neo-colonial global trade. As a result of gas poisoning, Animal has severe spine damage, which means he walks on four limbs rather than two and, as a result, associates himself with the animal rather than human world in the way that he expresses his body identity in public. Towards the end of the narrative, Animal decides to remain in his slum city rather than travel to America to undergo an operation that may improve his physical condition. Though Animal's journey is one of self-discovery, there is no acceptable society into which he can fit, and this is the sentiment expressed repeatedly in postcolonial novels that make use of the *Bildungsroman* genre. The individual is not required to shape himself or herself to fit into society because to do so is to remain subject to the colonial condition.

Far from reconciling with society, Saleem experiences a series of disconnections from society. These include disconnections caused by his telepathy, his discovery that he was swapped at birth, his incestuous desire for his sister, his amnesia, the death of his family, and, finally, his proposed removal to Kashmir. Notably, Kashmir remains outside the national narrative of independence and partition, as it remains a battleground for independence and operates slightly at odds with postcolonial independence. If a story that has all the basic elements required to construct a postcolonial *Bildungsroman* willfully subverts the genre, we need to ask whether there are problems inherent in the genre, making it irreconcilable with the postcolonial novel. Vazquez draws attention to some of these potential problems. He suggests that the dialectical process whereby the protagonist, who had hitherto exhibited a profound disagreement with his family or society but is able to resolve their disagreement and to establish a compromise, "does not respond to the necessities of women, racial and sexual minorities, or to the historical experience of the colonized peoples. As a result of the process of colonization, the postcolonial subject has been forced to stand in between two cultures: his own native civilization and the European traditions" (Vázquez 87).

These problems are apparent in *Midnight's Children*: Saleem is unable to reconcile his identity with that of his nation. Or, at least, he cannot locate a place within the nation in any way other than by describing the nation as unendingly fragmented and constructed from multiple and competing stories, and by claiming that his body, too, is destined to crumble into millions of fragments. There is no sense of closure or reconciliation at the end of a text that insists that, for the 'midnight's children'—that is, those born at India's independence and those following that generation—it is impossible "to live or die in peace" (*MC* 463).

Works Cited

Carrigan, Anthony. "'Justice is on our side'? *Animal's People*, Generic Hybridity, and Eco-crime." *The Journal of Commonwealth Literature* 47.2 (2012): 159–174.

Fitzgerald, Edward. Translator's Introduction and Notes. *Rubaiyat of Omar Khayyam*. 1879. *Project Gutenberg*. 10 Jul 2008. Web. 22 Jun 2009. <http://www.gutenberg.org/files/246/246-h/246-h.htm>.

Gentzler, Edwin. *Contemporary Translation Theories*. London: Routledge, 1993.

Huetius, Petrus Danielus. "De Optimo genere interpretandi" ("On The Best Way of Translating.") *Translation, History, Culture: A Sourcebook*. Ed. André Lefevere. London: Routledge, 1992. 86–101.

Jakobson, Roman. "On Linguistic Aspects of Translation." *The Translation Studies Reader*. Ed. Lawrence Venuti. London: Routledge, 2000. 126–132.

Lefevere, André. *Translation, History, Culture: A Sourcebook*. London: Routledge, 1992.

Munday, Jeremy. *Introducing Translation Studies: Theories and Applications*. 2nd ed. London: Routledge, 2008.

Rushdie, Salman. "'Errata'": or, Unreliable Narration in Midnight's Children." *Imaginary Homelands: Essays in Criticism, 1981–1991.* London: Granta, 1992. 22–25.

_____. *Midnight's Children.* 1981. London: Vintage, 1995.

Steiner, George. *After Babel.* Oxford: Oxford UP, 1992.

Vázquez, José Santiago Fernández. "Recharting the Geography of Genre: Ben Okri's *The Famished Road* as a Postcolonial Bildungsroman." *The Journal of Commonwealth Literature* 37.2 (2002): 85–106.

Wadensjö, Cecilia. *Interpreting as Interaction.* London: Longman, 1998.

Topographies of Nationalism in *Midnight's Children*

Ágnes Györke

Salman Rushdie's *Midnight's Children* is characterized by a textual pluralism that is truly unique. The novel has been called, for instance, a national epic, an Indian novel, a cosmopolitan narrative, as well as a postnational text. A number of critics claim that its narrative strategies show the influence of Western theories, such as postmodernism and deconstruction, while others maintain that they reflect the plural, garrulous, and rambling quality of Indian life (Sabin 275). It is a profoundly open text, which, like the writer, crosses all kinds of frontiers in search of the new, for "whatever nourishes" (Rushdie, "U2" 95). No doubt, *Midnight's Children* is also Rushdie's best novel; in Neil ten Kortenaar's words: "Rushdie has not yet equaled his achievement in the first half of *Midnight's Children*, and the closest he has come to doing so is in the second half of that same novel" (ten Kortenaar 5).

It is somewhat ironic that this versatile, hybrid narrative, which aims to challenge any kind of categorical idea and binary opposition, has produced a discourse that often relies on just such terms: critics, especially recently, have tended to assess the novel in the light of the approaches they prefer to advocate. Eric Strand, for instance, argues that the narrative erases alternative views of the nation that earlier Indian English novelists have envisioned by supporting a liberal-capitalist social model over Gandhian ideology (Strand 976–977). Reading *Midnight's Children* as an exclusively bourgeois text is, however, suggestive of a current critical interest in the repressed and the exploited. Coming from a post-communist country, where the legacy of the period in which Marxist aesthetics was the only supported horizon of interpretation still needs to be rethought, I am doubtful when works of literature are claimed to act as mouthpieces of preferred or rejected ideologies, regardless of their appeal to our sense of social justice.

In this chapter, I offer a textual analysis of *Midnight's Children*, exploring how the tropes of the politically independent Indian nation divide the narrative world of the novel into public and private domains, which I read as topographies of nationalism. Relying on the findings of Indian historiography and Western theories of the modern nation, I claim that *Midnight's Children*, apart from depicting the post-independence era as a hopeful, yet inevitably transitory period and the Emergency as a time of unavoidable decline, imagines the politically independent Indian nation as an ideal that is split between contradictory national discourses that revolve around the demands of the spiritual and the material.

Saleem's Historiography

As Partha Chatterjee points out, anticolonial nationalism in India, which emerged in the late nineteenth century, long before the formation of the independent nation state in 1947, divided the world into two domains: the material and the spiritual. Whereas the material was seen as "the domain of the 'outside,' of the economy and of statecraft, of science and technology, a domain where the West had proved its superiority and the East had succumbed" (Chatterjee 6), the spiritual remained an inner realm "bearing the 'essential' marks of cultural identity" (Chatterjee 6). Chatterjee does not claim that the aim of anticolonial nationalism was to challenge the superiority of science and technology, the legacy of Western modernity. Instead, Chatterjee asserts that it is quite the other way round: in the material domain, the achievements of the West had to be acknowledged and replicated. In the spiritual sphere, however, primarily associated with tradition, women, and a sense of purity, a distinct national culture had to be fashioned, which was the basis of the anticolonial struggle against Western modernity and its universalistic presumptions (Chatterjee 75).

This domain of sovereignty, which, as Chatterjee argues, existed long before the colonial society began its political battle with the imperial power, became all the more significant as the need to imitate Western accomplishments increased. It was perceived as the reservoir of cultural distinctness, yet it was also a profoundly elite realm: manufactured by the literate middle-class, the role of the nationalist elite was to produce a specifically Indian cultural identity. This assumption, however, led to a number of questions: can the voice of repressed groups be heard? Is cultural distinctness entirely the product of those who have the power to speak? Can repressed social groups contribute to the collective memory of a nation? Beginning in the 1980s, the time when Rushdie's novel was published, a number of South Asian critics, including Chatterjee, formed the Subaltern Studies Group to investigate these issues.

The novel's narrator—Saleem Sinai—is also aware of the fact that to speak is to assume power over the subject of his discourse. Saleem—born at the exact moment of India's independence at the stroke of the midnight hour on August 15, 1947 and, therefore, celebrated as the mirror of the nation, the embodiment of India— feels to have been "left entirely without a say" (Rushdie 9; further references preceded by *MC*) in the national project he is destined to represent. His narrative, nevertheless, attempts to compensate for this failure: the grandiose project of narrating his life story, entangled with the story of the independent nation, aims to demonstrate that he has a voice as well as a great number of stories to tell. Beginning with the narrative of his grandfather, Aadam Aziz, in the spring of 1915 in Kashmir, we see snapshots of history through a very personal perspective, tinged with humor and irony: the Indo-Pakistani war in 1965, for instance, or the Emergency declared by Indira Gandhi in 1975. The moment of independence, which Saleem recounts on the narrative's very first page, appears as a miraculous event, an inadvertent, yet inevitable incident, which defines the language the nation will speak in the novel.

To what extent does Saleem's narrative provide an alternative view of historical events? Is he a "historiographer" interested in the repressed, the subaltern? It is my contention that *Midnight's Children* primarily allegorizes a gap between the modern, material, and public Indian nation, influenced by Western models, and a spiritual, communal, and private alternative, which is akin to what Chatterjee calls the inner domain of national culture. In Rushdie's novel, however, this inner domain, allegorized by the 1,001 midnight's children, appears as a fragile and contaminated realm: it is neither the repository of an authentic national identity, nor is it a tool to be used in the struggle against Western ideas. Nonetheless, I argue that hidden, private spaces offer alternative visions of history in Rushdie's fiction, even though his narrators are aware of the fact that they do not possess the knowledge, or ability, to write a subaltern narrative of postcolonial modernity.

Rushdie has repeatedly argued that the primary aim of literature is to challenge official versions of truth; in "Imaginary Homelands," for instance, he states that "[w]riters and politicians are natural rivals. Both groups try to make the world in their own images; they fight for the same territory. And the novel is one way of denying the official, politicians' version of truth" (Rushdie, "Imaginary" 14). This is what happens in *Midnight's Children* as well: Saleem, left without a say in his very destiny, observes events from a critical distance. His portrayal of the state of Emergency, for instance, a period in which a number of laws were passed that limited personal freedoms (including forced sterilizations for the sake of population control), clearly shows that his sympathies lie with the disempowered and the repressed.

However, one cannot ignore the fact that Saleem grows up in an elite family, and it is also tempting to read his vision of India as a comment on the economic power of the upper-middle class after independence. Rushdie himself often reflects on the privileges he enjoyed due to his social position; he admits, for instance, that his success in England was primarily the result of his social class, his "freak fair skin" and his "'English' English accent" (Rushdie, "Imaginary" 18). Saleem, too, enjoys the comfort and the protection that his class provides. It is Shiva, his rival, and Parvati, the witch, along with characters such as Tai, Mary Pereira, Joseph D'Costa, Vanita, Padma, and Picture Singh, who embody a sense of subalternity in the novel (Morton 38–39; Jani 159–171; Katawal 94).

Furthermore, the very form that Rushdie chooses, the novel, is an imported medium in the Indian subcontinent. As Timothy Brennan argues, it is elitist and foreign "when compared to poem, song, television, and film. Almost inevitably it has been the form through which a thin, foreign-educated stratum (however sensitive or committed to domestic political interests) has communicated to metropolitan reading publics, often in translation (Brennan, "National Longing" 56). In the light of this argument, it is easy to see that statements, such as "*Midnight's Children* sounds like a continent finding its voice" (Blaise 1981) exaggerate to a great extent. Saleem's narrative cannot be regarded as an attempt to endow a continent with a voice; the very assumption would presume that India had been mute, lacking a speech of its own, before the novel was published (for a powerful counterargument see, for instance, Strand and Jani).

If *Midnight's Children* is a departure in literary history, it marks a turning point in the trajectory of transnational literatures, demarcating a renewed Western interest in the Indian subcontinent. It is important to note that India was not yet (or no longer) a subject important in the West (Goonetilleke 20) at the time when the novel was published. Publishers were afraid of the risk involved in financing Rushdie's book, since, as one claimed, "[t]he received wisdom in those days […] was that books on India didn't sell, big fat books on India didn't sell" (Goonetilleke 20). *Midnight's Children* has challenged this preconception and renewed the transnational mode of writing the nation, yet it never assumed to have the power, or ambition, to endow a continent with a voice.

This does not mean, though, that Saleem's narrative is entirely elitist; despite his grandiose attempt "to encapsulate the whole of reality" (*MC* 75), the novel remains a multivocal text. It is also important to note that Chatterjee, one of the leading authorities of subaltern studies, presumes that the elite and the subaltern are negotiable positions. Chatterjee should know this as he himself was accused of belonging to an elite class, together with Ranajit Guha, founder of the Subaltern Studies Group (Kopf 1281). The elite may turn towards indigenous traditions and become "subalternized," as Chatterjee point out (Chatterjee 37): the Brahmo leader, Keshub Chandra Sen (1838–1884) for instance, though born into one of the leading families of the new Bengali elite, became more conscious of the traditions of his people after having met the

Hindu religious leader, Ramakrishna (Chatterjee 37–46). So, the elite and the subaltern should not be conceived as binary opposites, and it is also necessary to be cautious of the tendency to think of the latter as the repository of truth and authenticity. The concept of "subalternization," i.e., a negotiation between empowered and repressed positions, offers a much more productive angle to read Saleem's vision of the politically independent Indian nation, too.

Between the Public and the Private

Though allegorical elements abound in *Midnight's Children*, two of these, as stated earlier, take a particularly central role in the narrative. First is the Midnight's Children's Conference, or MCC, founded by the children born between midnight and one a.m. on August 15, 1947, which has been read as the allegory of the politically independent nation by a number of critics (e.g., Kortenaar; Lipscomb; Strand). Second is Saleem's *body*, which acts as a mirror of the nation, according to the first prime minister of India, Jawaharlal Nehru (Györke 171–172), and which is seldom regarded as a trope that is distinct from, and perhaps even contradictory with, the allegory of the children. The differences between the structures of these allegories reveal a disparity in the way the nation addresses its subjects. It suggests there is a split between the official rhetoric, which Homi Bhabha calls pedagogical, and the performative image that the conference embodies (Bhabha 199): whereas Saleem's body is subdued by national pedagogy in the act of performing the Nehruvian, secular nation, the Midnight Children's Conference appears as a courageous, though hopeless, attempt to intervene in the official rhetoric of nationalism (Györke 139).

Relying on Jürgen Habermas's theory of the public sphere, Strand claims that the MCC is a bourgeois image, which comments on the elite's engagement with public affairs in post-independence India. It is not a private, repressed vision in his reading, and, above all, not a subaltern space, as David Lipscomb has claimed, but an elite rendering of the Indian public sphere based on Saleem's childhood fantasy. Strand makes no distinction between the public and the private domains, apart from the contrast posited between public life and private economy, which is, of course, an entirely different matter. In this, he is similar to Habermas, who understands "the protective space of the family's inner sanctum" as a realm that prepares "the grounds for entrance into public life" (Strand 995). However, it is my contention that we need to distinguish these domains when reading the novel, since the narrative repeatedly calls the reader's attention to its continuous struggle with, and negotiation of, the spaces they delineate in the act of mapping the nation.

Saleem claims, on the novel's very first page, that he has been handcuffed to history: "thanks to the occult tyrannies of those blandly saluting clocks I had been mysteriously handcuffed to history, my destinies indissolubly chained to those of my country" (*MC* 9). He represents the totality of the Indian nation, yet his body is subdued and "chained," literally. His photograph is published in *The Times of India* along with a letter by the Prime Minister, Jawaharlal Nehru, which, hanging on the bedroom wall while he is narrating his autobiography, reminds him of his "inescapable destiny […] forever fixed under glass" (*MC* 122). Saleem quotes Nehru's words:

> Newspapers celebrated me; politicians ratified my position. Jawaharlal Nehru wrote: 'Dear Baby Saleem, My belated congratulations on the happy accident of your moment of birth! You are the newest bearer of the *ancient face of India* which is also *eternally young.* We shall be watching over your life with the closest attention; it will be, in a sense, the mirror of our own' (*MC* 122, emphases added).

The language used here is reminiscent of the rhetoric of the modern nation described by Ernest Gellner, Benedict Anderson, and Tom Nairn, among other scholars, whose most original contributions to nationalism studies were produced before and shortly after the publication of *Midnight's Children* in 1981. In his influential account of the origin of nationalism, Benedict Anderson claims that print capitalism, the collective act of reading newspapers and novels in the eighteenth and nineteenth centuries, contributed to imagining the Western nation to a great extent. Similarly, Saleem, celebrated by newspapers, is addressed through this communal medium: his identity, "fixed under glass," is constructed publicly, without any personal, private contact. Furthermore, by becoming "the newest bearer of the *ancient* face of India which is also eternally *young*," he enacts the paradox that describes the temporality of the modern nation, according to Gellner and Nairn: the ambition to modernize, to move forward, and the need to rely on "cults of a particular past and tradition" (Nairn 71) at one and the same time.

Saleem is called to perform precisely this role: by embodying "the ancient face of India," his task is to renew, to revitalize the land. India becomes inscribed on his body publicly: in another episode, for instance, his teacher, the half mad Mr. Zagallo uses Saleem's face to explain the concept of human geography:

> 'See boys – you see what we have here? Regard, please, the heedeous face of these primitive creature. It reminds you of?'
>
> And the eager responses: 'Sir the devil sir.' 'Please sir one cousin of mine!' 'No sir a vegetable sir I don't know which.' Until Zagallo, shouting above the tumult, 'Silence! Sons of baboons! Thees object here' – a tug on my nose – '*thees* is human geography!'
>
> 'How sir where sir what sir?'
>
> Zagallo is laughing now. 'You don't see?' he guffaws. 'In the face of these ugly ape you don't see the whole map of *India*?' (*MC* 231, emphases original).

Saleem's nose is read as the "Deccan peninsula"; the stains on his face are Pakistan; and the drip from his nose, as one of the pupils suggests, is Ceylon (*MC* 231-232). What we see here is the antithesis of Nehru's congratulatory welcome: the bearer of the sacred face of India is seen as a "primitive creature," "an ugly ape." However, Zagallo also identifies his body with that of the nation, and, similarly to Nehru's, his act is performed publicly: Saleem's humiliation is a communal spectacle. His body is subdued by the public role imposed upon it, and this is the reason why he tries to find a hiding place in the private domain: in the family's washing-chest made of slatted wood (*MC* 152).

The public domain imagined by *Midnight's Children* is, then, akin to what Chatterjee calls the material world of nationalism: the realm of statecraft, science, and technology, which inherits the legacy of Western modernity. The body, disciplined by this domain, represents India as a public spectacle for all to see; no wonder that it splits under the burden of this heroic role – Saleem's body is fragmenting as he is narrating the novel, and, eventually, falls into pieces at the end. The act of imagining the Midnight's Children's Conference has to be understood in this context: its role is to counterbalance the ideological interpellation that the discourse of the modern, official nation imposes on the subject.

Saleem discovers the voices of the children when he is "nearly nine" years old (*MC* 152). He is hiding in the family's washing chest, which acts as the antithesis of the public realm in the novel:

> There are no mirrors in a washing-chest; rude jokes do not enter it, nor pointing fingers. The rage of fathers is muffled by used sheets and discarded brassieres. A washing-chest is a hole in the world, a place which civilization has put outside itself, beyond the pale; this makes it the finest of hiding-places (*MC* 156).

The washing-chest, a place which civilization has put "beyond the pale," seems to be situated at the very edge of the symbolic world, as opposed to the public domain of newspapers and photographs. It is associated with disgraceful secrets in the household of the middle class family: Saleem, as a voyeur, witnesses his mother's private confession when hiding there. The foul laundry and used underwear reminds the reader of other dirty entities in the narrative, such as Padma, for instance, the "dung goddess," who calls Saleem's narrative "writing-shiting" (*MC* 24), and who is often read as the representative of the subaltern in *Midnight's Children*, embodying the potency and power that Saleem lacks (Jani 159–166). The discovery of the children's voices is, then, not the result of the linear extension of the values and beliefs of Saleem's middle-class family; it is clearly an act of transgression in the narrative.

Saleem discovers the voices of the children in 1956, at the time when "Nasser sank ships at Suez" (*MC* 150) and the States

Reorganization Act was passed in India, which redesigned the country's internal map and led to a major redrawing of administrative boundaries, ensuring that "each of India's major regional languages would find its administrative reflection, while English and Hindi would remain joint national languages for purposes of legislation, law, and service examinations" (Britannica). The MCC, imagined to life at this time, is also engaged with linguistic issues: the very discovery of the voices is narrated in such terms: "Pain. And then noise, deafening manytongued terrifying, *inside his head*! […] Inside a white wooden washing-chest, within the darkened auditorium of my skull, my nose began to sing" (*MC* 162). A few pages later Saleem remarks that "[i]n 1956, then, languages marched militantly through the daytime streets; by night, they rioted in my head" (*MC* 167), suggesting that the children's community does not simply mirror the militant events happening in the public domain, but produces an inverted vision of these in the private sphere.

When Saleem claims that "below the surface of transmissions […] language faded away, and was replaced by universally intelligible thought forms which far transcended words" (*MC* 168) he attempts to create a community, which, despite the inevitable differences in language and social background and despite the awareness of exclusions and divisions—Shiva, for instance, will be barred from the conference after Saleem learns that he is the real midnight's child—is based on a pre-symbolic, spiritual principle. The language used here is the direct antithesis of the language of print capitalism: whereas Nehru relied on the publicity of the newspaper when he wrote to Saleem, which played a crucial role in imagining the nation to life in European modernity (Anderson 37–46), the tropes Saleem uses seem to evoke an unconscious, pre-symbolic realm: "I heard, beneath the polyglot frenzy in my head, those other precious signals, utterly different from everything else, […] those secret, nocturnal calls, like calling out to like… the unconscious beacons of the children of midnight" (*MC* 168). Later, however, when the children's "thought forms" are transformed into intelligible speech, the allegory loses its subversive potential (Györke 149–152), suggesting that it is the private, hidden domain that offers an alternative in Rushdie's fiction.

Spaces of Resistance

The trope of hidden, underground spaces, which contain some sort of subversive secret, recurs in a number of novels written by Rushdie in the 1980s. In *Shame* (1983), Sufiya Zinobia, the allegorical figure associated with repressed voices in Pakistan, is locked in an attic room, from which, despite the bricked up windows and huge bolts fastened to the door, she escapes (Rushdie, *Shame* 261). *The Satanic Verses*, published in 1988, also abounds in hidden locations; one of these, the Club Hot Wax, a daytime disco frequented by the Bangladeshi community in London, hosts wax statues of marginalized black historical figures such as Mary Seacole, Abdul Karim, Grace Jones, among others, as if it acted as the secret antithesis of Madame Tussaud's (Rushdie, *Satanic Verses* 292–293). The community ritually melts the effigy of Margaret Thatcher, which, apart from commenting on the narrative's pledge for alternative ways of musealizing history, also suggests that the space has a subversive potential.

In one of the essays written in defense of *The Satanic Verses*, "Is Nothing Sacred?", Rushdie puts literary works into a domain that is akin to the ones described above: allegorized as a hidden, "unimportant-looking" and "discretely positioned" little room (Rushdie, "Sacred" 428) inhabited by all kinds of voices. Literature is defined as "the one place in any society where, within the secrecy of our own heads, we can hear *voices talking about everything in every possible way*" (Rushdie, "Sacred" 429, emphasis original). The vision recalls the children's conference, and the analogy suggests that there is some truth in the claim that the MCC is rooted in Western traditions, since, no doubt, the allegory of the discretely positioned, little room indicates a profound belief in the values of liberal humanism. The affinity between the image in the essay and in the novel also suggests, however, that the children's community, the second allegory of India in *Midnight's Children*, is associated with a domain that is the most precious realm the writer can possibly imagine, and it is as dissociated from hegemonic discourses as its hidden, private location allows.

The MCC is, nevertheless, also rooted in Hindu imagery: the very opposition of the mind and the body, which splits the narrative of the nation in Rushdie's novel and is the basis of Indian spirituality, as Chatterjee claims. Quoting the biographer of Ramakrishna, he points out that the mind, the instrument of self-control and introspection, allows one to achieve a specific knowledge that is denied to Western people, who "missed the path to Self-knowledge and became materialists, identifying themselves with the body" (Chatterjee 48). Seen from this perspective, the image of the mind appears to be a fairly conventional trope in the novel: as the instrument of introspective spirituality, the children's conference challenges the secular, modernized public sphere, allegorized by the materiality of the body. Yet the narrative challenges this easy analogy in two important ways: first, it depicts the spiritual as a contaminated realm (it is by no accident that Saleem, whose head hosts the MCC, is the bastard son of the British landowner William Methwold and Vanita, one of his Indian servants), and, second, it redefines the relationship of women with this domain.

Whereas, as Chatterjee argues, women have primarily been situated in the inner realm of national culture as bearers of tradition, far removed from the arena of political contest (Chatterjee 117), in Rushdie's novel, the moment when Saleem discovers the children's voices exposes the hypocrisy of traditional gender roles in the middle-class Indian family. The very reason behind the fatal sniff that allows the noise of the children to invade Saleem's head is the appearance of his mother in the bathroom; Amina, obliged to marry Ahmed Sinai, since her ex-husband was unable to perform the sexual act, reminisces of her beloved Nadir Khan: "And her hands are moving. Lost in the memory of other days, of what happened after games of hit-the-spittoon in an Agra cellar, they flutter gladly at her cheeks; they hold her bosom tighter than any brassieres; and now they caress her bare midriff, they stray below decks..." (*MC* 161). The inner, domestic realm is not a domain that upholds tradition in the novel; it is indecorous and sexualized, making it impossible to think of the domestic, as well as the spiritual, as pure, uncontaminated entities.

The MCC disintegrates, and Saleem's body is fragmenting: apart from commenting on the historical events that follow independence (the Indo-Pakistani war, the Emergency), which Morton reads as instances of the terror and violence unleashed in postcolonial modernity (Morton 34), this motif also suggests that Saleem's nation is too ambitious. The novel imagines the politically independent India as an ideal that is split between contradictory discourses. By embodying the material and the spiritual domains, Saleem attempts to make whole what has been smashed; no wonder that he disintegrates under the burden of this role, similarly to his very narrative. It is the private and the hidden that has the potential to challenge hegemonic discourses in *Midnight's Children*, just as in *Shame* and in *The Satanic Verses*, which, undeniably, might not offer an alternative model for India in the public sphere, yet clearly suggest that it is reductive to read the Midnight's Children's Conference as the allegory of a nation under the spell of Western modernity.

Note

1. This research was supported by the European Union and the State of Hungary, co-financed by the European Social Fund in the framework of TÁMOP 4.2.4. A/2-11-1-2012-0001 'National Excellence Program'. I am also grateful to Central European University's Institute for Advanced Study for providing access to resources while I was writing the article.

Works Cited

Anderson, Benedict. *Imagined Communities: Reflections on the Origin and Spread of Nationalism.* 1982. 2nd ed. London: Verso, 1991.

Bhabha, Homi K. "DissemiNation: Time, Narrative and the Margins of the Modern Nation." 1990. *The Location of Culture.* Ed. Homi Bhabha. London: Routledge, 1994. 199–244.

Blaise, Clark. "A Novel of India Coming of Age." *New York Times.* New York Times, 19 Apr. 1981. Web. 31 Oct. 2013.

Brennan, Timothy. "The National Longing for Form." *Nation and Narration.* Ed. Homi K. Bhabha. London: Routledge, 1990. 44–70.

_____. *Salman Rushdie and the Third World: Myths of the Nation*. Basingstoke: Palgrave Macmillan, 1989.

Ecyclopædia Britannica. Britannica Electronic, n.d. Web. 31 Oct. 2013.

Chatterjee, Partha. *The Nation and Its Fragments: Colonial and Postcolonial Histories*. Princeton: Princeton UP, 1993.

Fugmann, Nicole. "Situating Postmodern Aesthetics: Salman Rushdie's Spatial Historiography." *REAL: Yearbook of Research in English and American Literature* 13 (1997): 333–345.

Gellner, Ernest. *Thought and Change*. London: Weidenfeld and Nicolson, 1964.

_____. *Nations and Nationalism*. Ithaca: Cornell UP, 1983.

Goonetilleke, D. C. R. A. *Salman Rushdie*. 1998. 2nd ed. Basingstoke: Palgrave Macmillan, 2010.

Györke, Ágnes. "Allegories of Nation in *Midnight's Children*". *Hungarian Journal of English and American Studies* 7.2 (2001): 169–190. *JSTOR*. Web. 31 Oct. 2013.

_____. "Rushdie's Postmodern Nations." *The AnaChronist* 15 (2010): 135–155.

Hassumani, Sabrina. *Salman Rushdie: A Postmodern Reading of His Major Works*. London: Associated UP, 2002.

Jani, Pranav. *Decentering Rushdie: Cosmopolitanism and the Indian Novel in English*. Columbus: Ohio State UP, 2010.

Katawal, Ubaraj. "In *Midnight's Children*, the Subalterns Speak!" *Interdisciplinary Literary Studies* 15.1 (2013): 86–102. *Project Muse*. Web. 31 Oct. 2013.

Kopf, David I. "Partha Chatterjee, *The Nation and Its Fragments: Colonial and Postcolonial Histories*". Review. *American Historical Review* 100.4 (1995): 1282–1282.

Lipscomb, David. "Caught in a Strange Middle Ground: Contesting History in Salman Rushdie's *Midnight's Children*." *Diaspora* 1.2 (1991): 163–189. *Project Muse*. Web. 31 Oct. 2013.

Morton, Stephen. *Salman Rushdie*. Basingstoke: Palgrave Macmillan, 2008.

Nairn, Tom. *The Break-Up of Britain: Crisis and Neonationalism*. London: Verso, 1981.

_____. *Faces of Nationalism: Janus Revisited*. London: Verso, 1997.

Rushdie, Salman. "Imaginary Homelands." 1982. *Imaginary Homelands: Essays and Criticism, 1981–1991*. Salman Rushdie. London: Granta, 1992. 9–21.

————. "Is Nothing Sacred?" 1990. *Imaginary Homelands: Essays and Criticism, 1981–1991*. London: Granta, 1992. 415–430.

————. *Midnight's Children*. 1981. London: Vintage, 1995.

————. *Shame*. New York: Knopf, 1983.

————. "U2." *Step Across This Line: Collected Nonfiction 1992–2002*. New York: Random House, 2002. 94–98.

————. *The Satanic Verses*. 1988. London: Vintage, 2006.

Sabin, Margery. "Not Fusion." Review of Amit Chaudhuri, *Clearing a Space: Reflections on India, Literature and Culture*." *Essays in Criticism* 59.3 (2009): 270–279. *Oxford Journals*. Web. 31 Oct. 2013.

Strand, Eric. "Gandhian Communalism and the Midnight's Children's Conference." *ELH* 72.4 (2005): 975–1016. *Project Muse*. Web. 31 Oct. 2013.

Swann, Joseph, "East Is East and West Is West? Salman Rushdie's *Midnight's Children* as an Indian Novel." 1986. *The New Indian Novel in English: A Study of the 1980s*. Ed. Viney Kirpal. New Delhi: Allied, 1990. 251–262.

ten Kortenaar, Neil. "*Midnight's Children* and the Allegory of History." *ARIEL* 26.2 (1995): 41–62.

————. *Self, Text, Nation in Salman Rushdie's* Midnight's Children. Montreal: McGill Queen's UP, 2004.

Williams, Mark, "The Novel as National Epic: Wilson Harris, Salman Rushdie, Keri Hulme." *The Commonwealth Novel since 1960*. Ed. Bruce King. Houndmills: Macmillan, 1981. 185–197.

"A Collective Fiction": The (De)construction of Nehruvian India in *Midnight's Children*

Raita Merivirta

The Nehruvian Background

Jawaharlal Nehru (1889–1964), one of the main architects of modern India, argued for a pan-national Indian identity and an Indian cultural nation, but significantly, he also advocated unity in diversity, "a model committed to protecting cultural and religious difference rather than imposing a uniform 'Indianness'" (Khilnani 167). This was the model on which independent India was built when Nehru served as Prime Minister (1947–1964). After his death—and especially in the 1970s—the Nehruvian model started to erode. In both his "Indian" novels and in his non-fiction, Salman Rushdie manifests a deep commitment to the Nehruvian idea of India. In an early essay, he wrote:

> For a nation of 700 millions to make any kind of sense, it must base itself firmly on the concept of multiplicity, of plurality and tolerance, of devolution and decentralization wherever possible. There can be no one way—religious, cultural, or linguistic—of being an Indian; let difference reign (Rushdie, "Assassination" 44).

Rushdie is also very critical of the rule of Nehru's daughter, Indira Gandhi, in the 1970s, which, he asserts, betrayed the Nehruvian legacy. However, though he celebrates the Nehruvian idea, Rushdie also examines the failures and fault lines of Nehruvian India in his works and presents criticism of Nehru and 'his' India. In *Midnight's Children*, Rushdie's idea of India is markedly Nehruvian, but while portraying the nation in formation, Rushdie also depicts some of the oversights, failures, and problems of that project. This article examines how Nehruvian India is constructed, deconstructed, and assessed in *Midnight's Children*'s version of India's history.

Independent India is described in *Midnight's Children* as 'a collective fiction', 'a new myth' constructed by nationalist discourse that draws on the ancient Indian civilization and tradition as well as Western political ideas. The novel's main protagonist and narrator, Saleem Sinai, notes how, with independence, there was:

> a new myth to celebrate, because a nation which had never previously existed was about to win its freedom, catapulting us into a world which, although it had five thousand years of history, although it had invented the game of chess and traded with Middle Kingdom Egypt, was nevertheless quite imaginary: into a mythical land, a country which would never exist except by the efforts of a phenomenal collective will—except in a dream we all agreed to dream; it was a mass fantasy shared in varying degrees by Bengali and Punjabi, Madrasi and Jat, and would periodically need the sanctification and renewal which can only be provided by rituals of blood. India, the new myth—a collective fiction in which anything was possible, a fable rivalled only by the two other fantasies: money and God (Rushdie, *Midnight's Children* 130; further references preceded by *MC*).

Saleem describes Nehru's India here, the pervasiveness and mass appeal of the idea of India as a unified nation and sovereign political entity, a nation-state based on secularism and pluralism. In Saleem's—as well as Nehru's—story of the nation-state, the state gives territorial shape to the pre-existing community of the Indian cultural nation, but for the state to come into existence, not only political will, but a shared sense of Indian identity is needed. In *Midnight's Children*, Rushdie traces the development of this political nation.

Becoming Indian

Nehru occupies a central position in *Midnight's Children* from the beginning. Saleem's birth at the stroke of midnight on August 15, 1947, when India became independent, is narrated in parallel with Nehru's famous "Tryst with Destiny" speech; in effect, Nehru seems almost to be narrating the birth of Saleem. The connection between Nehru and Saleem is cemented when the former writes a letter to the latter:

Dear Baby Saleem, My belated congratulations on the happy accident of your moment of birth! You are *the newest bearer of that ancient face of India* which is also eternally young. *We* shall be watching over your life with the closest attention; it will be, in a sense, the mirror of our own (*MC* 143, emphases added).

Nehru's "we" here is clearly the Indian government's "we": Nehru's cabinet and administration will be watching over Saleem, whose life often parallels that of the newborn state. Josna E. Rege, a scholar of Indian colonial and postcolonial literature, argues that "the letter links the unlimited potential of the newborn infant both with that of the nascent state, with all its future glory lying before it, and with the India of timeless antiquity" (350). I would argue that it goes even further than that: the letter equates Saleem and the new state, and it connects them as "the newest bearer of that ancient face of India" (*MC* 143). As Saleem, in his allegorical form, embodies the state, his life mirrors the fortunes, misfortunes, and changes in the Indian government. Similarly, Saleem's ancestry is the ancestry of the state.

Saleem explains that the point at which his life "really began" (*MC* 4) was the early spring of 1915, when his grandfather, Aadam Aziz, the young, German-educated doctor recently returned from Europe, experienced a crisis of faith. Saleem chooses to trace his lineage from this particular grandfather, his maternal grandfather who, it turns out later, is actually not even biologically related to him. Literary scholar Neil ten Kortenaar argues that this is "because Saleem can identify with young Aziz and with his dreams of secularization and modernization" (37). I suggest that it is because in the novel, the birth of the idea of an Indian *political nation* is traced back to the late 1910s. Saleem describes the ideological formation and lineage of the state: the idea originally was advanced and advocated by modernized and somewhat Westernized Indians, such as Aadam Aziz. Though he later becomes a firm supporter of Mian Abdullah and the Free Islam Convocation, representing secular Muslim nationalism "sympathetic to, but not entirely represented by, the mainstream nationalism of the Congress" (Srivastava 57), Aadam Aziz seems to be Nehru's man through and through. He is actually quite like Nehru in age, Kashmiri origins, agnosticism, and Western education, and his politics are not dissimilar either. On an allegorical level, Aziz seems to embody the Nehruvian strand of secular political nationalism.

Though Saleem's family history mirrors the development of the Indian political nation, Rushdie's novel is not a nation-building narrative, but an exposition of such narratives; he is not writing a mythic or nationalist account of the nation's origins and development, but he is exploring how the political nation and the state came to be created and narrated by Nehru and other Indian leaders and historians. Rushdie's project is to look at the nation and state as they came to be, to examine their supporting nation-building narratives, and to prod and poke them, exposing problems and fault lines.

In Saleem's version, the story of the Indian state begins in 1915, the year Mahatma Gandhi returned to India from South Africa, though, significantly, neither Gandhi nor his arrival in India is mentioned in the novel at this point. Instead of concentrating on Gandhi and his role in leading India to independence, Saleem focuses on the Nehruvian ideals of modernization and secularization.

Aziz's crisis of faith—he can neither believe nor disbelieve either—is soon followed by a conversion to nationalism, which reflects Benedict Anderson's argument of the birth of nations when religiosity wanes. Aziz balances between his belief in modern Western science/medicine and the traditional wisdom and ancient practices of Tai the boatman, between his newly acquired Western education and Indian tradition, represented here by Naseem, and the landowner's daughter Aziz is treating. Though it seems that Rushdie thinks a dose of modernity, here represented by secularism and science/medicine, was needed to predispose Indians to the idea of a political nation that ultimately led to the birth of the Indian state, he also emphasizes the importance of the Indian cultural nation and the underlying, unifying civilization, much like Nehru, who "discovered a basis for unity both in a shared historical past of cultural mixing" (Khilnani 154). The marriage of Aadam Aziz and Naseem Ghani is a union of Western-derived modernity and Indian tradition and culture, which proves to be a fertile ground for the burgeoning Indian nationalism.

Nalini Natarajan (170) notes that when the young Aadam Aziz first meets and treats Naseem, "she is shown to him through holes in a sheet. As he treats her in parts he begins to imagine her as a whole. This coincides with his imagining a 'whole' Indian identity for himself, instead of his regional Kashmiri one." Aadam Aziz's process of becoming *Indian* is sealed in Amritsar, where the newlywed couple stops on 7 April 1919 on their way to Agra. Saleem notes that, at that time, though his grandfather apparently sympathizes with the people of British India and their plight,

> Aziz, with Tai in his head, does not feel Indian. Kashmir, after all, is not strictly speaking a part of the Empire, but an independent princely state. He is not sure if the *hartal* of pamphlet mosque wall newspaper is his fight, even though he is in occupied territory now (*MC* 32, emphasis added).

In the days before the massacre, Aziz is still influenced by old allegiances and kinships and his identity is largely regional. He is a Kashmiri, the idea of India as a political entity is still alien to him. The Indian subcontinent was, at the time of course, politically fragmented under local princes and kings and other parts under British rule. Yet, while most of the people of the subcontinent still clearly identify more with their region than with some pan-Indian idea, some of them are starting to feel the call of a common cause, the struggle for political rights and self-rule. The *hartal* described by Saleem refers to a traditional Indian method of protest by suspending all activity for a day. Such passive action was suggested by Gandhi as a moral response to the oppressive Rowlatt Acts that were passed in March 1919. The Rowlatt Acts allowed judges to try political cases without juries and gave the provincial governments the power of internment without trial. Naseem has trouble understanding this political use of *hartal*, and even Aadam is not fully convinced.

Arrests had followed anti-Rowlatt Acts meetings in Amritsar, causing rioting. As a consequence, mass meetings were prohibited, though this was not commonly known. On April 13, 1919, British

Brigadier-General Reginald Dyer broke up a prohibited meeting by ordering his men to shoot point-blank at the unarmed crowd of some 10,000 Indians in the enclosed Jallianwalla Bagh, a public garden. The multitude was gathered there on the occasion of a religious festival. After 1,650 bullets were fired, 379 people were killed and another 1,137 were injured.

The massacre has a profound effect on the young and honeymooning Aadam Aziz's identity. Aziz is in the thick of the crowd being fired at in Jallianwalla Bagh and is saved only by a sneeze and his consequent fall. The clasp of his doctor's bag, which has the word 'Heidelberg' inscribed on the bottom of it, brands his chest with a bruise that will not fade during his lifetime. Aziz explains later: "I started off as a Kashmiri and not much of a Muslim. Then I got a bruise on the chest that turned me into an Indian. I'm still not much of a Muslim, but I'm all for Abdullah. He's fighting my fight" (*MC* 40). What happened in Amritsar in April 1919 was enough to turn him, a middle-class Kashmiri into an Indian, his regional identity giving way to pan-Indian national identity. As Saleem puts it, "[s]tained by the bruise of a Heidelberg bag's clasp, we throw our lot in with India" (*MC* 124).

Historian Stanley Wolpert explains that "[m]illions of [...] Indians turned at this time from loyal supporters of the British Raj to nationalists who were no longer content to follow its orders or trust in the 'fair play' of its officials" (*MC* 300). Experiencing the worst excesses of colonial rule and being imprinted by Western modernity awakens nationalist feelings in Aadam Aziz, who joins millions of others in the subcontinent in becoming Indian in a political sense. In *Midnight's Children*, the ancient civilization of the subcontinent is now reimagined as a community with political potential by people like Aziz: educated, modernized, upper-middle class, upper caste elite of the subcontinent; they identify a cultural nation that needs to be turned also into a political nation. Aadam Aziz, like other secular nationalists, believes in a unified India and continues, years later, to support Free Islam Convocation leader Mian Abdullah against the Muslim League's demand for a separate country and the formation of the confessional Muslim State of Pakistan.

Following the Nehruvian line, Aadam Aziz is drawn towards secularism and modernization. In his eagerness to modernize and facilitate progress, Aadam burns his wife's veils. Subsequently, "[b]uckets are brought; the fire goes out; and Naseem cowers on the bed as about thirty-five Sikhs, Hindus, and untouchables throng in the smoke-filled room" (*MC* 33). The great Indian religions come together in the aftermath of the massacre, which helped to create an Indian identity for the people of the subcontinent, who had, until then, identified themselves first and foremost as Hindus, Muslims, and Sikhs as well as Bengalis, Punjabis, and Kashmiris. Natarajan reads this exposure of Naseem 'to the multiplicity of the Subcontinent' as "a signal for the melting pot of secular modernity" (*MC* 171). This is confirmed by Aadam's instruction to his wife: "Forget about being a good Kashmiri girl. Start thinking about being a modern Indian woman" (*MC* 33). Nehru's pluralist and secular idea of India, an India with "a civilizational tendency towards unification that would realize itself within the frame of a modern nation state" (Khilnani 166), requires that regional identities are subordinated to a new national one and that secularism and modernity are embraced by easing up on old traditional and religious ways, such as wearing a veil.

The Nehru Years

From the political awakening and the emerging construction of pan-Indian identity after the Amritsar Massacre, the novel's narrative jumps forward in time more than two decades. This means, as Timothy Brennan points out, that "the very staple of a major branch of Indo-English historical fiction, Gandhi's National Movement" is absent (84). This essay argues that the reason for the absence of Mahatma Gandhi from the story of Saleem Sinai after the Massacre is the fact that, in contrast to the industrial modernity and the West-derived nation state that Nehru envisioned, Gandhi favored a more indigenous type of society, with a focus on villages, religion, and traditional Indian values. Gandhi's ideology is omitted from Saleem's story of Nehruvian India, where dams and factories constitute the 'temples of the future' and modern secularism provides the nation-state its ideology, since the focus of the novel is on the formation of the Nehruvian secular ideology and the future nation state.

The foundation of this state is laid when Aziz's daughter Mumtaz—the offspring of Western-derived modernity and Indian tradition and culture as well as an embodiment of the Nehruvian strand of secular nationalism—marries the merchant Ahmed Sinai, an allegory of the Indian middle classes, and takes a new name, Amina. The wedding takes place in June 1946, the month in which the British Cabinet Mission proposed a plan to divide India into Hindu-majority India and Muslim-majority Pakistan, after the previous month's plan, which envisaged a united India, has fallen through. The Cabinet Mission visited India between March and June 1946 to negotiate the transfer of power to Indians. Discussions were held with the leaders of the Congress Party and All-India Muslim League about framing a new constitution for India and forming an interim government. The negotiations fell through in July 1946, and the popular agitation for Pakistan began with a "Direct Action Day" on August 16, 1946.

In early 1947, when the partition of India is officially accepted, Amina Sinai makes a public announcement about the child she is expecting. This happens in conjunction with declaring her secular principles and religious tolerance by saving the Hindu peepshow man Lifafa Das from the attack of an angry mob in the Old Delhi Muslim neighborhood. The Sinais soon leave these Muslim Quarters behind and move to multicultural Bombay. They settle on one of the houses on Methwold Estate with other Indian English-speaking, middle-class families of different religions.

The take-over of power in India by the upper-middle classes in the summer of 1947 is figured in ironic terms when the newly married, middle-class couple Amina and Ahmed take over and inhabit the house of William Methwold, who stands for the British from whom the state inherited its ruling classes, administrative and political systems, and its army. Saleem explains that "Methwold's estate was sold on two conditions: that the houses be bought complete with every last thing in them, that the entire contents be retained by the new owners; and that the actual transfer should not take place until midnight on August 15th" (*MC* 109). With the transfer of power, British rulers are replaced with 'brown Englishmen,' and nothing seems to change for the Indian masses, as the new elite expect the birth of the Indian state within the trappings of the old power. The outward structures of power are handed over "intact" to "suitable persons" (*MC* 111), such as the Sinais, by the British. More specifically, power is transferred from British men to Indian upper-middle-class men. While Rushdie takes almost for granted that the new, independent India is a secular state, home to Hindus, Muslims, Sikhs, Christians, Jains, and Parsis and does not really examine communalism, he takes issue with the inequality and differences in the citizen status between Indians of differing economic classes after Independence.

Much of the criticism in the novel about the class-based political inequality in independent India is presented through Ahmed Sinai who, like so many other Indian businessmen, "goes white" after Independence. Saleem describes "going white" as "a disease which leaked into history and erupted on an enormous scale shortly after Independence" (*MC* 46) when the "pigmentation disorder [...] afflicted large numbers of the nation's business community" (*MC* 212). Amina's husband represents the middle-class businessmen who benefited most from the transfer of power and prospered in independent India. The middle classes, the rich peasants, and the capitalists were "the main beneficiaries of the social system and economic development since 1947" (Chandra 24). Neelam Srivastava argues that "the class that came to identify most closely with Nehru's secular and developmentalist ideology was the English-speaking upper-middle-class elite that had stood most to gain from state-planned economic development" (7). The middle classes took the reins of the government and civil service and the subalterns largely remained subalterns, despite universal franchise and the outlawing of untouchability and caste-based discrimination by the Constitution of India in 1950.

At the precise hour of Independence, two fellow midnight's children, Saleem and Shiva, are born. Saleem and Shiva represent the division of the political nation after Independence, the haves and have-nots, the ones with political power and the individuals who are not full members of society. The babies are swapped at birth and Saleem, born of Indian (Vanita) and British (William Methwold) parents, comes to represent the Indian state, cared for mainly by the educated elite, the middle-class citizens, making the state ultimately their project. Shiva, on the other hand, whom Rushdie has described as Saleem's "kind of dark side," (*MC* 4) is raised in the slums by Wee Willie Winkie. Shiva, Saleem's Other, is pushed to a marginal existence in the underbelly of the independent state. He stands for the segment of Indians who were not integrated into the new nation state, the people who came to live in its margins, the people whom the nationalist project failed. The relation between the 'elite citizens' and the rest of the population that inhabits Indian territory becomes a significant theme in the otherwise positively described Nehru years.

Like Saleem explains, the one-thousand-and-one magical midnight's children, born in India within the first hour of Independence "can be made to represent many things, according to your point of view" (*MC* 240). And he continues: "they can be seen as the last throw of everything antiquated and retrogressive in our myth-ridden nation, whose defeat was entirely desirable in the context of a modernizing, 20th-century economy; or as the true hope of freedom, which is now forever extinguished" (*MC* 240). It is clear that for Saleem, as well as for Rushdie, the children were "the true hope of freedom" that was "forever extinguished" in the mid-1970s. In an interview, Rushdie has described the midnight's children as "a kind of metaphor of hope and possibility, which, one day, was destroyed. A metaphor of hope betrayed and of possibilities denied" ("*Midnight's Children* and *Shame*" 6). The midnight's children represent all the excited hope and political will of the early Nehru era.

Saleem convenes the *Midnight's Children*'s Conference in his head to discuss and debate matters, having discovered that his magical power is to be able "to act as a sort of national network, so that by opening my transformed mind to all the children I could turn it into a kind of forum in which they could talk to one another, through me [...] in the lok sabha or parliament of my brain" (*MC* 271). Here, the state allegory is perhaps most clear as excited debates take place in a kind of parliament provided by Saleem/the state. As Jean Kane argues, the parliament "represents the utopian promise of a just, democratic, and unified government" (*MC* 100). Furthermore, the nine-year-old Saleem has started to hear in his head the voices of not just other midnight's children, but of millions of his fellow countrymen: "Telepathy, then: the inner monologues of all the so-called teeming millions, of masses and classes alike, jostled for space within my head" (*MC* 200).

In Nehru's India, the "masses and classes alike" were jostling for space, the future seemed bright and full of promise, democratic, and just governance possible. Though the promises and the hopes represented by midnight's children were often utopian, the reality in Nehruvian India did sustain these hopes and even fulfilled some of the promises, at least where the middle classes were concerned.

Shiva, however, is alienated from middle-class politics and debates fiercely with Saleem. Shiva wants the two of them to be the uncontested leaders of the group, whereas Saleem, blinded to the realities of the masses by his middle-classness and his family's access to full citizenship and its benefits, is idealistically after a 'sort of loose federation of equals, all points of view given free expression' and strives for meaning, a purpose for their federation (*MC* 263). Shiva, representing the subalterns, who are not heard in the nation's podiums, retorts:

> What *purpose*, man? What thing in the whole sister-sleeping world got *reason,* yara? For what reason you're rich and I'm poor? Where's the reason in starving, man? God knows how many millions of damn fools living in this country, man, and you think there's purpose! Man, I'll tell you—you got to get what you can, do what you can with it, and then you got to die. That's reason, rich boy. Everything else is only mother-sleeping *wind* (263–264).

Brennan argues that "the contest between Saleem and Shiva is further portrayed as a debate between parties in a parliament chamber. It takes place in the arena of Midnight's Children's Conference, a microcosm of the Indian government" (*MC* 102). In my reading, Saleem and Shiva's debates bring forth the differences

Critical Insights

in political, economic and social possibilities between economic and social classes in Indian society. "The arena of Midnight's Children's Conference, a microcosm of the Indian government," is dominated by middle-class politics and values, represented here through Saleem's character, and the most potent opposition is quickly shut out, as the idealistic Saleem and the materialistic realist Shiva cannot see each other eye to eye. Eventually, the two part ways, and Shiva is no longer heard on the arena of the Midnight's Children's Conference/Indian government nor does he have a place in the institutions of Indian political or civil society.

The exclusion of Shiva from the Midnight's Children's Conference in 1958 is a critical mistake, which endangers the idealistic, optimistic, and until now, somewhat democratic conference and reinforces the dominance of the middle classes. The end of the Nehruvian consensus was coming to end.

After more than a decade of euphoric nation-building, development of science and technology, economic growth, prosperity, and high-powered foreign relations, which generated a sense of well-being and self-esteem, the 1960s brought with them crises and changes in India's international and national politics. Saleem convenes the Midnight's Children's Conference once more in October 1962, but the Conference disintegrates as China humiliates India in a short demonstration war in the North, signaling the end of the Nehru era. Saleem notes:

[A]s the midnight children lost faith in me, they also lost their belief in the thing I had made for them. Between October 20th and November 20th, I continued to convene—to attempt to convene—our nightly sessions; but they fled from me, not one by one, but in tens and twenties; each night, less of them were willing to tune in; each week, over a hundred of them retreated into private life. In the high Himalayas, Gurkhas and Rajputs fled in disarray from the Chinese army; and in the upper reaches of my mind, another army was also destroyed by things—bickerings, prejudices, boredom, selfishness—which I had believed too small, too petty to have touched them (*MC* 357–358).

Saleem describes a loss of faith in the state, the parliament, and in what democracy can do in India. This happens at the same time as the war with China, which broke Nehru's heart and India's confidence. The war with China disillusioned India about its own powers and capabilities. The last day of Saleem's old life is November 20, when the Chinese defeat Indian troops; the following day, the day of the ceasefire, Saleem's nose is operated on to drain his inflamed sinuses and clear it, bringing about a permanent break with the other children.

The brief but disastrous war with China was a shocking wake-up call for Jawaharlal Nehru and for India. The war crushed Nehru's hopes of great Asian unity and peaceful relations and shook his idealism drastically. Nehru's health deteriorated rapidly after the war. He suffered a stroke in January 1964 and passed away four months later. Saleem links the death of the founder of his family, Aadam Aziz, in January 1964, with the death of Nehru, thus confirming the connection between the two men: "after the death of my grandfather, Prime Minister Jawaharlal Nehru fell ill and never recovered his health. This fatal sickness finally killed him on May 27, 1964" (*MC* 334). The deaths of these two founding fathers are closely connected and mark the end of the Nehruvian era: "my grandfather was the founder of my family, and my fate was linked by my birthday to that of the nation, and the father of the nation was Nehru" (*MC* 334).

The End of an Era

Nehru, the leading figure of Indian political life from Independence until his death in 1964, was a staunch advocate of democracy, and he enjoyed the trust and support of millions of his countrymen. Yet, as Arvind Rajagopal states, "Nehruvianism, held to represent the consent of the majority, in fact involved only a small minority, comprised of the educated middle and upper classes" (*MC* 45). Despite its democratic and pluralist ideals, Nehruvian India did not manage to incorporate the poor and the subalterns—represented in the novel by Shiva—as true citizens, full members of society with equal opportunities. *Midnight's Children* points out that the lower classes have fallen through the cracks. The lower classes in Nehruvian India may have had the right to vote and they may have been politicized, but the middle classes held the power and dominated the polity and civil society.

Yet it is worth noting that, despite the fact that *Midnight's Children* includes criticism of the project of state formation and points out deficiencies in the system that did not extend full citizen's rights to all members of the nation, the Nehru era is remembered and described mainly in a very positive light in the novel. Nehru's idea of India is clearly approved of and even emulated, and Nehru's ideology is not criticized. Saleem's childhood appears happy, some minor events notwithstanding, and also the other midnight's children prosper in Nehruvian India. The Nehru era is thus contrasted strongly with the very different India under Nehru's daughter Indira Gandhi.

Works Cited

Anderson, Benedict. *Imagined Communities: Reflections on the Origin and Spread of Nationalism.* 1983. Revised Edition. London: Verso, 1991.

Brennan, Timothy. *Salman Rushdie and the Third World: Myths of the Nation.* Houndmills, Basingstoke and London: Macmillan, 1989.

Chandra, Bipan. *In the Name of Democracy: JP Movement and the Emergency.* New Delhi: Penguin Books India, 2003.

Kane, Jean M. "The Migrant Intellectual and the Body of History: Salman Rushdie's *Midnight's Children.*" *Contemporary Literature* 37.1 (1996): 94–100.

Khilnani, Sunil. *The Idea of India.* 1997. New York: Farrar, Straus, Giroux, 2001.

Natarajan, Nalini. "Woman, Nation, and Narration in *Midnight's Children.*" *Rushdie's* Midnight's Children: *A Book of Readings.* Ed. Meenakshi Mukherjee. Delhi: Pencraft International, 1999.

Rajagopal, Arvind. *Politics After Television: Religious Nationalism and the Reshaping of the Indian Public.* Cambridge: Cambridge UP, 2001.

Rege, Josna E. 'Victim into Protagonist? *Midnight's Children* and the Post-Rushdie National Narratives of the Eighties. *Studies in the Novel* 29.3 (1997): 342–375. *JSTOR.* Web. 16 Dec. 2013.

Rushdie, Salman. *Midnight's Children*. 1981. New York: Penguin Books, 1991.

_____. "The Assassination of Indira Gandhi." 1984. *Imaginary Homelands: Essays and Criticism 1981–1991*. London: Granta Books in association with Penguin Books, 1992. 41–46.

_____. "*Midnight's Children* and *Shame*." University of Aarhus. 7 Oct. 1983. Lecture. *Kunapipi* 7.1 (1985): 1–19.

Srivastava, Neelam. *Secularism in the Postcolonial Indian Novel: National and Cosmopolitan Narratives in English*. London: Routledge, 2008.

ten Kortenaar, Neil. *Self, Nation, Text in Salman Rushdie's* Midnight's Children. Montreal and Kingston: McGill-Queen's UP, 2004.

Wolpert, Stanley. *A New History of India*. 6th ed. New York: Oxford UP, 2000.

Indian Oral Narrative in Postmodern Historiography: A Reading of *Midnight's Children*

Madan M. Sarma

Midnight's Children and Postmodern Literature

The 1981 publication of Salman Rushdie's *Midnight's Children* marks the beginning of a new phase in Indian fiction in English. This phase witnessed daring innovations in the narrative as the new crop of novelists displayed greater confidence and ingenuity in the use of the English language and a greater urgency to negotiate with the vastness of India in their works of fiction.

Apart from its thematic novelty, what made *Midnight's Children* stand out in the 1980s were its metafictional character and its use of diverse narrative modes, including the ones associated with Indian oral narratives, magic realism, and (post-) modernist fragmentation. However, Rushdie's use of magic realism is somewhat different from that which comes across in the novelist Gabriel García Márquez's classic magical realist novel *Cien años de soledad* (*One Hundred Years of Solitude*). This point will be taken up in the latter part of this chapter. *Midnight's Children* is a metafiction because, unlike a conventional realistic novel, it revels in its own fictionality and deliberately and consistently draws attention to itself—its very constructedness. It is consciously self-reflexive: "… I must interrupt myself. I wasn't going to today, because Padma has started getting irritated whenever my narration becomes self-conscious, whenever, like an incompetent puppeteer, I reveal the hands holding the strings" (Rushdie 65; further references preceded by *MC*). In fact, postmodern texts are self-reflexive and are often marked by a playful and parodic tone.

Critics have described *Midnight's Children* as a multifaceted narrative that is "at once an autobiographical Bildungsroman, a picaresque comedy, a surrealist fantasy, a political and existential allegory, a topical satire, and a stylistic experiment" (Naik and

Narayan 203). Literary theorist Linda Hutcheon sees the novel as a historical metafiction, a form of postmodern fiction that works towards "a critical return to history and politics" (Hutcheon 61). She distinguishes this form of fiction from the realistic historical novel and suggests that, whereas the protagonist of a historical novel is or should be a type, that of a historiographic metafiction happens to be an ex-centric, a marginalized character who may play the key role in the fictional history. Hutcheon talks of some kind of conflation of history and fiction in historiographic metafiction. Literary scholar Michael McKeon rightly points out that evidence for both the separation and the conflation of history and fiction could be noticed even in the realistic novels of earlier periods (McKeon 808). According to Hutcheon and other critics, postmodern fiction problematizes the entire idea of historical knowledge. At the same time, as Hutcheon argues: "Postmodern fiction suggests that to rewrite or to re-present the past in fiction and in history is, in both cases, to open it up to the present, to prevent it from being conclusive and teleological" (Hutcheon 834).

In *Midnight's Children* one notices such postmodern features as the adoption of an apparently flippant attitude toward historical developments, a playful parody of events and (historical) personalities, the juggling and fictionalization of facts, and the celebration of fragmentation. Self-parody and trivialization of historical moments are obviously the features of postmodern irreverence for historical truth. Such trivialization and deliberate and extreme playfulness in narrating historical events and agents may undermine the role of the marginalized human agents, although such peripheral figures are given key roles in this novel. Though his tone is playful and ironic, the historiographer Saleem seems to emphasize the role of the subaltern in important phases of the Indian nationalist movement against colonial rule, including the initial phase of the Hindu-Muslim communal divide. As postcolonial scholar Nicole Weickgenannt Thiara points out: "Significantly, the invented anti-Partition Free Islam Convocation is under the dynamic and electrifying leadership of a subaltern, namely the Delhi magician Mian Abdullah, who is popularly referred to as the Humming bird" (Thiara 21).

Protagonist Saleem creates, or attempts to create, the impression that he is in control of the historical events and presents himself as the one responsible for a number of crucial historical moments and twists and turns. For instance, he asserts: "Let me state this quite unequivocally: it is my firm conviction that the hidden purpose of the Indo-Pakistani war of 1965 was nothing more or less than the elimination of my benighted family from the face of the earth" (*MC* 338). He flouts reasoning or cause and effect relationships and considers himself to be the prime mover of historical events: "the war happened because I dreamed Kashmir into the fantasies of our rulers; furthermore, I remained impure, and the war was to separate me from my sin" (*MC* 339). He claims that his chanting of a rhyme in the broken Gujarati language to mock its speech rhythm was responsible for a language riot in Bombay, as his rhyme was adopted by the anti-Gujarati protest marchers as their song of war (*MC* 191–192).

Chutnification of History

Saleem uses the Indian term *chutney* as a metaphor for historiography, indicating the juxtaposition of disparate ingredients and a loss of hierarchy. He questions and challenges the historiographic claims of authentic representation of the past. For his deliberate "chutnification" of history by blurring the boundaries between fiction and history, Saleem works on his memories, fantasies, and dreams, and tries to create a narrative around the recent history of the subcontinent, especially India. Rushdie's protagonist and perhaps his alter ego Saleem is inexorably "handcuffed to history," his "destinies indissolubly chained to those" of his country—his nation, India—because both were born at the stroke of midnight of August 15, 1947. This coincidence is behind Saleem's obsession with the idea of presenting his own life or the lives of his grandfather and father in relation to that of the nation. In the process, he tends to ignore certain phases in India's anti-colonial struggle (e.g. the 1920s).

Saleem is an autobiographer (*MC* 443), the grand biographer of the nation, and a chronicler of his time at the same time because, while narrating the story of his life, he unfolds the history of country pertaining to the pre-independence and post-independence periods. As Søren Frank says: "Before his personal disintegration, Saleem attempts to produce a meaningful personal identity, mainly through the correspondences he creates between his personal story, his family's story, and the history of the Indian subcontinent" (Frank 134). Saleem's evocation of the parallel between himself and India is justified on the grounds that he is born at the exact moment of modern, independent India's birth. While narrating the history of the nation, he presents various events in such a manner as to make his role the central one.

While conventional historians write or reconstruct history by accessing archives and gathering information from various sources to find the truth, Saleem's sources are his memory—"my new, all-knowing memory" (*MC* 88), telepathy and his "powers of sniffing-out-the-truth" (*MC* 307). However, memory has its own advantages and disadvantages, which Saleem admits to his listener Padma. Saleem assures her that he is telling the truth. Saleem's truth is memory's truth-distorted, embellished, pared by memory: "'I told you the truth,' I say yet again, 'Memory's truth, because memory had its own special kind. It selects, eliminates, alters, exaggerates, minimizes, glorifies, and vilifies also; but in the end it creates its own reality, its heterogeneous but usually coherent version of events'" (*MC* 211).

What is more important is that Saleem's narrative may prove to be the source materials for future historians:

> It is possible, even probable, that I am only the first historian to write the story of my undeniably exceptional life-and-times. Those who follow in my footsteps will, however, inevitably come to this present work, this source-book, this Hadith or Purana or *Grundrisse*, for guidance and inspiration (*MC* 295).

As Saleem becomes aware of the disintegration of his body, he begins to write his autobiography and, in the process, rewrites or reassembles the materials/sources for writing the history of India. This rewriting takes the form of narration to Padma.

Midnight's Children and the Indian Oral Traditions

Rushdie here is concerned with alternative historiography for presenting, which he adopts what colonial literature researcher Kumkum Sangari calls "a non-mimetic mode" that cannot be seen as "continuous with postmodernism" (Sangari 912). This non-mimetic mode, or what Frederick Luis Aldama calls "magicorealism," is informed by the (primarily oral) narrative tradition preserved in the Indian epics, puranas, and folk tales. At the same time, the narrator resorts to postmodernist strategies of fragmentation, deliberate fallibility, and uncertainty.

The Sanskrit epics, the *Ramayana* and the *Mahabharata* were preserved and transmitted as oral texts, at times giving rise to a number of folk versions in different parts of India (often resulting in total transformation of the story, especially of the smaller text of the *Ramayana*). As rightly pointed out by Sangari: "The informality of the epic structure—the scope for interpolation, digression, accretion, in addition to its self-ascribed status as history or *itihaas* (for example the *Mahabharata*)—has allowed it in the past to represent ideological collectivities as well as to permit the expression of contesting world views" (Sangari 913). The *Mahabharata* is described as an *itihaas* of great merit. The word *itihaas* originally meant an event of the past, and later, it came to mean myth, legend, and story (Kapoor 953). Much later, however, the word came to mean history in a number of Indian languages.

The flexibility (rather than "informality") of the epic structure of the *Mahabharata* and the *Ramayana* (to a lesser extent) allows digressions, interpolations, and embedding of one story in another, as well as a multitude of characters and events of different periods in the past. Though the *Ramayana* contains a number of episodes that are not intimately connected to the main plot, such incorporation is more abundant in the *Mahabharata*, which, with 100,000 *slokas* (verses), is really a storehouse of folk tales, myths, and legends. The *Mahabharata* has such instances where what happened to a character or even to his family in the distant past, even in another life, might have repercussions in his or his family's present. Births and deaths are often prophesied in the *Puranas*. The "daivavani," or oracle, predicted the birth of Lord Krishna as the eighth child of Daivaki. Such features are utilized by the narrator of *Midnight's Children* mainly for parodic purposes. Saleem pompously claims: "Believe it or not, I was prophesied twice" (*MC* 113). The epics contain both historical and fictional materials; places, persons referred to, and certain events mentioned in the *Ramayana* and the *Mahabharata* have been found to be factually correct.

The puranas (ancient lore), written in Sanskrit, "expounding ancient Indian theogony, cosmogony, genealogies, and accounts of kings and rishis, religious beliefs, worship" also contain tales, legends, anecdotes, and fables (Kapoor 1,458). In *Midnight's Children*, the Kashmiri boatman, Tai, is a puranic figure, ageless, all-seeing, a witness to an almost mythical past. So he can claim that "I have watched the mountains being born; I have seen emperors die. [...] I saw that Isa, that Christ, when he came to Kashmir" (*MC* 16). Much later, Padma's excursion to locate herbs for Saleem's treatment helped the latter to connect himself "with the world of ancient learning"; Saleem gets an idea of the vastness of time measured in Hindu mythology by referring to a typical day for Brahma, the supreme creator (*MC* 194).

Saleem's attempt to trace his genealogy in the first book of the novel has Puranic parallel. Towards the end, however, this genealogy is "completely subverted when he discloses that, instead of being the true son of Amina and Ahmed, he is in fact a simulacrum in the genealogies of the Aziz and the Sinai families" (Frank 135). So Saleem's genealogy appears to be a parody of Puranic concern for authentic genealogy.

The oral character of the *Mahabharata* can be perceived from its first canto, the *Adviparva*. Saleem confuses the narrative of this epic with that of the *Ramayana*. Padma's absence for two days (in the chapter "Accident in a washing-chest") makes the narrator miss his "necessary ear"—so he says: "When Valmiki, the author of the *Ramayana*, dictated his masterpiece to elephant-headed Ganesh, did the god walk out on him half-way?" (*MC* 149).

In the Adiparva of the *Mahabharata*, the sage Vyasa, the author-compiler of the epic, says to the elephant-headed god, Ganesh: "O guide of the *Ganas*! be thou the writer of the *Bharata* which I have formed in my imagination, and which I am about to repeat." Ganesh agrees to write on the condition that his pen will not "for a moment cease writing." Vyasa knows that there would be occasions when he would be required to pause and think before dictating to Ganesh. So he lays down one important condition for the scribe: "Wherever there be anything thou dost not comprehend, cease to continue writing" (Ganguli). In *Midnight's Children*, Padma occasionally plays the role of Ganesh, though she is illiterate and can only listen and react to Saleem's narration. She plays an important role: she goads him on to continue his story.

The epic the *Mahabharata* has numerous interpolations, chain stories, episodes, and a multitude of characters from different times and places. Miraculous and fantastic coexist with the real in the epic. The fantastic is not mere embellishment or entertainment. The focus has all along been on the underlying (symbolic) meaning or truth. Rushdie uses fantasy as a method to produce what he describes as "intensified images of reality" (Haffenden 246). The serial nature of folk tales is noticed in many texts in Indian languages and also in Sanskrit texts, such as *Panchtantra* from the second century, *Brihadkathasangraha* from the fifth century, *Kathasaritsagara* and *Brihadkathasarita* both from the eleventh century. Gunadhya's *Brihadkathasangraha*, written originally in the Paisachi Prakrit language, was later translated into Sanskrit and lost forever. Only some stories were preserved and made their way into the *Alif Laila wa-Laila,* or the *Arabian Nights.*

Apart from the in itself allusive number of the one-thousand-and-one midnight's children, Saleem alludes to the *Arabian Nights* on a number of occasions. In the novel's opening chapter, Saleem says that he has many stories to tell, stories involving "an excess of intertwined lives events miracles places rumours" (*MC* 9). As he is crumbling and disintegrating, he must tell his story/stories fast; he cannot count on having one-thousand-and-one nights: "I must work faster than Scheherazade" (*MC* 7). Saleem takes up his incomplete narrative, which he "left yesterday hanging in mid-air—just as Scheherazade […] used to do night after night!" (*MC* 24).

Literary critic Meenakshi Mukherjee has drawn our attention to the sharing of myths by both narrators and listeners of oral tales: "The sharing of a common mythology between the narrator and the audience is a general condition of the oral tradition of story telling" (Mukherjee 131). Both Saleem, a Muslim, and Padma are aware of the mythological significance of the names Ganesh, Padma, Shiva, Buddha, and Ravana. Ravana has always been a symbol of demonic forces because it was he who abducted Sita, the epitome of virtue and chastity in Hindu mythology. So the destructive gang of "never do wells" is referred to as the Ravana gang even by the Muslims (*MC* 85).

Any conflict between good and evil immediately reminds even a Christian woman like Mary Pereira of the epic conflict between the Pandavas and Kauravas in the *Mahabharata* (*MC* 245). Saleem realizes that the new phase in India's history, beginning on August 15, 1947, is not new at all, since it is just a flitting instant in the age of darkness, the mythical *Kali-Yuga*, lasting for several hundred thousand years. And like the entire *Yug*, this phase too is ruled by confusion and brittle morality (*MC* 194).

Storytelling

Saleem is not only an autobiographer but also an objective chronicler as well as a story teller. At the age of thirty-one, Saleem decides to write his story. Quite early in the narrative he declares: "And there are so many stories to tell, too many, such an excess of intertwined lives events miracles places rumours, so dense a commingling of the improbable and the mundane!" (*MC* 9). The words "miracles" and "improbable" are notable in view of the narrator's allegiance to the ancient story telling tradition and magic realism.

Traditionally, storytelling sessions are marked by interruptions and digressions. As Mukherjee observes: "The digressive method of storytelling is perhaps the oldest device in narrative literature" (Mukherjee 131). In *Midnight's Children*, too, narrator Saleem is occasionally interrupted and forced to digress. First, he goes back to 1915 to his grandfather Aadam Aziz's time. Then there is a little digression as he goes on to narrate the story of boatman Tai. After narrating the events of 1919, Saleem comes to 1942, in order to highlight what appeared to him to be the major historical events.

Saleem's narration does not follow a strict sequence; he narrates the events or episodes in the order in which they are brought to the surface by his memory. This necessitates breaking of linearity, which is noticed in oral narratives and also in the narratives of Indian epics. In the epics, interpolations or digressions were added to the original work, disrupting the linear movement of the plot. A similar strategy has been used by the narrator of *Midnight's Children*. Padma, his lone audience, is not ready to allow him to digress or break the familiar linearity: "But here is Padma at my elbow, bullying me back into the world of linear narrative, the universe of what-happened-next" (*MC* 38). She interrupts to protest: "You get a move on or you'll die before you get yourself born" (*MC* 38). She is an attentive listener who does not like the leisurely pace (like the oral storytellers) adopted by Saleem to tell his story, "To me, it's a crazy way of telling your life story," she cries, "if you can't even get to where your father met your mother" (*MC* 38).

Padma raises objection to the narrator's remarks about her name (*MC* 32). She does not hesitate to comment on some of the characters (for example, Mian Abdullah) and events (*MC* 46), but as she becomes more attentive, Saleem the storyteller "warms" his theme. Padma's "contradictory love of the fabulous" (*MC* 38) and her idiosyncrasy allow her to readily accept the fact that Mian Abdullah could ceaselessly hum like an engine or a dynamo (*MC* 46). At times, she nods in agreement with a character's observation conveyed to her by Saleem: "'We have been alive too long, and we know.' (Padma is nodding her head in agreement.)" (*MC* 47). She makes an occasional observation about a character and even worries about him or her: "'Poor girl,' Padma concludes, 'Kashmiri girls are normally fair like mountain snow, but she turned out black. Well, well, her skin would have stopped her making a good match, probably"; she even sympathizes with Mumtaz, the dark girl and predicts what the family would do after discovering her relationship with Nadir Khan (*MC* 57). Sometimes, she grows impatient with the pace of the narrative and also with what appeared to be mere digressions. She says, "I don't want to know about this Winkie now; days and nights I've waited and still you won't get to being born" (*MC* 102). The narrative delay irritates her and Saleem imagines that she was "stirring her vats like a whirlwind, as if that would make the time go faster" (*MC* 106). Finally, she is satisfied: "'At last', Padma says with satisfaction, 'you've learned how to tell things really fast'" (*MC* 109). Padma's gullibility is revealed as the twist in Saleem's story of his life confuses her about his being "fathered by history" (*MC* 118). Padma could even be jealous of (or angry with) written words (*MC* 122). As sulking Padma stays away, Saleem realizes that her "paradoxical earthiness of spirit" keeps his feet on the ground and that her ignorance and superstition are necessary counterweights to his "miracle-laden omniscience" (*MC* 150).

Sangari talks about the "fabulous realism" of *Midnight's Children.* The self-conscious narrator deliberately highlights the fantastic elements in his revelations: "I am coming to the fantastic heart of my own story" (*MC* 195). This is quite unlike the fantastic in the traditional oral narratives, where the fantastic moves seamlessly with the real. Saleem describes the fantastic feats and capabilities of the midnight's children who had "exotic multiplicity of gifts" (*MC* 198): one who never forgot what he heard or saw, one had the power to cure any ailment by touch, another could fly above the birds just by closing eyes, one could prophesy the future, while another could step into mirrors and re-emerge through any reflective surface. The narrator uses Puranic mythology to name the characters as Parvati, Shiva, Narada, Markendaya, and so on. He admits the metaphorical and allegorical connotations of these children and their fantastic faculties. He first says: "I have stated before that I am not speaking metaphorically," but a little later he claims: "Reality can have metaphorical content; that does not make it less real" (*MC* 200).

Saleem's narrative does not maintain the usual linearity of folk tales. Rather, it adopts a method that is similar to the epic strategy of going back in time, coming back to the present, and then again looking for resonances of the present in certain incidents of the past. Conventions of folk tales, such as referring to an indefinite, indeterminate period in the past are used to convey the ironic

---

stance of the narrator. Such playfulness stands out against Saleem's fastidiousness with time and place, as in the following: "Once upon a time there was a mother who, in order to become a mother, had agreed to change her name" (*MC* 213). Or in the intertextually playful passage in which the narrator leaves out the last two words of the traditional fairy tale ending—"ever after"—"And we all lived happily...."—but even then his story "does indeed end in fantasy" (*MC* 326). This is a reference to the sham democratic election in Pakistan, a country where "reality quite literally ceases to exist" (*MC* 326).

Creative Take on Narrative Tradition

In *Midnight's Children* Rushdie also uses magic realism as a device for foregrounding the postcolonial historical, social, and ideological contexts of the work that incorporates and modifies the past in an effort to give it a new and different meaning as historiographic metafiction usually does. As already hinted, in García Márquez's classic work of magic realism *One Hundred Years of Solitude*, magic realism is interwoven with realistic narration. The way the narrator describes the events does not give the reader the impression that the former had any doubt about the possibility of the things really happening as described. For example, the following example of magic realistic incidents can be cited from *One Hundred Years of Solitude*:

> ...Remedios the beauty gave off not breath of love but a fatal emanation...[when Remedios and her friends] went into the plantings the air became impregnated with a fatal fragrance. 'The men who were working along the rows felt possessed by a strange fascination, menaced by some invisible danger, and many succumbed to a terrible desire to weep' (García Márquez 240).

One may find an echo of this passage in *Midnight's Children*: "He took to drifting slowly past the Aziz household, releasing the dreadful fumes of his body across the small garden and into the house. Flowers died; birds fled from the ledge outside old Father Aziz's window" (*MC* 27).

The following passage from *Midnight's Children*, then, reminds one of a passage in García Márquez where the mother of the children of the Buendía family makes sweets that cause insomnia:

> Amina began to feel the emotions of other people's food seeping into her—because Reverend Mother doled out the curries and meatballs of intransigence, dishes imbued with the personality of their creator; Amina ate the fish salans of stubbornness and the birianis of determination (García Márquez 139).

In this and other instances, Rushdie's narration takes the magic realist path. However, in Rushdie's novel, magical happenings are narrated in a matter of fact tone, as if there were nothing unusual about them. The author describes them as naturally as he talks. At no point does the narrator draw the reader's attention to those features of the text that might sound unusual or incredible.

In a self-reflexive novel like *Midnight's Children*, however, the narrator may emphasize the deliberateness of the use of the device or mode of magic realism. Thus we see a slightly different use of the mode of magic realism in such novels. Rushdie's narrator refers to his "miracle-laden omniscience" (*MC* 165) and announces: "I am coming to the fantastic heart of my own story, and must write in plain unveiled fashion, about the midnight children" (*MC* 195). Miraculousness of some of the incidents have been deliberately foregrounded: the narrator states that each of the one thousand and one children born during the first hour of August 15, 1947 were "endowed with features, talents, or faculties which can only be described as miraculous" (*MC* 195). The narrator is occasionally troubled by the thought that he may be disbelieved, and on one occasion says: "Please believe that that I am falling apart [...]. I'm literally disintegrating" (*MC* 37). Only in a few instances, the magical seems to be smoothly woven into the everyday: "I can reveal most of the secrets of my neighborhood, because the grown-ups lived their lives in my presence without fear of being observed, not knowing that, years later, someone would look back through baby-eyes and decide to let the cats out of their bags" (*MC* 129).

In Rushdie's narrative one often hears the narrator's urban, sophisticated voice assume an ironic tone that goes against the naturalness of both traditional oral narrative and magic realism (as practiced by García Márquez): "I mean quite simply that I have begun to crack all over like an old jug—that my poor body, singular, unlovely, buffeted by too much history, subjected to drainage above and drainage below, mutilated by doors, brained by spittoons, has started coming apart at the seams" (*MC* 32). At times, however, Rushdie's excessive use of metaphorical language might have come from his deliberate ploy of imitating and distorting the way conversations are usually structured and thoughts are expressed in many Indian languages.

As Sangari points out, there is a conflation of an oral narrator with a modernist narrator in *Midnight's Children*, leading to "an interesting parodic result" (Sangari 913). This is quite apparent towards the end of the novel, where the narrator refers to the declaration of Emergency, marking "the beginning of a continuous midnight" (*MC* 419). This historical moment coincides with the birth of Saleem's son, who too was "mysteriously handcuffed to history" and who was "the child of a father who was not his father; but also the child of a time which damaged reality so badly that nobody ever managed to put it together again" (*MC* 420). The oral narrative strategies help the narrator to capture the bewildering variety and complexity of Indian society, with it numerous castes, creeds, beliefs, and cultures often overlapping other cultures. These oral narrative strategies also help to reveal political turmoil over land and water rights and, above all, language, with its secular ethos.

Edward Sackey talks about a number of African novelists drawing on the narrative of African tradition for structure, theme, and style, and suggests continuation of the oral traditions in "dialectic tension within the novel form" (Sackey 389). While, the African novelists like Ayi Kwei Armah and Ngũgĩ wa Thiong'o worked toward "the Africanization of the novel form" (Sackey 390), one feels that, in Rushdie, the adoption and creative use of the oral and written narrative tradition of India and his combining of narrative strategies culled from this tradition with magicorealism or magic realism do not signal any such attempt at Indianization.

In spite of the narrator's attempt to make creative use of the indigenous narrative tradition, the overall tone of the entire narration appears to be modern, quizzical, ironic, half-believing himself and, in the process, turning the oral folk narrative upside down. Sangari observation seems to be relevant here: "The totalizing and meandering potential of his chosen form cohabits uneasily with a modernist epistemology of the fragment, the specific perspectivism of a bourgeois subject" (Sangari 915). Perhaps this and the extreme playfulness preclude the possibility of going beyond mere problematizing the very possibility of historical knowledge to attempt a more balanced revisioning of history.

Works Cited

Aldama, Frederick Luis. *Postethnic Narrative Criticism: Magicorealism in Oscar "Zeta" Acosta, Ana Castillo, Julie Dash, Hanif Kureishi and Salman Rushdie.* Austin: U of Texas P, 2003.

Frank, Søren. *Migration and Literature: Günter Grass, Milan Kundera, Salman Rushdie, and Jan Kjærstad.* New York: Palgrave Macmillan, 2008.

García Márquez, Gabriel. *One Hundred Years of Solitude.* 1967. Trans. Gregory Rabassa. New Delhi: Penguin India, 1981.

Haffenden, John. "Salman Rushdie." 1983. *Novelists in Interview.* Ed. John Haffenden. London: Methuen, 1985.

Hutcheon, Linda. "Historiographic Metafiction." 1988. *The Theory of the Novel: A Historical Approach.* Ed. Michael MacKeon. Baltimore and London: The Johns Hopkins UP, 2000. 830–850.

_____. *A Poetics of Postmodernism: History, Theory, Fiction.* New York and London: Routledge, 1988.

_____. *The Politics of Postmodernism.* New York & London: Routledge, 1989.

Kapoor, Subodh, ed. *The Hindus: Encyclopaedia of Hinduism.* Vols. 2 and 3. New Delhi: Cosmo Publications, 2000.

Naik, M. K. and Shyamala A. Narayan. *Indian English Fiction.* New Delhi: Pencraft International, 2009.

Mahabharata, The. Transl. Kishori Mohan Ganguli. 22 Jan. 2005. Web. 20 Dec. 2013. <http://www.sacred-texts.com/hin/maha/>.

McKeon, Michael. "The New Novel, the Postmodern Novel." *The Theory of the Novel: A Historical Approach*. Ed. Michael McKeon. Baltimore & London: The Johns Hopkins UP, 2000. 803–808.

Mukherjee, Meenakshi. *The Twice Born Fiction: Indian Novel in English*. 1971. Delhi: Pencraft International, 2001.

Rao, K.Raghavendra. "The Novel on History as 'Chutney': Unriddling Salman Rushdie's *Midnight's Children*." *Perspectives on Indian Fiction in English*. Ed. M. K. Naik. New Delhi: Abhinav Publications, 1985. 150–160.

Rushdie, Salman. *Midnight's Children*. 1981. London: Vintage, 1995.

Sackey, Edward. "Oral Tradition and the African Novel." *Modern Fiction Studies* 37.3 (Autumn 1991): 389–407. *JSTOR*. Web. 10 Feb. 2009.

Sangari, Kumkum. "The Politics of the Possible." 1987. *The Theory of the Novel: A Historical Approach*. Ed. Michael McKeon. Baltimore and London: The Johns Hopkins UP, 2000. 900–922.

Thiara, Nicole Weickgenannt. *Salman Rushdie and Indian Historiography: Writing the Nation into Being*. New York: Palgrave Macmillan, 2009.

Bombay in *Midnight's Children*

Lotta Strandberg

Saleem and the Urban-Rural Binary in India

Bombay literature today is as frequent as any global-city literature. The vagabonds, the dandies, the romantics, the political conflicts, and different forms of urban violence, and so on, all find their unique representation in Bombay literature.

Released in 1981, *Midnight's Children* signals the start for Salman Rushdie's sustained engagement with the city, a theme which he continues in 1988's *The Satanic Verses*, 1995's *The Moor's Last Sigh*, and 1999's *The Ground Beneath Her Feet*. How Bombay is represented in *Midnight's Children* is not straightforward, and anthropologist Thomas Blom Hansen has argued that the novel is a story, which unfolds in Bombay but is not a story about Bombay (Hansen 91). However, the story only partly unfolds in Bombay, and is, as I intend to show, actually a story about Bombay and part of a diverse Bombay literature.

When first-person narrator Saleem Sinai tells the story of himself and his family, it is a story of cities, of displacements, and relocations. Saleem and his family are linked to the cities they reside in, and each city on their journey brings its contribution to history to the table. The novel begins in Srinagar in Kashmir, long before Saleem's birth. We learn that his grandparents move from Srinagar to Amritsar and later to Agra. His parents, on the other hand, make the journey to Delhi and Bombay, where Saleem is born. Together with his family, Saleem moves to Rawalpindi in Pakistan and back to Bombay, only to return to Pakistan and Karachi. Here, he loses his family, an event that has a devastating effect on him, and we find him somewhere in the Pakistani countryside without memory or emotions. He has assumed a dog-like shape, become a scout in the Pakistani army, and participates in the war in East-Pakistan, today's Bangladesh. Dwelling in the jungles of the Sundarbans, he regains his memory and human shape and returns first to Delhi and Benares

(Varanasi) and then to Bombay, where we encounter him in the narrative present as he unfurls the story to his only audience, Padma.

To deprive the main character of its human traits by making it dog-like and robotic, as it resides in rural terrains, is a vested statement, which speaks directly to the heart of the Indian independence struggle, nationalism, and identity. Traditionally, the agricultural countryside has been privileged to urban spaces. It is an important reservoir of ideological and political imaginary for the development of Indian national consciousness, as it is seen to harbor the original Indian culture, unblemished by colonialism.

This rural pastoral is an ingredient in Indian independence movements, namely Gandhianism. Its centrality is emphasized by many important Indian literary figures, such as the Bengali writers Rabindranath Tagore (1861–1941) and Bankim Chandra Chatterjee (1838–1894). Later, the Indian film industry did little to remedy the bias with films like *Mother India* (dir. Mehboob Khan, 1957). Also, the importance of Maoism in Indian politics and the Subaltern Studies Group on the Indian intellectual arena continued the focus on the Indian villages, assigning agency and political determination to rural India. Even *Midnight's Children* has its share of nostalgia for an uncontaminated past, when Saleem repeatedly turns to the precolonial/pre-Bombay romantic fishermen-scene: *"in this primeval world before clocktowers, the fishermen—who were called Kolis—sailed in Arab dhows, spreading red sails against the setting sun. They caught pomfret and crabs, and made fish-lovers of us all"* (Rushdie 100; further references preceded by *MC*).

By contrast, the city represents an odd combination of both colonial past and modernity. Rashmi Varma, a researcher of the postcolonial city, has convincingly demonstrated how immensely popular films like *Shri 420* (dir. Raj Kapoor, 1955) produced an image of Bombay as "a place of relentless exchange and enterprise, where values are expressed in terms of money and where emotions are commodities" (Varma 2004, 68). Rushdie's intervention with the dog-like Saleem draws attention to the urban-rural binary divide in India, and the way the rural poor have been hailed and championed for political purposes, such as the independence struggle, and equally abused and exploited for other purposes, such as warfare.

This chapter intends to show how Rushdie, in *Midnight's Children*, addresses three vital questions about the metropolis Bombay, which also divides this essay into three different sections. The first section places Rushdie's engagement with Bombay within the discourse of globalization and asks how does Rushdie contributes to versifying the debate in globalization studies about the relationship between the global, the national and the urban? The second section addresses the particular postcolonial aspects of Bombay in *Midnight's Children* by asking how Bombay is represented in the novel. Finally, the essay moves to analyze how *Midnight's Children* presents a notion of Bombay that is flavored by a specific diasporic patina. Jointly, these three aspects provide an analysis of how important the city as an urban milieu is for Rushdie's work and for a reading of *Midnight's Children*.

Globalization

Globalization studies have suffered from the division of academic disciplines, which predominantly has favored the nation-state (Sassen). The nation, culture, or languages are dominant ports of entry for researchers in both the social sciences and humanities, which have resulted in compartmentalized foci on research topics. However, as sociologist Saskia Sassen comments, the assumption that the "nation-state is a closed unit and that the state has exclusive authority over its territory" (Sassen 4) cannot effectively serve the study of globalization, which, in its essence, is transnational and transgresses such boundaries. Since the 1990s, attempts have been made to remedy this problem by focusing on movement and fluidity between spaces. As a concrete example of how globalization could be addressed, anthropologist Arjun Appadurai analyses five different themes significantly defining global cultural formations; that is, the global flows of people (ethnoscapes), technology (technoscapes), finances (financescapes), the production and dissemination of information (mediascapes), and ideas (ideoscapes). These five themes impact each other and jointly constitute "imagined worlds, that is, multiple worlds that are constituted by the historically situated imaginations of persons and groups spread around the globe" (Appadurai 33). This seems to be fruitful way to circumvent the nation-state, which he believes is not a sustainable entity (Appadurai 32–36).

Moving in another direction, globalization studies have focused on the city; its economies, its culture, and its politic as an arena for these flows. Again, transgressions became the focal point as the city itself became blurred; the city-limits, which traditionally were marked by walls and gates, and thus indisputable, seem to evaporate, and even suburbia appears to be swallowed up by the 'city-region' or the metropolis, which extended its tentacles beyond both region and nation-state (Roy 820). Rushdie intervenes in these discussions by focusing on tensions between the global, the national, and the metropolis. Like Chinese boxes, one location is embedded in the other, but unlike Chinese boxes, they do not fit together easily. By depicting and scrutinizing the flows and transgressions between them, Rushdie provides a fruitful intervention to the study of globalization.

Midnight's Children is a novel about the birth of a nation, its aspirations, hopes and failures, and it is an astute political critique of the post-independence politics of India. The travel itinerary of Saleem's family, presented earlier, reveals some important aspects of the novel. The vagabond life-style of Saleem and his family allows them to be at the very locations where Indian history is made. Rushdie uses location and relocation as a way to claim first-hand observations or narrator presence of history-in-the-making. Like prime minister Jawaharlal Nehru, Saleem's grandfather, Aadam Aziz is a secular, Western-educated Kashmiri; he happens to be in Amritsar during the massacre in 1919, when British troops shoot into an unarmed crowd of Indian protesters, killing hundreds of people; it is a decisive moment for Indo-British relations. However, since the storyteller Saleem is born only on page 130, the telling of the events before his birth has to find some other form of justification, and Saleem argues that everything "really began, some 32 years before anything as obvious, as *present*, as clockridden, crime-stained birth" (*MC* 4, emphasis in the original). He draws attention to his Kashmiri background and his grandfather's similarities with Nehru. Saleem emerges as the mediascape of these eye-witness accounts in the "business of remaking (his) life" (*MC* 2). The most obvious temporal coincidence is, of course, Saleem's own birth. Together with the independent India and originally 1,000 other midnight's children, he is born at midnight on August 15, 1947. This connection between the Aziz-Sinai family history and the history of the nation-state merges the domestic narrative with a public one (Gurnah 94).

Saleem's family's move to Bombay resembles a myriad of similar relocations; it is the hope of a prosperous future and financial gains to be made as the British are about to leave Bombay. Ahmed Sinai, Saleem's father, wants to partake of the financescape of the metropolis, and not even the humiliation of enacting William Methwold's colonial charade can diminish the pleasure of being part of this future. After partition, Muslim assets are frozen, which not only paralyzes the father, but also makes him impotent, as is clear from the following dialogue between Ahmed and Amina: "'The bastards have shoved my balls in an ice-bucket!' […]. 'Oh my goodness, jamun, I thought you were just talking dirty but it's true! So cold, Allah, so coooold, like little round cubes of ice!'" (*MC* 153-154). The family is on the verge of bankruptcy, and there are no means to bribe the court in order to get the funds released. In resourceful decisiveness, Amina Sinai, Saleem's mother engages in another branch of the diverse and multidimensional financescape of the city, as she pursues her luck in gambling on horses.

If cities are central arenas, in which history is enacted, it implies that as Rushdie allegorizes Indian history, it is condensed to the cities and to Bombay in particular. The postcolonial researcher Vassilena Parashkevova notes a certain duplicity: on the one hand, Bombay functions as a frame that shapes Saleem's history of India, while on the other, it is a framed narrative, which seems to be contained within this history (Parashkevova 52). Even though, narrating the allegory of the nation, Bombay is the lens through which this history is perceived and interpreted. As Saleem's birth is celebrated in the *Times of India*'s Bombay edition, the entire *Midnight's Children*

---

is narrated through the prism of Bombay. Consequently, Rushdie creates a disjuncture between two incompatible spaces. Bombay can never fully represent the nation-state India, and India can never fully represent the metropolis Bombay. This tension is re-enacted on various levels throughout the novel.

The Postcolonial City

A significant disadvantage with the research on the metropolis, or global city, is that it has been developed by studying London, New York, or other Western cities. Western modernity, the conceptualization of global cities and their possibilities and challenges, exclude most non-Western cities and set the agenda for research, urban planning, and the imaginary of urban life (Roy 828). Cities in the rest of the world usually go under the label 'cities of the global South' or 'mega-cities.' They are perceived to be uncontrollably set for self-destruction due to chaos, poverty, disease, violence and pollution (Roy 820).

To assess and categorize the modernities of postcolonial cities proves to be difficult with the existing analytical apparatus within globalization studies. A more inclusive theorizing needs to address its historical, political, cultural, economical, and geographical contexts, as they have all partaken in the creation and development of postcolonial urban modernity. A postcolonial metropolis is, as Varma argues, formed by layers of "imperial legacies and nationalist re-inscriptions of spatial practices"; it demonstrates the complexity of representing 'difference,' which shape both its material and the symbolic relations (Varma 1). Varma focuses on citizenship and feminist citizenship in particular, when she analyses different forms of belonging in the postcolonial city. This leads her to conclude that the opposition between nation and city, familiar from globalization studies, can be overcome by not seeing them as antagonist entities but as "interlocking and mutually constitutive spaces" (Varma 8). While I have no quarrel with this argument, however, location remains essential for citizenship and migration. Diasporic communities create new relationships, and as long as the nation-state formally defines citizenship and provides residence permits, it is *not* a "mutually constitutive" relationship, but an authoritarian one. Habitation in the metropolis will then, to some extent, always be in opposition and resist the circumscription of the nation-state. The question of belonging is thereby also contested. This problematic relationship is the topic for Rushdie's engagement with Bombay.

In *Midnight's Children*, Rushdie provides his own reading of the city of Bombay as a postcolonial urban modernity. Through a variety of entries to the city, he provides a reading of a vibrant, multilayered, and dynamic Bombay, in which history, politics, and culture impact and mold each other, thus creating the city-space called Bombay.

Among the midnight's children, Saleem has an alter ego, Shiva; alluding to Shivaji, the seventeenth-century Indian warrior king, and/or Shiv Sena, a Hindu nationalist organization. Shiva is born in the same hospital, but to very different life conditions. While Saleem is born into an upper-middle class Kashmiri family, Shiva becomes an orphan early in life and has to fend for himself in the streets of Bombay. As it turns out, the Christian midwife Mary Pereira, who wanted to impress her socialist boyfriend and make an effort for the underprivileged, swapped the two boys at the nursery. When the truth about swapping of the two infants is revealed, the Sinai family agrees in consensus to disregard it. Saleem tells us that:

> [W]e all found that it *made no difference!* I was still their son: they remained my parents. In a kind of collective failure of imagination, we learned that we simply could not think our way out of our pasts… if you would have asked my father (even him, despite all that happened!) who his son was, nothing on earth would have induced him to point in the direction of the accordionist's knock-kneed, un-washed boy. Even though he would grow up, this Shiva, to be something of a hero (*MC* 131, emphasis original).

The Sinais are unanimous in their decision, and Shiva, whose future is also at stake, is not consulted. The consolidated class-barriers cannot be transgressed even by blood lineage. The condescending tone reveals an upper-class arrogant attitude, but also an Anglophone Westernized disconcertedness toward elements in the Indian society, which would stand out as particularly Indian or Third World-like, such as, the dirt and the poverty of the metropolis of 'the global South.'

The two boys occupy totally different habitats, where transgressions are awkward and unwanted. Together with his soon-to-die father, the accordion player Wee Willie Winkie, Shiva visits Methwold Estate where his father performs. Shiva's visits end abruptly when, after being mocked, he, in revenge, throws a stone that blinds a boy. For Saleem, situated in his upper-class surroundings, the streets of Bombay appear threatening. Indeed, for all men residing at Methwold Estate, Bombay is overtly articulated as the land of opportunities, but the public Bombay is simultaneously a menace. For example, Dr. Narlikar, who tries to make business with Saleem's father, sees a potential in tetra-pod wave breakers. When local lingam worshippers appropriate the tetra-pod placed on display, he angrily attacks them, only to be beaten to death by a demonstrating language mob.

As a child, Saleem seldom ventures into the streets of Bombay, but two accounts of such attempts are particularly highlighted. First, he inadvertently plunges into a Maharathi language demonstration on a bicycle and, when asked to say something in Gujarati, offers a rime. According to his own account, this sets off the Maharathi-Gujarati language dispute, which ultimately leads to the creation of the two states, Maharashtra and Gujarat: "In this way I became directly responsible for triggering off the violence which ended in the partition of the state of Bombay" (*MC* 219). In his comments on Saleem's taking the responsibility for this split, the novelist and literary scholar Abdulrazak Gurnah suggest that Saleem suffers from an obsessive delusion of self-centrality (Gurnah 103–104). I believe the matter is even more complicated.

Out of fear of personal loss, that is, out of fear that Shiva would discover the truth about the exchange of babies at the hospital, Saleem turns off the communication centre in his head for the Midnight's Children's Conference. As a consequence, each of the children is left to fend for himself or herself, and the potential of the council is never realized. So indeed, Saleem is partly responsible for the failure of the midnight's children's generation. For this, Saleem takes no blame. Instead, he focuses on the language quarrels in Bombay. I would argue that it is transference Saleem is suffering from, rather than sustaining a delusion of centrality. However, the important question is, why? As Bombay is the frame through which Saleem shapes the history of India, he interprets everything through this lens. He is not to blame for the language riots, but he is responsible for closing down the council and thereby also the potential of a collective effort with tremendous potential to change India and the world. The ideal with global outreach crumbles under individual interests and personal benefits. This transference between India, the nation, and Bombay articulates the tension between the nation-state and the city, which the novel addresses.

A second encounter with the streets of Bombay is no less disconcerting for Saleem. His anxiety in front of the streets of Bombay is articulated precisely, when he enters them, not when he describes them from a distance. He hides in the trunk of his mother's car as she departs to meet her former husband, Nadir Khan, now resurrected as the communist Qasim the Red, at the Pioneer Café. Peeking in through the windows of the café, Saleem feels threatened and uncomfortable amid the inhabitants of the street. This displays a similar upper class, socialist attitude, where the masses are best admired at a distance, which is not an Indian attitude at all but quite universal.

Many scholars have noted how Rushdie uses allegory and metaphor to connect Saleem's life story to the history of India as one of the most awarding and interesting aspects of his narrative style, which makes the novel witty, resourceful, and sharp in tone. In short, it is a fabulous reading experience, full of invention. Furthermore, it is a necessary narrative strategy. Given that Saleem hardly ever exits his upper-class milieu, except for the above-mentioned occasions and some cinema visits, his perspective cannot sufficiently—nor effectively—describe Bombay. To remedy this, Rushdie uses the means of Bombay's cultural world: its cinema and its language. Bombay is transmitted to storyteller Saleem through various sources, which enables him to re-tell the city from diverse spectra and with all-inclusive of references. Shiva and the other council members are essential because it is through them that Saleem gets access to sections of the multi-layered society, which otherwise would be unreachable for him with his upper-class allegiance in the segregated postcolonial city.

The Bombay cinema is an important register for understanding the representation of the city in *Midnight's Children*. Cinema is, without contest, Bombay's most important art form. In addition, the Indian film industry is the biggest in the world, producing around 3,000 movies a year, of which twenty percent are produced in Bombay. The eminent scholar of Rushdie and Indian cinema, Vijay Mishra, goes as far as to contend that Bollywood holds the key to the cultural logic of Indian modernity. It is by way of Bombay that this cultural logic is developed and formulated. What is more, he argues that Bombay cinema permeates the representation and the narrative structure in *Midnight's Children*.

The domestic melodrama is the generic script for Saleem's narrative style, where his family members enact the characters of the melodrama. The easily recognizable hero and villain; the voluptuous narrating style; themes, like the swapping of babies and sudden loss of memory; and characters, ranging from ominous mothers to snake-charmers certainly point in that direction. The importance of films, such as *Awaara* (dir. Raj Kapoor, 1951), *Shri 420* (1955), and *Mother India* (1957) has been recognized by many scholars (e.g. Stadtler 2012 and Mishra 2013), and Rushdie himself admits the direct influence of Bombay cinema (Rushdie 9–10). Saleem famously comments: "Nobody from Bombay should be without a basic film vocabulary" (*MC* 30). This is undeniably true for *Midnight's Children*, as Rushdie uses techniques, such as montage and close-up, wide-shot, and fading-out:

> Close-up of my grandfather's right hand: nails knuckles fingers all somehow bigger than you'd except. Clumps of red hair on the outside edges. Thumb and forefinger pressed together, separated only by a thickness of paper. In short: my grandfather was holding a pamphlet. It had been inserted into his hand (we cut to a long-shot [...]) as he entered the hotel foyer (*MC* 30).

It is a narrative style influenced not only by cinema vocabulary, together with the incomplete sentences, the omnipresent narrator Saleem seems to be operating a camera, which creates a suspense and generates an energy in the storytelling.

Stuti Khanna, an expert on Rushdie and the city, holds that Bombay's contradictions and multitonality is linked to spatiality, rather than identity politics. Whereas the literary scholar Neil ten Kortenaar correctly demonstrates that an important aspect of Rushdie's humorous style is that the metaphor is taken literary (ten Kortenaar), Khanna's textual analysis goes directly to the core, analyzing signs, advertisements, jingles, and spaces, and how and where they are used in the novel. She argues, for example, that a sign in a shop conveys the social strata of the clientele; who is welcome to enter and who is not, the aspirations of the owners as well as the atmosphere of the joint. This, she contends, invokes Bombay in a way other cities are not represented. *Midnight's Children* is littered with similar references, in which a sign, advertisements, and even hybrid words join forces to create a notion of the whole of Bombay.

Diaspora and Bombay

It is not only Saleem who occasionally feels threatened by the city of Bombay; Bombay is also a menace to itself. Rushdie's energetic and excessive descriptions create a force that drives the story. The multitude of fragments; the bits and pieces of signs, advertisements, slogans, names of streets and buildings, references to Bombay cinema, the multiple and diverse images create, in a hectic, never-ending narrative, and demonstrate a desire to convey the whole Bombay, even the smallest part of it. Every aspect has to be chutneyfied and pickled and preserved for eternity. In itself, this is an enormous undertaking and an attempt to grasp, fix, and stabilize the postcolonial Bombay, which is set in constant transformation. It is also a task for a diasporic writer.

Saleem returns to Bombay at age thirty with the anticipation of recovering the city he once left, but this excitement is soon replaced by the realization that the city has changed. The street and shop names are no longer the same, even his sanctuary, the Methwold Estate, is replaced by new urban skyscrapers. Saleem's recognition— "yes, it was my Bombay, but also not mine" (*MC* 520–521)—can be contrasted with Rushdie's own comment in the essay "Imaginary Homelands": "'it's my present that is foreign, and that the past is home, albeit a lost home in a lost city in the midst of lost time [...] gripped by the conviction that I, too, had a city and a history to reclaim" (Rushdie 9–10). This tension between the recognition of not belonging, while at the same time claiming belonging is an essential part of the diasporic imaginary.

Cracking is a crucial *leitmotif* in *Midnight's Children*, starting from the cracking of India, followed by the cracking of first the state of Bombay and then Pakistan, and accentuated in the cracking of Saleem, as his body falls to pieces. On a meta-level, there is also a fear of an invincible crack between the author and Bombay. The eminent postcolonial critic, Homi Bhabha, mixes his personal accounts of Bombay with his reading of *Midnight's Children*, pointing at the energy Bombay transmitted through Saleem's excessive and chant-like invocation. He concludes his article by insisting that he is a 'Bombayite' because to be a Bombayite is a "frame of mind" that is enacted through the food he eats and serves his guests, through the love for street sounds and gossip, through being able to be surprised by a good story. And he continues:

> I will always protest against poverty, dirt, property prices, corruption, and privilege because I am a Bombayite. I will never fail to jump the queue, demand special treatment, further corrupt an already corrupt bureaucracy because I am a Bombayite. I will condemn petty nationalisms, regionalisms, and ethnic and communal intolerance because as a Bombayite I know that the world is a place large enough for diverse identities, cultures and affiliations. As a Bombayite I admire the sheer spirit of survival, even as I complain that pavements are for walking not sleeping. Being a Bombayite is a *frame of mind*, and yes, I will always be a Bombayite (Bhabha 727, emphasis added).

To my knowledge, Bhabha is an Indian citizen, but it is with Bombay he here pledges his allegiance. Unlike Saleem, who only claims a partial belonging to the city and recognizes a certain alienation, Bhabha insists on belonging. This energetic and persistent assertion of identity and belonging is hardly anything one would come across among the people actually living in Bombay, but then, few of them would be asked the question of whether they are Bombayites.

In what is, without doubt, the best work on Indian diaspora writing, *Literature of the Indian Diaspora: Theorizing the Diasporic Imaginary,* Mishra argues that Rushdie in *Midnight's Children* attempts to diversify and challenge any homogeneous or authoritarian versions of history and that the text is highly self-aware and embeds the questions of history and identity in its aesthetic design (Mishra 213–217). Indeed, Rushdie's Bombay is under threat. The awareness that memory is not fact, that it is partial and comes in bits and pieces makes the narration of the past equally fragmented. An awareness of the fact that locations not lived are locations not experienced expresses both the longing for belonging and the trauma of not belonging to a continuously changing city due to urban planning, increased population, rising fundamentalism, terrorism, monsoon rains, time, people, language—in short, due to everything—is quintessential to diasporic aesthetics.

Bombay and the Problematization of Belonging

It is obvious that any form a theoretical development regarding the Third-World global cities has to recognize the particularities and specialities in question. No community and no city are without a past, which shapes and structures the city. Rushdie takes this issue to task when he collides the history of India with the city of Bombay. The outcome is the partial destruction of the storyteller.

The diasporic location of the storyteller adds to the tension between the nation-state and the city and problematizes belonging. It is likely that, as long as cities are located within nation-states, a certain tension between the nation-state and global city will prevail, but if we are to believe Appadurai, nation-states are a less sustainable structure than the global city and that the global city surely will outlive the nation-state. Nevertheless, diaspora is a condition that will prevail, regardless of the destiny of the nation-state.

Works Cited

Appadurai, Arjun. *Modernity at Large. Cultural Dimensions of Globalization*. Minneapolis: U of Minnesota P, 1996.

Bhabha, Homi K. "Bombay. Salman Rushdie Midnight's Children 1981." *The Novel. Forms and Themes*. Ed. Franco Moretti. Vol. 2. Princeton, NJ: Princeton UP, 2006. 721–727.

Gurnah, Abdulrazak. "Themes and Structures in Midnight's Children." *The Cambridge Companion to Salman Rushdie*. Ed. Abdulrazak Gurnah. Cambridge: Cambridge UP, 2013. 91–108.

Hansen, Thomas Blom. "Reflections on Salman Rushdie's Bombay." *Midnight's Diaspora: Critical Encounters with Salman Rushdie*. Ed. Ashutosh Varshney. Ann Arbor: U of Michigan P, 2008. 91–111.

Khanna, Stuti. "Art and the City. Salman Rushdie and His Artists." *Ariel. A Review of International English Literature*. 37.4 (2006): 21 43. *Ariel*. Web. 16 Dec. 2013.

Khanna, Stuti. "Language and the Postcolonial Colonial City: The Case of Salman Rushdie." *The Journal of Commonwealth Literature*. 46.3 (2011): 397–414.

Mishra, Vijay. *Literature of the Indian Diaspora: Theorizing the Diasporic Imaginary*. London: Routledge, 2007.

_____. "Rushdie and Bollywood Cinema." *The Cambridge Companion to Salman Rushdie*. Ed. Abdulrazak Gurnah. Cambridge: Cambridge UP, 2013. 11–28.

Mukherjee, Meenakshi, ed. *Midnight's Children. A Book of Readings*. Delhi: Pencraft International, 2003.

Parashkevova, Vassilena. *Salman Rushdie's Cities. Reconfigurational Politics and the Contemporary Urban Imagination*. New York: Continuum, 2012.

Roy, Ananya. "The 21st-Century Metropolis: New Geographies of Theory." *Regional Studies* 43.6 (2009): 819–830. Web. 16 Dec. 2013. <www.sas.upenn.edu>.

Rushdie, Salman. "Imaginary Homelands." 1982. *Imaginary Homelands. Essays and Criticism 1981-1991*. 1991. Ed. Salman Rushdie. London: Granta Books, 1992. 9–21.

_____. *Midnight's Children*. 1981. New York: Random House, 2006.

Sassen, Saskia. *A Sociology of Globalization*. New York: W. W. Norton & Company: 2007.

Stadtler, Florian. "Nobody from Bombay Should Be Without a Basic Film Vocabulary. *Midnight's Children* and the Visual Culture of Indian Popular Cinema." *Salman and Visual Culture. Celebrating Impurity, Disrupting Borders*. Ed. Ana Cristina Mendes. New York: Routledge, 2012. 123–138.

ten Kortenaar, Neil. "Midnight's Children and the Allegory of History." *Rushdie's Midnight's Children. A Book of Readings*. Ed. Meenakshi Mukherjee. Delhi: Pencraft International, 2003. 28–48.

Varma, Rashmi. "Provincializing the Global City. From Bombay to Mumbai." *Social Text*. 22.4 (2004): 65–89. *Project Muse.* Web. 16 Dec. 2013.

_____. *The Postcolonial City and Its Subjects*. New York: Routledge, 2012.

Fictions of the Self: The Reader, the Subject, and the Text in *Midnight's Children* and *The Satanic Verses*

Liani Lochner

Problematic Subjectivity

Even though ideas, texts, even people, "once their sacredness is established, seek to proclaim and preserve their own absoluteness, their inviolability" (Rushdie 416), Salman Rushdie ("Sacred" 416) argues in his essay "Is Nothing Sacred?," it "is the product of the many and complex pressures of the time in which the act occurs." After the *fatwa* was announced, he wrote this in defense of his right to critique, in *The Satanic Verses*, what he calls "the eternal, revealed truths of religion" (Rushdie 418; further references preceded by *SV*). There is a difference, however, in Rushdie's engagement with history in the novels published before and after the so-called Rushdie Affair; Shailja Sharma, a scholar of diasporic literatures, argues that Rushdie's earlier novels "were formed by his obsession with history and the way its elusive quality constantly betrays those certainties we die to believe" but for the later Rushdie, the "years of the fatwa and its aftermath have stripped away any academic sense of history and its power" (Sharma 139). Moreover, the post-9/11 Rushdie seems to spurn his commitment to "the many truths of freedom" at risk from totalitarian societies' "truth of power" (Sharma 215) by seeking, as postcolonial critic Priyamvada Gopal notes in her commentary on Rushdie's knighthood, to associate violence solely with Islam and freedom as the domain of the West.

This is as polarizing as the argumentative positions of freedom of speech and blasphemy—ostensibly two monolithic counterparts—also imposed during the Rushdie Affair. The 2005 publication of twelve cartoons of the Prophet Muhammad in the Danish newspaper, *Jyllands-Posten*, resulted in a new eruption of impassioned debates around the world on freedom of expression, blasphemy, and the nature of modern Islam, as well as several violent conflicts causing numerous deaths. Yale University Press, after consulting several experts, decided to publish Jyette Klausen's book on these events, *The Cartoons that Shook the World*, without the accompanying cartoons to avoid "an appreciable chance of violence" (Donatich). According to the director of Yale University Press, John Donatich, making a claim for the public responsibility of the artist based on his presumed intention,

> the cartoons are deliberately grotesque and insulting, gratuitously so. They were designed to pick a fight. They meant to hurt and provoke. At best, they are in bad taste. The Press would never have commissioned or published them as original content ... there was an argument to be made that printing the cartoons and accompanying illustrations would simply perpetuate the misunderstandings and reignite the very conflict that it intends to analyze in a balanced and nuanced way (Donatich).

Donatich's argument is exemplary of a response that forecloses on the possibility of public discussion exceeding blasphemy and freedom of speech as the terms of debate.

It is an understatement to say that these polarizations are, to borrow a phrase from *The Satanic Verses*, "polluted by history" (*SV* 297). As Talal Asad, Wendy Brown, Judith Butler, and Saba Mahmood's discussion in *Is Critique Secular? Blasphemy, Injury and Free Speech* shows, they bring into conflict two very different conceptions of subjectivity and belonging. Freedom of speech as articulated in secularism, each of these thinkers argues, is based on the idea of the subject as self-owning, which is contrasted by the way of life that Islam (and other religions) represents wherein the subject is dispossessed in relationship to a transcendent power. For Asad (30): "The right to choose how to dispose of what one owns is integral to the liberal subject, and the subject's body, affections, and speech are regarded as personal property because they constitute the person" (30). This is in contrast to Islamic devotional literature, as Mahmood points out, in which "Muhammad is regarded as a moral exemplar whose words and deeds are understood not so much as commandments but as ways of inhabiting the world, bodily and ethically" (75). Free speech is seen as injurious when it tries to disrupt this "living [embodied] relationship" between the religious subject and God, which perhaps can explain why Rushdie's dramatizing of the prophet's family in the brothel scenes were considered particularly offensive.

The positions of freedom of speech, as opposed to blasphemy, expose two very different normative frameworks through which the subject is viewed, or through which subjects become visible, but more pertinently for my argument here is how—and here I am again drawing on Butler—understanding blasphemy as an injury to "the sustaining relation" of the religious subject to her God is also to critique the secular view of the subject as self-owning. In other words, the idea of competing frameworks suggests that existence is fundamentally social, and therefore, the subject is always given over to the other; or put differently, the subject is always dispossessed. To take it even further, the notion of the self-owning, or self-identical subject, requires an act of violence.

While Gayatri Spivak perhaps says it best when she states that to read *The Satanic Verses* "as if nothing has happened since late 1988" (106) when it was published is an attempt to do the "impossible," the novel seems to stage, and therefore subvert, the idea of the self-possessed liberal subject. In other words, the novel puts into question the notion of freedom articulated by the later Rushdie himself, which as Gopal rightly points out, seems to have narrowed to a purely Western concept. In this, *The Satanic Verses* seems to build on ideas of history, language, and the subject, and the subject in history and language introduced and explored in *Midnight's Children*, the first novel that put Rushdie on the world stage. This work is, in many ways, the literary precursor to both *The Satanic Verses* and the Rushdie Affair.

On the one hand, *Midnight's Children* enacts the ideological function of a nationalist discourse in a similar fashion to *The Satanic Verses*' staging of the totalizing nature of a racist nationalism through a politics of exclusion. On the other hand, it is in the excesses of identity that these novels undermine both notions of the subject: as self-owning or as fundamentally dispossessed in relation to a transcendent power. Furthermore, if we understand *subjectivation* as the linguistic constitution of the social subject, then it becomes significant that the "earlier" Rushdie advocates the kind of literature that does not purport to be the last word, but rather "about the way in which different languages, values and narratives quarrel, and about the shifting relations between them, which are relations of power" ("Is Nothing Sacred?" 420).

Saleem in Search for Identity

Narrator Saleem Sinai's celebrated assertion that he is "handcuffed to history" (*MC* 9) is often quoted by critics who read *Midnight's Children* as an allegory of the birth and growing pains of the Indian nation-state (as well as, to a lesser extent, that of Pakistan and Bangladesh), a reading which finds the meaning of Saleem's narrative in an extra-discursive and historical context—for example, Abdulrazak Gurnah writes that Saleem's multiplicity, "Hindu mother, English father, brought up Muslim by a Catholic ayah [...] is also a metaphor for polyglot and multifaith Bombay, itself an example to India" (*MC* 101). While this is certainly an intended and well-explored aspect of the novel, this movement is consistently interrupted by the narrative's own insistence on its textuality, on its allegorical function. Saleem's coming into being is represented as constitution in language: "What had been (at the beginning) no bigger than a full stop had expanded into a comma, a word, a sentence, a paragraph, a chapter; now it was bursting into more complex developments, becoming, one might say, a book—perhaps an encyclopedia—even a whole language" (*MC* 100).

Rushdie is drawing attention to both the nation's writing of itself and the interpellation of its subjects, which constitutes their social identity *and* the individual's responses to, and possibilities for exceeding, that hailing. Saleem gives an account not only of himself, but also of those discourses of the nation (and religion and family) that constitute his social being. His narrative reveals, as Butler writes, regarding the notion of confession, the "crucible of social relations" within which the "telling and showing" take place: "And when we do act and speak, we not only disclose ourselves but act on the schemes of intelligibility that govern who will be a speaking being, subjecting them to rupture or revision, consolidating their norms, or contesting their hegemony" (Butler 132).

Saleem's narrative repeatedly affirms the link between writing and meaning or identity; in fact, the narrator's voice is most obtrusive when it expresses this desire. As he states early in the novel, "I must work fast ... if I am to end up meaning—yes meaning—something" (*MC* 9). This introduces a complex and nuanced exploration of the individual subject's relation to history. Initially, Saleem exhibits a seemingly monomaniacal drive to see himself as the main signifier of history: "I was already beginning to take my place at the centre of the universe," he writes, "and by the time I had finished, I would give meaning to it all" (*MC* 126–127). That this project is doomed to failure is suggested early on when the narrator asks, when faced with the "problem of defining itself," what "can a baby do except swallow all of it and hope to make sense of it later?" *MC* 130).

Saleem's search for identity in *Midnight's Children* is presented not only in the relation between the subject and historical events, but more importantly, in the relation between the individual and others, with whom he shares the past and present. His self-possessed "I" is confronted by the "I"s of the other midnight's children "whose insistent pulsing eventually broke through the fish-market cacophony" (*MC* 168) of the voices he hears. He admits that the "spirit of self-aggrandizement which seized" him was motivated by the desire to believe himself in control of "the flooding multitudes" (*MC* 175). Moreover, he expels from his narrative his rival and double, Shiva, who was cheated of his birthright as the truthful heir to the wealth of Saleem's parents by Mary Pereira's deception. For Saleem, who ignores the other characteristic of the deity Shiva is named after—"the god of destruction, who is also the most potent of deities" (*MC* 221)—represents the death of his self-owning identity. The revelation of Shiva's birthright will not only destroy his claims to be at the centre of both national history and that of his family, but also be a violent incursion on his self-possessed "I."

It is crucial to Saleem's progression that he experiences the exclusionary violence of the excision of his own history. Hit in the head by his family's flying spittoon during a bombing, which destroys his parents' house in Pakistan in that country's war with India, Saleem finds himself "abandoning consciousness, seceding from history" (*MC* 351):

> as I look up there is a feeling at the back of my head and after that there is only a tiny but infinite moment of utter clarity while I tumble forwards to prostrate myself before my parents' funeral pyre, a miniscule but endless instant of knowing, before I am stripped of past present memory time shame and love, a fleeting but also timeless explosion in which I bow my head yes I acquiesce yes in the necessity of the blow, and then I am empty and free, because all the Saleems go pouring out of me [...] restored to innocence and purity (*MC* 343).

"Emptied of history" (*MC* 350), an amnesiac, he becomes powerless against the dictates of historical forces: "the buddha learned the arts of submission, and did only what was required of him. To sum up: I became a citizen of Pakistan" (*MC* 350). He becomes a tracker working for West Pakistan against East Pakistan's secession.

The subjection of the individual to history is a reoccurring theme in Rushdie's writing, in which the collapse of the distinction between religion and politics is represented as ideology. History, Rushdie claims, is marked by the effort of different groups to subject others to the principles of a certain worldview. Thus, he writes in *The Satanic Verses*, "Ideology is destiny" (*SV* 432) and in *Shalimar the Clown*, "Ideology was primary" (Rushdie, *Shalimar the Clown* 265). The words of Alicja Cone, wife of Holocaust survivor Otto Cone in *The Satanic Verses*, are repeated almost verbatim in *Shalimar the Clown* by Pyarelal, who fears the Islamist extremist threat to the village of Shirmal: "'Our natures are no longer the critical factors in our fates,' he claims. 'When the killers come, will it matter if we lived well or badly? Will the choices we made affect our destiny? [...] It would be absurd to think so'" (Rushdie, *Shalimar the Clown* 295), parroting Alicja's declaration that "'our pathetic individual self doesn't have a thing to do with it, only to suffer the effects'" (*SV* 432), further affirmed by Rushdie: "Their characters were not their destinies" (Rushdie, *Shalimar the Clown* 304).

In *Midnight's Children*, Saleem's memory-loss means both submission and a total unselfconsciousness. Significantly, he expresses his being in a phrase that prefigures protagonist Chamcha's words and his struggle for identity in the *Satanic Verses*, discussed later in this chapter. "'Don't try to fill my head with history,' he tells Ayooba, who prompts him to remember a "mother father sister" somewhere, "'*I am who I am*, that's all there is'" (*MC* 351, emphasis added). Saleem recounts the story of this self-identical buddha only in the second person. When his interlocutor, Padma, tells him that she is happy he fled the war, he writes, "But I insist: not I. He. He, the buddha. Who, until the snake, would remain not-Saleem; who, in spite of running-from, was still separated from his past; although he clutched, in his limpet fist, a certain silver spittoon" (*MC* 360). Saleem reclaims the buddha as part of his self, in the first person, only after the snake-bite which restores the tracker to history:

> the buddha, who was head-to-foot numb, seemed not to have noticed … but *I* was stronger than the snake-poison. For two days *he* became as rigid as a tree … *I* was rejoined to the past, jolted into unity by snake-poison, and it began to pour out through the buddha's lips. As his eyes returned to normal, his words flowed so freely that they seemed to be an aspect of the monsoon […] because he was reclaiming everything, all of it, all lost histories, all the myriad complex processes that go to make a man (*MC* 364–365, emphases added).

Saleem is returned to Bombay by Parvati-the-Witch, one of the midnight's children, where he is confronted with the emergency regulations imposed by the Widow, an allegorical stand-in for Indira Gandhi. This "puts an end to Saleem's delusion of responsibility for India's history," Gurnah claims, "as he comes to grasp his impotence under the onslaught of Mrs. Gandhi's sterner form of history-making and her desire for power" (Gurnah 96).

Seemingly, Saleem and the other children are put beneath history, as the Widow's sterilization project destroys the multiplicity and possibility they represent for India's future. This is countered when Saleem finally allows his double, Shiva, his rightful place in his own story by adopting his rival's son as his own. Representing both "that tribe of fearsomely potent kiddies, growing waiting listening, rehearsing the moment when the world would become their plaything" (*MC* 447–448), and "the people" of the magician's slum where he was born, Aadam is "more my heir than any child of my flesh would have been" (*MC* 447), according to Saleem. In the final moments of his narrative, Saleem gestures towards both his role in, and his dispossession in his control over, the history and future of India.

Chamcha's Desire for Purity

The model for the dispossession of the secular subject represented by Saleem in *Midnight's Children* is further explored in Chamcha's exploration of identity in *The Satanic Verses*. His attempted metamorphosis, "from Indianness [into] Englishness" (*SV* 41) is predicated upon the belief that he has managed to execute a movement between two purities, in other words, that his incarnation into a "proper" Englishman has meant the death of his Indian self. Chamcha's choice and conceptualization of an English identity are clearly influenced by India's colonial history, as is evident from his mantra based on what constitutes "Proper London": "Bigben Nelsonscolumn Lordstavern Bloodytower Queen" (*SV* 38). While this is undoubtedly an intended and well-explored aspect of *The Satanic Verses*, Chamcha's transformation is motivated by more than the colonial subject's desire to be "'more English than'" (*SV* 53). As the narrator promises, "The mutation of Salahuddin Chamchawala into Saladin Chamcha began, it will be seen, in old Bombay, long before he got close enough to hear the lions of Trafalgar roar" (*SV* 37). His metamorphosis is an attempt to deny his father his paternity by seeking to become "the thing his father was-not-could-never-be, that is, a goodandproper Englishman" (*SV* 43). Losing his faith in his father as a "supreme being," he becomes a "secular man." The irony of his taking on the creator role himself, to become a being of his own making, is that his very attempt at orphaning himself is birthed in the rebellion against his father; as the narrator reveals, "Of what did the son accuse the father? [...] Of turning him into what he might not have become" (*SV* 69). This reveals the violence of any attempt at self-identity, which is possible only with the destruction of that which exceeds the bounds established by the self-owning subject.

The same exclusionary violence in the construction of identity is evident in the brief histories we are given of various other characters, and, more importantly, in the racist nationalism Chamcha is confronted with; each case depends on the erasure of history. Like Polish prison camp survivor and English immigrant, Otto Cone, Chamcha wants to "make [the past] as if it had not been" (*SV* 295) by changing his name and adopting a new language. However, like Otto Cone, "keeping the heavy drapes almost permanently drawn in case the inconsistency of things caused him to see monsters out there," Chamcha seems to be aware "of the fragility of the performance" (*SV* 298).

Chamcha rejects everyone, including Hyacinth, his black physiotherapist, and other Indians, who do not belong in his understanding of a white, homogenous Britain. The police arrive at the precise moment when he, after his fall from the heavens, denounces his culture: "'Damn all Indians,' he cried [...]. '*What the hell*. The vulgarity of it, the *sod it sod it* indelicacy. *What the hell*. That bastard, those bastards, their lack of *bastard* taste'" (*SV* 137, emphases original). Picked up for illegal immigration, he is confronted with the racism he has directed at others. His transformation into a goat, the devil, is the result of their "power of description"—he is called a "Packy billy" (*SV* 163) and "Beelzebub" (*SV* 167); this abuse is justified by the racial slur that "he looks like the very devil, what were we supposed to think?" (*SV* 164).

The idea of a homogenous Englishness is made possible only through the abjection of that which is Other, based on a misrecognition of the immigrant as a scapegoat figure, the source of all social ills. This is reminiscent of philosopher Jacques Derrida's observation that "there's no racism without a language":

The point is not that acts of racial violence are only words but rather that they have to have a word. Even though it offers the

---

excuse of blood, color, birth—or rather, because it uses naturalist and sometimes creationist discourse—racism always betrays the perversion of a man, the 'talking animal.' It institutes, declares, writes, inscribes, prescribes. A system of marks, it outlines space in order to assign forced residence or to close off borders. It does not discern, it discriminates (Derrida 292).

Racist discourse inaugurates its subjects in space and time, but again, this is the idea of the subject as self-identical. Furthermore, this Othering of the immigrant figure is based on a misrecognition of a shared vulnerability or, moreover, an attempt to insure the vulnerability of the idea of a homogenous English society against the threat of the immigrant. It is telling, therefore, that Chamcha's transformation back into human form later in the novel takes place in Club Hot Wax, where waxwork figures of the suppressed history of England—the history of migrant communities' contributions to society—dance with other migrants.

Chamcha progresses from stating, "I am *no longer myself*"— which refers to his constructed identity—to "or not only. I am the embodiment of wrong, of what-we-hate, of sin" (*SV* 256) to "*I am ... that I am*" (*SV* 289). In Christian mythology, this phrase is interpreted as God's affirmation of unpredicated existence, for when Moses in the Bible asks God whom he should tell people sent him, God answers, "I am that I am." French Marxist philosopher Louis Althusser, in comparing the interpellation of individuals as subjects in ideology to the power of divine naming, reads this declaration as a statement of "the Subject *par excellence*, he who is through himself and for himself" (53). In Althusser's formulation, then, interpellation is always effective because the speaker, or God, is the originator of the discourse that enacts the individual into social being. Read through Foucault's understanding of power as dispersed, however, Althusser's interpellative call has no clear origin; according to Butler, it becomes a citational utterance, which relies on context and convention to be effective (32–34). Interpellation is, therefore, subject to failure, as it does not always enact what it names; furthermore, it is possible for the subject to respond to the interpellative call in ways not intended by the law. Crucially, though, the subject can never achieve an "instrumental distance" from the injurious names that he or she is called; agency comes from mobilizing "the power of injury," as Butler writes (123). The interpellative call, which constitutes the subject's discursive identity, or which inaugurates its social existence through subjection to the law, is, therefore, also enabling.

In *The Satanic Verses*, Rushdie uses the statement, "I am that I am," as an affirmation of the self, through which, it is suggested, it is possible to reclaim insults and turn them into strengths. "He would enter into his new self," Chamcha decides, "he would be what he had become: loud, stenchy, hideous, outsize, grotesque, inhuman, powerful" (*SV* 288–289). This does not imply that the subject is self-identical, however, but that identity, to a certain extent, involves the activity of self-definition. In Chamcha's case it also means self-acceptance; the kind of monomania he exhibits can be a destructive force, whereas openness results in survival: "Captain Ahab drowned, [...] it was the trimmer, Ishmael, who survived" (*SV* 435).

Chamcha's redemption, therefore, lies not in being above history or in being subjugated by it, but in being reinserted into historical existence. In *The Satanic Verses*, love—described as "the yearning towards, the blurring of the boundaries of the self, the unbuttoning, until you were open from your adam's-apple to your crotch" (*SV* 314)—becomes an essential experience for Chamcha's next regeneration. This is not the pure love he requires from, or enacts with, Pamela, marked by a blind absolutism that subjects the individual to an ideal version of the Other. Pamela represents everything Chamcha thinks Englishness should be: "I was blood Britannia. Warm beer, mince pies, common-sense, and me" (*SV* 175), she bitterly remarks to Jumpy Joshi. She becomes the "custodian of his destiny" (*SV* 49), without whom his entire attempt at metamorphosis would fail. Pamela is, of course, also engaged in a self-identical project, marrying an Indian man as a revolt against her own culture, even toasting the success of her project with the words "I am that I am" (*SV* 182). Rather, Chamcha falls in love with his father, who is on his deathbed after "long angry decades" (*SV* 523); this form of love makes a particular demand of openness of the self, signaling Chamcha's redefinition of his self not in opposition to, but in relation to, and as a relation of, his father. Not only does he become a creature of "history and blood" (*SV* 523) again, but he relinquishes the idea of identity as self-owning and realizes the relationality of his existence.

Chamcha becomes whole by "confronting the great things about human beings, [...] the great issues of birth and love and death," Rushdie claims in an interview: it is through "learning how to deal with them" that he qualifies, by the end of the novel, to be called "a human being" (Ball 103). This is reminiscent of Butler's formulation, in *Giving an Account of Oneself*, that "our willingness to become undone in relation to others constitutes our chance of becoming human. To be undone by another is a primary necessity, an anguish to be sure, but also a chance [...] to vacate the self-sufficient 'I' as a kind of possession" (Butler 126).

Chamcha's return to Bombay at the end of the novel has struck many critics as a false note; Brian May argues that "Saladin's ultimate achievement of happy unity with the Indian culture of his early youth" come about "only with his severance from the Western culture of his adulthood" (26). It is clear, however, that Chamcha's salvation comes in the acknowledgement that human beings are made up of "conflicting selves jostling and joggling within these bags of skin" (*SV* 519). More important than the hybridized, historicized being this suggests, it also points to existence as fundamentally social. Self-possession necessitates the rejection of and protection against that which is abjured; letting go of possession enables an affirmative community that no longer needs this kind of protection because there is no more outside.

Public Challenges to Self-owning

Saleem's account of himself, in *Midnight's Children*, is his final attempt at meaning-making, the subject writing himself into historical being. His narrative drive is an attempt to resist the pressures of history, which are causing him to crack: "I mean quite simply that I am falling apart [...], that my poor body, singular, unlovely, buffeted by too much history [...] has started coming apart at the seams"

(*MC* 37). Unlike his initial claims to centrality, however, the final product reveals an individual situated, not above or below, but in, and dispossessed by, history. Furthermore, he relinquishes control over his own text, acknowledging not only mistakes, but also the fundamental importance of Padma, his listener—and by extension, the reader—to the meaning of his narrative. When she briefly leaves him, he finds that he is unable to maintain control over his narrative: "In her absence, my certainties are falling apart" (*MC* 166). When he makes errors in key historical dates and facts, he asks, "Does one error invalidate the entire fabric? Am I so far gone, in my desperate need for meaning, that I'm prepared to distort everything—to rewrite the whole history of my times purely in order to place myself in a central role? Today, in my confusion, I can't judge. I'll have to leave it to others" (*MC* 166).

The initial response to *The Satanic Verses* called on the social responsibility of the author as public intellectual; claims that Rushdie should have known better and was committed to a politics of offense—while perhaps true—assume a certain realism in the text's representations. Edward Said, who defended Rushdie's right to free expression, argues that it is the novel's "knowing intimacy with the religious and cultural material it so comically and resourcefully plays with" (Said 165), which outraged many Muslims. He continues that: "There is also the further shock of seeing Islam portrayed irreverently" by a writer who "writes both in and for the West," and that the cultural context "is horrifically and even ludicrously inhospitable to such transgressions" (Said 165). Like the reading of *Midnight's Children*, this locates meaning in the text's extra-discursive spaces; Rushdie's need to defend himself in effect foreclosed any other reading.

Similarly to *Midnight's Children*, however, the construction of meaning is constantly foregrounded in *The Satanic Verses*. Rushdie creates a narrator who, even though he assumes the identity of a deity, refuses not only to assist the reader with the interpretation of events, but also to impose his will on the characters: "I'm saying nothing. Don't ask me to clear things up one way or the other. The rules of Creation are pretty clear: you set things up, you make them thus and so, and then you let them roll. Where's the pleasure if you're always intervening to give hints, change the rules, fix the fights? [...] I'm leaving now" (Rushdie, *SV* 408–409). The idea of "one one one"—that there exists a supreme being of "terrifying singularity" as expressed by "I am that I am"—is further destabilized by the narrator's frequent interjections: "Who am I? Who else is there?" (Rushdie, *SV* 4) and again later, Who am I?" (Rushdie, *SV* 10). The comments of this essentially secular deity (and, therefore, not a deity at all) on his own role in the events in the novel undermine the possibility of extracting a final truth from the text; the reader, like the characters, is forced to make her own decisions, to create her own meanings. As the narrator reveals regarding Gibreel's struggle, "I'm giving him no instructions. I, too, am interested in his choices—in the result of his wrestling match" (Rushdie, *SV* 457).

Rushdie's alignment with the United States' so-called War on Terror has made him into a viable and visible speaking subject in Western discourses on terrorism, which often depend on an Orientalized representation of Islam. The public statements of this Rushdie are in marked contrast to the staging of *subjectivation* in his earlier novels; as portrayed in *Midnight's Children* and *The Satanic Verses*, existence is fundamentally social, constantly challenging any subject's attempt at being self-owning. It is in forging a recognition of the subject's vulnerability towards the Other that these novels challenge freedom of speech and blasphemy as the only terms of debate on the place of religion in the public sphere.

Works Cited

Althusser, Louis. "Ideology and Ideological State Apparatuses (Notes Towards an Investigation)." 1970. Trans. Ben Brewster. *On Ideology*. 1971. London: Verso, 2008. 1–60.

Asad, Talal. "Free Speech, Blasphemy, and Secular Criticism." *Is Critique Secular? Blasphemy, Injury, and Free Speech*. By Talal Asad, Wendy Brown, Judith Butler, and Saba Mahmood. Berkeley, CA: U of California P, 2009. 20–63.

Butler, Judith. *Bodies That Matter: On the Discursive Limits of 'Sex'*. New York: Routledge, 1993.

_____. *Excitable Speech: A Politics of the Performative*. New York: Routledge, 1997.

_____. *Giving an Account of Oneself*. New York: Fordham UP, 2005.

_____. "The Sensibility of Critique: Response to Asad and Mahmood." *Is Critique Secular? Blasphemy, Injury, and Free Speech*. By Talal Asad, Wendy Brown, Judith Butler, & Saba Mahmood. Berkley, CA: U of California P, 2009. 101–136.

Derrida, Jacques. "Racism's Last Word." 1983. Trans. Peggy Kamuf. *Critical Inquiry* 12 (1985): 290–299.

Donatich, John. "Statement by John Donatich." September 9, 2009. *Yale Alumni Magazine* Nov. –Dec. (2009). Web. 20 Dec. 2013. <http://yalepress.yale.edu>.

Gopal, Priyamvada. "Sir Salman's Long Journey." *The Guardian* 18 June (2007). Web. 12 Oct. 2013. <http://guardian.co.uk>.

Gurnah, Abdulrazak. "Themes and Structures in *Midnight's Children*." *The Cambridge Companion to Salman Rushdie*. Ed. Abdulrazak Gurnah. Cambridge, UK: Cambridge UP, 2007. 91–108.

Mahmood, Saba. "Religious Reason and Secular Affect: An Incommensurable Divide?" *Is Critique Secular? Blasphemy, Injury, and Free Speech*. By Talal Asad, Wendy Brown, Judith Butler, and Saba Mahmood. Berkeley, CA: U of California P, 2009. 64–100.

May, Brian. "Memorials to Modernity: Postcolonial Pilgrimage in Naipaul and Rushdie." *ELH* 68 (2001): 241–165.

Rushdie, Salman. *Midnight's Children*. London: Vintage, 1981.

_____. *The Satanic Verses*. London: Vintage, 1988.

_____. "In Good Faith." 1990. *Imaginary Homelands: Essays and Criticism, 1981-1991*. Salman Rushdie. London: Granta, 1991. 393–414.

_____. "Is Nothing Sacred?" 1990. *Imaginary Homelands: Essays and Criticism, 1981-1991*. Salman Rushdie. London: Granta, 1991. 415–429.

_____. "An Interview with Salman Rushdie." Interview by John Clement Ball. *Conversations with Salman Rushdie*. Ed. Michael Reder. Jackson, MI: Mississippi UP, 2000. 101–109.

_____. "Messages from the Plague Years." Part II of *Step Across This Line: Collected Non-fiction, 1992-2002*. Salman Rushdie. London: Vintage, 2003. 211–258.

_____. *Shalimar the Clown*. London: Jonathan Cape, 2005.

Said, Edward W. "Statement", 22 Feb. 1989. Rpt. in *The Rushdie File*. Eds. Lisa Appignanesi and Sara Maitland. Syracuse, NY: Syracuse UP, 1990. 164–166.

Sharma, Shailja. "'Precious Gift/Piece of Shit': Salman Rushdie's *The Satanic Verses* and the Revenge of History." *Scandalous Fictions: The Twentieth-Century Novel in the Public Sphere*. Eds. Jago Morrison & Susan Watkins. Basingstoke, UK: Palgrave Macmillan, 2006. 136–149.

Spivak, Gayatri Chakravorty. "Reading *The Satanic Verses*." 1989. *What Is an Author?* Eds. Maurice Biriotti & Nicola Miller. Manchester, UK: Manchester UP, 1993. 104–134.

The Play with the Connotations of Sexuality in *Midnight's Children*

Jūratė Radavičiūtė

Subversive Play with Synecdoches

The focus of this chapter is to analyze the subversion of synecdoche's traditional usage in Salman Rushdie's novel *Midnight's Children*. Synecdoche is the central means of rhetoric used in the novel. The indeterminacy of the interpretations of synecdoche can be explained by the postmodern nature of the novel, where chance and instability are favored over order and hierarchy. The very idea of a strict synecdoche, which is a figure of speech, where a part stands for a whole, a whole for a part, an individual for a class or a material for the thing, implies a striving for order, hierarchy, and subjugation. Postmodernism aims to subvert and undermine similar strong impositions of order. In my analysis of the novel, I will focus on highlighting how the principal symbols in the novel—such as those of the nose, voice, and hair—acquire a variety of unusual connotations because of the subversion of their traditional meanings.

I will carry out the analysis with the view to the concept of play as a strategy of writing and reading of a text. Although the strategy is not a postmodern invention, semiotician Roland Barthes highlights a set of features that distinguish a postmodern form of play. First, he points out that a postmodern text lacks a hierarchical structure, which enables the writer or the reader to construct/interpret the text in an infinite variety of ways. Second, Barthes notes that, although the postmodern text has no center, it still has a framework that holds the elements of the text together; a close reading of such a text reveals that the system is perceptible and comprehensible (Barthes 31–33).

Discussing the role of play in a postmodern text, Roland Barthes uses the term bricolage to identify the method that a postmodern writer uses to create a literary work. Bricolage is the term, which philosopher Jacques Derrida introduces in the postmodern theory to describe the improvisation of a creator or a *bricoler*, who produces something new and unexpected, using the means close at hand

(Derrida 360). The reader, while using the well-known traditional interpretations of the images prevalent in the novel, will have all his expectations subverted. The undermining of the connotations of the images that emerge from different traditions, mainly European and Indian, creates a unique blend of new meanings that a particular image puts forward.

Since the system of images in *Midnight's Children* is highly complicated, I will focus on the synecdoches of the nose, voice, and hair. These synecdoches are repeatedly used in the novel, and they are attributed to its central characters. Moreover, the synecdoches acquire a variety of connotations throughout the novel through their connections with other constituent parts of the text. However, the metonymies, which comprise the imagery system in the novel are not limited to the ones mentioned above; therefore, a number of them will be mentioned alongside the dominant images, which comprise the overall figurative language of the novel. I will analyze the images with respect to the means used to compose them as well as to the multiple connotations prevalent in the novel.

A Nose Is More than Just a Nose

The synecdoche of the nose, which is central to the imagery of *Midnight's Children*, traditionally carries the meaning of sexuality. The discussion of the meanings it acquires in the novel, with a view to the subversions the meanings undergo, will be presented here. The article will also explore how the connotations of the synecdoches of the hair and voice contribute to the interpretation of sexuality and the ways the above-mentioned figures of speech supplement the connotations of the nose in the case of its absence.

Traditionally, the nose symbolizes a male sexual organ. The portrayal of Aadam Aziz contains references to two interpretations of sexuality: reproduction and pleasure. To begin with, the connotation of reproduction, at the initial stage of the novel, Tai, the boatman, predicts: "That's a nose to start a family on, my princeling" (Rushdie, 9; further references preceded by *MC*), and his prediction comes true, as Aadam Aziz becomes a father of five children. Moreover, a frequent reference to Aadam Aziz as a patriarch is also justified, for his influence on the family is not limited to mere reproduction: each child is affected by different qualities of the father. His rebellious nature is mirrored in Mumtaz's stance against an angry Muslim mob ready to tear apart a Hindu street-seller; in Emerald's fleeing to Major Zulfikar without her dupatta and, consequently, without any shame; in Hanif's realistic film scripts, which ruin his career and end in his suicide; and a number of other instances.

Regarding physical pleasure, Aadam Aziz faces a failure, as he is unable to convince his Muslim wife that sexual intercourse might be related to pleasure. She blames his views on his formative years in Europe and flatly refuses to compromise her position. This clash, as the narrator points out, "set the tone for their marriage, which rapidly developed into a place of frequent and devastating warfare under whose depredations the young girl behind the sheet and the gauche young Doctor turned rapidly into different, stranger beings" (*MC* 38).

The estrangement of wife and husband manifests itself in multiple forms within the novel: starting with minor complaints concerning education, social activity, and finishing battles result in starvation periods, leading to exhaustion or months of silence.

Saleem Sinai is the character closest in his views and destiny to Aadam Aziz; he is also the character whose personality is dominated by the qualities attributed to the nose. In a way, he inherits Aadam Aziz's characteristics; however, his destiny, to be raised in a family that is not his by birthright, has an effect on Aadam Aziz's inheritance. The connotations, which are introduced in his portrayal, undergo major alterations if compared to those attributed to Aadam Aziz, although the key link to the concept of sexuality is retained.

The traditional connotation of the image is subverted in the portrayal of Saleem Sinai. In contrast to Aadam Aziz, Saleem is physically impotent. This fact is constantly emphasized in the novel. In the first book, Saleem contemplates his relationships with Padma and bitterly admits:

And Padma is a generous woman, because she stays by me in these last days, although I can't do much for her. That's right [...] I am unmanned. Despite Padma's many and varied gifts and ministrations [...] despite everything she tries, I cannot hit her spittoon (*MC* 45).

Saleem's impotence threatens their relationship, and, at some point, Padma temporarily leaves the factory without any explanation. From Saleem's point of view, this might have been caused by her distress over "the futility of her midnight attempts at resuscitating my 'other pencil,' the useless cucumber hidden in my pants" (*MC* 165).

The reference that Saleem here makes to a "pencil" is not accidental: having lost his sexual potency after castration, he replaces his lost sexual potency with writing. Therefore, another explanation he comes up with, regarding Padma's fleeing, is her jealousy of the book he is writing: "Is it possible to be jealous of written words? To resent nocturnal scribblings as though they were flesh and blood of a sexual rival?" (*MC* 165). The importance the writing has to Saleem seems to be as significant as family is to Aadam Aziz: overlooking any obstacles on his way to completing the story (deteriorating health, dramatic relations with Padma), Saleem is overcome by the desire to finish it before his death.

The period of Saleem's impotence coincides with his maturity. However, the description of his childhood years contains references to other significations related to sexuality: self-awareness, sin, and physicality. Saleem spends his teenage years in Karachi, where his nasal qualities acquire the sharpness they have never displayed before. Estranging himself from his family, Saleem surrenders to the world of senses and his experiences form his personality:

So, from the earliest days of my Pakistani adolescence, I began to learn the secret aromas of the world, the heady but quick-fading perfume of new love, and also the deeper, longer-lasting pungency of hate [...]. Having realized the crucial nature of morality, having sniffed out that smells could be sacred or profane, I invented, in the isolation of my scooter-trips, the science of nasal ethics. Sacred: purdah-veils, halal meat, muezzin's towers, prayer mats; profane: Western records, pig-meat, alcohol (*MC* 427–442).

The quest for self-awareness is completed when Saleem visits a whore. The name of the whore, Tai Bibi, refers to the name of the boatman Tai, who prophesied the future of Aadam Aziz. Similar to those of the boatman, the powers of Tai Bibi rest in the knowledge of the world and people. Exploring the world through the olfactory powers of his nose, Saleem is attracted to Tai Bibi because of her ability to reproduce any smell in the world: "my ancient prostitute possessed a mastery over her glands so total that she could alter her bodily odors to match those of anyone on earth. Ecrines and apocrines obeyed the instructions of her antiquated will" (*MC* 443).

In addition to Tai Bibi's knowledge of the world, Saleem is attracted by an opportunity to explore the secrets of his own sub-consciousness that Tai Bibi is able to reveal through the manipulation of smells. When the initial embarrassment is conquered with the help of the whore, Saleem plunges into the world of the forbidden:

> she succeeded in reproducing the body odours of his mother his aunts, oho you like that do you little sahibzada, go on, stick your nose as close as you like, you're a funny fellow for sure […] until suddenly, by accident, yes, I swear I didn't make her do it, suddenly during trial-and-error the most unspeakable fragrance on earth wafts out (*MC* 444).

The climax of the visit is reached when Tai Bibi reproduces the smell that Saleem has not asked her for: the smell of her sister Jamila, and, from his expression, he understands that it is the smell he has secretly been searching for. This discovery of love finalizes his quest: having rushed from the whore's room in shame, Saleem never returns to explore the city again. However, the forbidden and shameful feeling is not forgotten, and another smell, a lusty smell of a hashashin wind, provides Saleem with an opportunity to confess his love to Jamila.

The smell of shame and horror, which Saleem's confession produces, inflicts dramatic consequences: Jamila takes revenge upon Saleem by signing him up for the army. Devoid of family and prospects of love, Saleem numbs: he is no longer able to communicate, remember, or feel. The only sense he possesses in this period is smell, which becomes so sharp that he turns into a man-dog. The acuteness of his sense of smell at this stage coincides with the increase in his sexual potency. The only female of the unit, a latrine cleaner, chooses him over other soldiers, explaining that, despite his being numb or perhaps because of that, she likes having sex with him. In contrast, Saleem participates in the intercourse purely physically: he does not feel any emotions towards the girl.

Saleem recovers other senses only after months spent in the jungles, and this transformation coincides with the complication of his sexual life. In love with Jamila, he is not able to respond to Parvati's advances despite her devotion, magic, and moral pressure. His pretended impotence turns into the real defect when a sterilization campaign gets started in the slums of Delhi. Saleem's castration inflicts a number of consequences: besides impotence, it starts the process of his personality's disintegration. Therefore, the narrator compares the vasectomy procedure to the drainage of hope. If Saleem manages to supplement his lost sexual potency with writing, the lost hope is never replaced; therefore, the process of disintegration cannot be stopped.

In summary, a multitude of meanings related to sexuality are attributed to the nose. Two central characters in the novel bear big noses: Aadam Aziz and Saleem Sinai. If the meanings related to Aadam Aziz are relatively stable: patriarchy/sexual potency and physical pleasure, the significations attributed to Saleem Sinai undergo certain transformations, symbolizing different periods of his life. The period of Saleem's adolescence is dominated by sensuality as a means to increase self-awareness and recognition of the outside world. Different experiences, guided by his hypersensitive nose, enrich him with feelings of lust and sin. The height of his sexual potency coincides with the elimination of emotions. The recovery of memory and feelings some time later leads him to the complication of sexual relationships and finally to castration and impotence. Saleem partially supplements the absence of sexual potency with the process of writing. However, the supplementation is not complete, for the disintegration of his personality, inflicted by castration, appears to be irreversible.

The Power of Voice

Another synecdoche related to sexuality is that of the voice, to which sexual attraction is generally attributed, especially when related to female characters (Price and Kearns 514). The image connotations are revealed through the depiction of Mian Abdullah/ the Hummingbird and the Brass Monkey/Jamila Singer. Although the latter image is of secondary importance and does not offer a great variety of interpretations in respect to the concept of sexuality, the connotations of the voice continue and enrich some connotations that are related to the nose, but are not developed to a greater extent.

A link between sexuality and the natural world is scarcely noted in the contexts related to the nose. However, in the episodes of Saleem turning into a man-dog, devoid of human feelings and memories, the narrator emphasizes an increase in his sexual potency and sexual attraction, for the only female character selects him over other soldiers. Regarding the voice, the connection between sexuality and nature is of major significance.

Mian Abdullah is the first character closely related to the image of the voice to appear in the novel. His nickname, the Hummingbird, is a double reference: first, it refers to the unique qualities of his voice, and second, it refers to his connection to the natural world. The description of his voice highlights certain qualities of the voice, which are elaborated on further in the novel:

> it was a hum that could fall enough to give you toothache, and when it rose to its highest, most feverish pitch, it had the ability of inducing erections in anyone within its vicinity [...]. Nadir Khan, as his secretary, was attacked constantly by his master's vibratory quirk, and his ears jaw penis were forever behaving according to the dictates of the Hummingbird (*MC* 55).

In addition to the physical effect the hum has on people, this excerpt highlights its longer lasting overall impact. The most obvious example to illustrate this is the story of the Hummingbird's secretary. Therefore, even after Mian Abdullah's death, having married Aadam Aziz's daughter Mumtaz, Nadir is incapable of having sexual relationships with her, despite their mutual affection. In terms of the impact, the narrator often emphasizes the magic power, which Mian Abdullah's voice has on anyone: his political supporters, such as the Rani of Cooch Naheen, who is unable to oppose his request to organize an assembly in Agra, although she knows that it is the stronghold of Mian's opponents; other politicians, who are otherwise fierce opponents, unite into one organization at his request.

The connection between the power of Mian Abdullah's voice and the natural world is most effectively depicted in his death scene. Unable to fight the assassins, sent by his political opponents, with the power of his voice, the Hummingbird turns to the natural world for help:

> Abdullah's humming rose out of the range of our human ears, and was heard by the dogs of the town. In Agra there are maybe eight thousand four hundred and twenty pie-dogs […] all of these turned and ran for the University […]. They went noisily, like an army, and afterwards their trail was littered with bones and dung and bits of hair […] afterwards the killers were so badly damaged that nobody could say who they were (*MC* 58–59).

The battle between humans and animals inflicted by the power of the voice is mirrored in the Brass Monkey's story, too. In contrast to Mian Abdullah, the Brass Monkey is involved in the fight for animals, whose lives are threatened by a draught and Evie Burns's gun. The portrayal of the fight in its power equals that of the dogs' fight for Mian Abdullah's life:

> like a blur the Monkey descended on Evie and a battle began which lasted for what seemed last like several hours […]. Shrouded in the dust of the circus ring they rolled kicked scratched bit, small tufts of hair flew out of the dust cloud, and there were elbows and feet in dirtied white socks and knees and fragments of frock flying out of the cloud; grownups came running, servants couldn't pull them apart (*MC* 312).

The battle with Evie marks the part of the Brass Monkey's life, when she is recognized for her superhuman powers of communication rather

---

than her voice. The power of the latter is recognized in her teenager years; and then her nickname, the Brass Monkey, is replaced by that of the Bulbul of the Nation. Jamila's voice possesses the power to cast a spell even greater than Mian Abdullah's. In her performances, no one can resist it, and its power is constantly compared to that of a magician:

> her voice wafted out through the window and silenced the traffic; the birds stopped chattering and, at the hamburger shop across the street, the radio was switched off the street was full of stationary people, and my sister's voice washed over them […] (*MC* 435).

The sexual attraction of Jamila's voice is irresistible; although her body is hidden from the public behind a silk chadar, she receives "one thousand and one firm proposals of marriage a week" (*MC* 435–436). However, the sexual attraction, which the voice possesses, is opposed to the sternness of Jamila's inner self, for she firmly rejects all marriage proposals. The conflict could be interpreted with the view to the concept of *simulacra*, elaborated by sociologist Jean Baudrillard, for the fatal attraction of Jamila's voice is due to the image that is created around her voice and is not related to her true self. Jamila does not succumb to the influence of the image; however, the people around her, including her family members, appear to be under the influence of the image. The novel contains two stories, which exemplify the impact the image has on people and the consequences it inflicts on them.

The first victim of Jamila's voice is Mutasim the Handsome, the power of whose looks is compared to the power of Jamila's voice. As the narrator points out, "he was so good-looking that, whenever he traveled around Kif, girls with silver nose-jewellery fainted in the heat of his beauty" (*MC* 446). He falls in love with Jamila at the first instance of hearing her voice. However, his dramatic attempts to see Jamila, and his insistent marriage proposals, fail; as a result, he volunteers for the army and dies a martyr.

The second victim of the love for Jamila is Saleem, whose declaration of love leads to Jamila's betrayal. She signs him up for the army when he falls ill, which results in Saleem's becoming numb:

deprived of human emotions or memories, and later on, incapable of having sexual intercourse with anyone, similar to Nadir Khan, Mian Abdullah's secretary. On the other hand, Jamila herself is victimized by the powers her voice possesses. In the course of her increasing popularity, she loses all her connections with the people who are significant to her: her family is killed during a bombing, and Saleem is signed up for the army. Finally, what remains for her is her voice, which replaces her personality.

In general terms, the image of the voice in *Midnight's Children* acquires two distinctive significations in terms of sexuality: power and connection to the natural world. Two main characters, whose individualities are determined by the image of the voice, are Mian Abdullah, the Hummingbird, and the Brass Monkey, or Jamila Singer. The portrayal of Mian Abdullah highlights the aspect of power in terms of control and purposefulness and the connection with the natural world. Jamila's characteristics emphasize the aspect of the sub-conscious: in contrast to Mian Abdullah, she does not have any objectives, which could be reached using the powers of her voice, and she herself is partially victimized by its power: the voice starts to dominate her personality, replacing her old self with the image that is imposed to her by the media. After her betrayal of Saleem that recalls the Brass Monkey she has once been, the rest of the references to Jamila are primarily allusions to her voice in relation to its media-attributed functions.

Playing with Hair

The final image, related to the concept of sexuality, is the hair, with which sexual attraction and fertility are associated meanings; these connotations are traditionally linked to female characters (Ferber 91–92). The characters whose personalities are dominated by this image are Nadir Khan, Methwold, and the Widow. The following analyzes the undermining of hair's traditional significations with respect to this image.

First, the portrayal of Nadir Khan subverts the concept of love. This character displays the qualities traditionally attributed to female characters: he is passive, romantic, and loyal in his amorous relationships with Mumtaz; a physical aspect is eliminated from his sexuality. His womanly nature is emphasized in the description of his hair: "he had long hair, poetically long, hanging lankily over his ears" (*MC* 300). Although his factual impotence is due to the causes, which do not depend on him, it becomes apparent, in the course of events, that Nadir's failure as a man is a circumstance of his character rather than chance. This statement could be exemplified with the scene of the meeting of Mumtaz and Nadir at the Pioneer Café:

> What I saw at the end: my mother's hands raising a half-empty glass of Lovely Lassi my mother's lips pressing gently, nostalgically against the mottled glass, my mother's hands handling the glass to her Nadir-Quasim; who also applied to the opposite side of the glass, his own poetic mouth. So it was that life imitated bad art [...] (*MC* 301–302).

The meeting, in which any physical contact fails to be accomplished, the indirect kiss is only the simulacrum of a physical act that is completed. However, while the kiss causes a physical resentment when it is shown in the film, reproduced in the life outside the cinema, it symbolizes the failure of an image to become a legible replacement for a real act. It also marks the failure of Nadir Khan to comply with the implications, which are attributed to his hair.

In contrast, Methwold, another male character, whose hair plays an important role in defining his character, is purposeful and is capable of using the benefits, which hair offers. The attractiveness of his hair is emphasized in Methwold's first description:

> he had a head of thick black brilliantined hair, parted in the centre [...] whose ramrod precision made Methwold irresistible to women, who felt unable to prevent themselves wanting to rumple it up [...]. It was one of those hairlines along which history and sexuality moved (*MC* 125).

The description reveals the active nature of Methwold in addition to the sexual attraction his hair possesses. In contrast to Nadir Khan's lanky hair, which reveals his passiveness, Methwold's thickly brilliantined hair points to his purposefulness and his ability to recognize potential opportunities and use them. Methwold's purpose is to leave his mark in India before emigration, after the declaration of its independence. Before moving to Europe, he imposes his rules of behavior on the purchasers of his estate; in addition, using the sexual attraction of his hair, he seduces a local Indian's wife and leaves her pregnant.

His physical potency is different from all the other significations of sexual attraction attributed to different images, as all of them are related to impotence rather than potency. However, the novel provides an explanation for this contrast. On his last visit to the estate, Methwold reveals his secret:

> white hand dangled above the brilliantined black hair; long tapering white fingers twitched towards centre-parting, and the second and final secret was revealed, because fingers curled and seized hair; drawing away from his head, they failed to release their prey; and in the moment after the disappearance of the sun Mr. Methwold stood in the afterglow of his Estate with his hairpiece in his hand (*MC* 153).

The false hair appears to be more significant in terms of sexual attraction than the real hair of Nadir Khan. This play with the significations which are traditionally attributed to certain symbols is most clearly exposed in the portrayal of Methold. It appears that it is not the hair but the personality of the man who wears the hair which is significant. The irresistible attraction of the hair appears to be caused by Methwold's understanding of the powers that hair displays and ability to manipulate his knowledge.

Purposefulness is a defining feature of one more character related to the image of hair, and that is the Widow. A physical characteristic, which Methwold and the Widow share is the centre-parting of their hair. Similarly to Methwold, the centre-parting is a noticeable characteristic of her hair, for it is highlighted by the difference in color of each part: white or green on one side and black on the other. In terms of sexuality, the difference in color hints at the traditional interpretation of the concept of a widow as eliminated from the process of reproduction by the death of her husband. A negative connotation of the concept is stressed when the Widow is compared to a witch from fairy-tales:

> High as the sky the chair is green the seat is black the Widow's arm is long as death its skin is green the fingernails are long and sharp and black [...]. And children torn in two in Widow hands which rolling rolling halves of children roll them into little balls the balls are green the night is black (*MC* 288).

In terms of sexuality, the excerpt relates the Widow to castration. In the process of castration, Saleem and other midnight's children are robbed of potency: both sexual and creative. They are drained of the miraculous powers they were awarded at birth. However, although the process of castration is irreversible, a hope remains because Shiva, one of the midnight's children, has given birth to numerous children before being castrated, while Saleem supplements his lost sexual potency with writing, which is the book of the generation of midnight's children.

Summarizing, the image of hair reveals a number of meanings related to the concept of sexuality. First, through the portrayal of Nadir Khan, the aspect of the passive sexual attractiveness is revealed. When related to a male character, it acquires a negative connotation of weakness, or inablity to reverse fate. Second, Methwold introduces the aspect of active sexual attractiveness, which is useful for a purposeful person. What is more, the aspect of consciousness in manipulating the power is characteristic of this character, too. Finally, the Widow, the only female character related to the image of hair, adds the signification of castration to the concept of sexuality in the novel.

Provocative Simulations

In general terms, my analysis of the connotations, which are attributed to the concept of sexuality, reveals that Rushdie employs a number of strategies to approach the traditional interpretations of the images of the nose, voice, and hair. He portrays a number of characters, including Aadam Aziz and Jamila Singer, who reveal the connotations of the images hinging on their traditional interpretations. On the other hand, in their portrayal, the writer also introduces the elements, which subvert the above mentioned interpretations: a cultural clash between Aadam Aziz and his wife or a media-determined personality of Jamila can serve as the cases in point.

The novel also includes a number of protagonists who undermine the traditional interpretations, such as Saleem Sinai or the Widow, both of whom introduce the connotations of impotence and castration. Similarly, the portrayal of Methwold and Nadir Khan illustrates an ironic treatment of the traditional interpretation of the hair as an instrument for attracting the opposite sex. Methwold's irresistible sexual attraction appears to be due to his baldness; whereas Nadir Khan's womanly hair signifies his impotence.

Frequent subversions of the expected traditional connotations form a clear mark of a postmodern text. The opposition to the inherited modes of thinking and traditional discourse, as well as the opposition to the newly emerging postmodern world has been lately producing a new kind of writing, based on the paradoxes brought about by simulacra. *Midnight's Children* is one of the clearest and most provocative examples of this kind of writing.

Works Cited

Barthes, Roland. *Empire of Signs.* 1970. Trans. Richard Howard. New York: Hill and Wang, 1982.

Baudrillard, Jean. *Simulations.* Trans. Paul Foss, Paul Patton, and Philip Beitchman. New York: Semiotext(e)/ Foreign Agent Series, 1983.

Derrida, Jacques. *Writing and Difference.* 1967. Trans. Alan Bass. London: Routledge Classics, 2007.

Ferber, Michael. *A Dictionary of Literary Symbols.* Cambridge: Cambridge UP, 2007.

Price, Simon and Emily Kearns. *The Oxford Dictionary of Classical Myth and Religion.* Oxford: Oxford UP, 2004.

Rushdie, Salman. *Midnight's Children.* 1981. London: Vintage, 2006.

The Role of the Women Characters in the Nature/Nurture and the Optimism/Pessimism Questions in *Midnight's Children*

Celia Wallhead

From the beginning of Salman Rushdie's *Midnight's Children*, the reader is led to believe that the protagonist and narrator, Saleem Sinai, is someone other than who he turns out to be. The name Sinai belongs to his identity as an individual nurtured in a middle-class Muslim family in Bombay, but his bloodline is quite the opposite. Furthermore, he controls his narration in order to delay the confession of the error he and the reader were in, so that narrator, narratee, Padma, and reader alike appear to make a belated discovery. The novel prioritizes narrative strategy and is influenced by Laurence Sterne's *Tristram Shandy*. Central to Sterne's work is the idea of how difficult it is to tell a story, even if you know the "facts" because you have lived them. Not everything is what it seems—in personal life or history.

The midway chapter, "At the Pioneer Café," is central to *Midnight's Children* in more than one way. Overtly, Saleem has proof of the infidelity of women in the person of his mother, but more far-reaching than that, as Saleem fundamentally enters the mind of Shiva, it shows Saleem Sinai and Shiva in their true colors, though we cannot say that they reveal their true natures. Nature and nurture have been mixed up, and the poor boy, Saleem, turns out to be optimistic, since he was nurtured in a comfortable family, while the rich boy, Shiva, had no nurturing and grew up to be bitter, cynical, and pessimistic. The optimism/pessimism paradigm functions not only on an individual, domestic plane, but, as Rushdie has Saleem see himself as personifying the new nation of India, born at midnight on August 15, 1947, the narrative ploy is used to discuss the future of the new nation.

In this chapter, I am going to examine the roles played by women in the life of the protagonist, from the historical character of Indira Gandhi through the females of his "adopted" family, his real family, and all other females who have affected his life, for as Saleem recounts:

> Women have always been the ones to change my life: Mary Pereira, Evie Burns, Jamila Singer, Parvati-the-witch must answer for who I am; and the Widow, who I'm keeping for the end; and after the end, Padma, my goddess of dung. Women have fixed me all right, but perhaps they were never central—perhaps the place which they should have filled, the hole in the centre of me which was my inheritance from my grandfather Aadam Aziz, was occupied for too long by my voices. Or perhaps—one must consider all possibilities— they always made me a little afraid (Rushdie 266; further references preceded by *MC*).

The Bloodlines

In *Midnight's Children,* the contemporary historical situation of the Indian subcontinent is very central. If we include Saleem's putative grandfather, Aadam Aziz, born in 1890, and the projections into the future of the families involved and the nation-states of India, Pakistan and Bangladesh, it can be said that the novel gives an overview of the subcontinent throughout the twentieth century.

In the previous quotation, Saleem speaks of his grandfather, but because of the switching of the babies at birth, the character, whom we know as Saleem Sinai, is not a Sinai at all, but a changeling from an apparently poor family, thus he can have no biological inheritance from Aadam. Figure 1 shows the true blood lines of Saleem, son of Englishman William Methwold and Vanita (wife of the accordionist called Wee Willie Winkie, whose real name is unknown) who died giving birth to him at midnight on August 15, 1947.

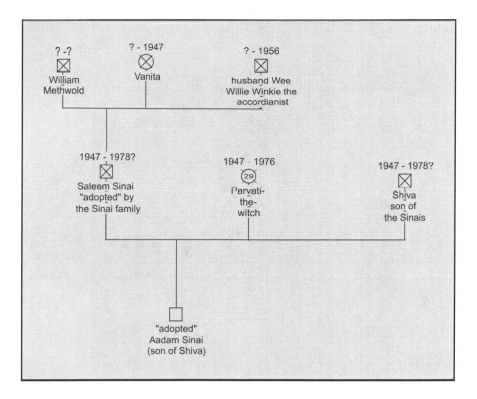

Figure 1: Saleem Sinai's Bloodline

Saleem's "sky-blue eyes" (*MC* 169) no doubt come from Methwold, also his height, light skin (compared to that of his putative mother, Amina Sinai), and prominent nose, "the legacy of a patrician French grandmother—from Bergerac!" (*MC* 126) jokes Saleem. Just as Methwold was bald (*MC* 153), Saleem is nicknamed "Baldy" (*MC* 158), after his teacher Emil Zagallo has pulled his hair out, though, dying at the age of thirty-one, he has little time to reveal the presence or absence of the genes of his English father with regard to his head of hair.

While physical attributes are usually self-evident, intellectual qualities may be harder to define and require time to assess their recurring characteristics. An added complication in the formation of Saleem's identity is that he is made up not only of the binary of nature and nurture, but he is endowed with magical gifts, powers, which can be attributed to neither. This supernatural element, wrought within the magical realist mode of the novel, is as much a narrative device as a strategy for character development. Saleem's ability to hear in his head almost six hundred different voices—those of the one-thousand-and-one midnight children, who survived to their tenth birthday—combined with his sense of smell, whereby he can sniff out all manner of secrets, is a strategy for extending the scope and opening the character out to the wider world. One wonders also if the magical realist dimension of superhuman powers is a metaphor for the idea that each individual brings something new to their makeup, whereby something new enters the world. It is, therefore, difficult to separate Saleem's intellectual capacities into discrete attributes emanating from their threefold source: whatever mental prowess he may have inherited from Methwold (a product of millions of years of natural selection), his excellent education (spiritual and secular) in his "adopted" middle-class Muslim family, and his magical powers—together with the element of chance, beginning from the substitution at birth.

In comparison to the evident masculine physical features contributed by Methwold, what his mother Vanita might have contributed to her ugly son seems obscure or non-existent, certainly not her seduction. In his early life, Saleem was oblivious to the fact that Vanita was his true mother, so when he blames women for destroying his life, she is obviously not on the list: "From ayah to Widow, I've been the sort of person *to whom things have been done*" (*MC* 330, emphasis original). Most of the traumatic things that have changed the course of his life have been perpetrated quite deliberately by women: "Mary's crime," "Evie's push," his "mother's infidelity," Masha Miovic's "goads," Aunty Pia, who "was becoming the next in the long series of women who have bewitched and finally undone me good and proper" (*MC* 330–335). The word "bewitched" is probably here a prefiguration of the two witches to come in the narration: Parvati-the witch and the Widow (Indira Gandhi).

Although I am going to concentrate on Saleem, for the purposes of comparison, we need to assess the possible genetic inheritance of his rival, Shiva. Figure 2 sets out the bloodlines in the family tree of Shiva, the Aziz-Sinai family. That Saleem grew up to be tall did not surprise the Sinai family, as his height was attributed to his putative grandfather, Aadam Aziz, but the genes were really Methwold's. Aziz bequeathed his height to Shiva, who was born already "of a remarkable size" (*MC* 156) and with his true father Ahmed Sinai's knobbly knees (*MC* 157). The latter referred to a heritage of "Mughal blood" to impress an incredulous Methwold and "invent a family pedigree" (*MC* 147). Saleem was surrounded by women, so he sought out fathers: "Ahmed Sinai, Hanif Aziz, Sharpsticker sahib, General Zulfikar"—even Picture Singh, in the absence of his real father, William Methwold. His "grandfather" Aadam Aziz had "a certain vulnerability to women" due to the "hole at the centre of himself caused by his (which is also my) failure to believe or disbelieve in God" (*MC* 382). Saleem has inherited nothing from Dr. Aziz, but his true grandson, Shiva, has inherited his weakness for women, claiming to have sired 20,000 children (half that number, according to Saleem) by upper-class wives (*MC* 571). His namesake, Shiva, is the God of Procreation, and this is his form of revenge for being brought up poor. But Shiva is also the God of Destruction and, as such, contributes to the destruction of the midnight children.

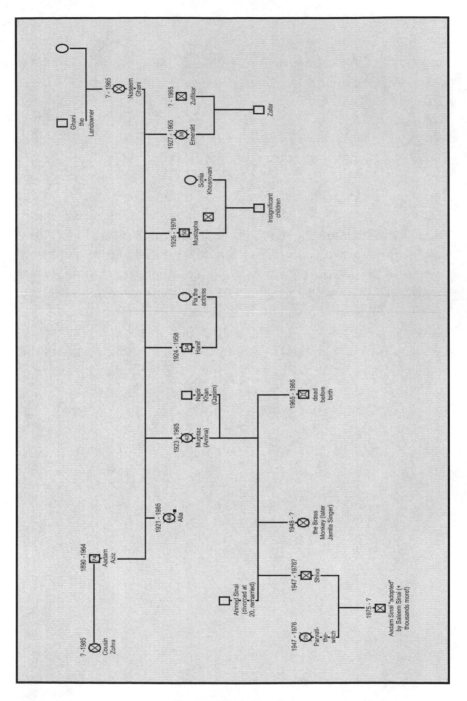

Figure 2: Shiva's Bloodline

The Communities and the Nation

If Saleem has inherited little from biological mother Vanita, his identity must be composed more from factors related to his nurturing. I am going to examine the female members of his "adopted" family, the Sinais, then the servants and the neighbors and women external to his family, with whom he came into contact, in order to see what influence they exerted over his upbringing and early manhood. To do so, we must evaluate their particular outlooks.

In her 1999 essay "Woman, Nation and Narration in *Midnight's Children*," Nalini Natarajan studies the way in which women are presented and seen in the novel, especially in relation to the concept of "Mother India." She identifies the role of the body of woman in the focus of what is seen (the scopic), both in terms of the flag and in terms of the cinematic viewpoint of Hindi cinema. In my analysis, I am going to focus *not* on how the women are seen by the male gaze in terms of their country/countries, but how the *women* see these, how they envision India/Pakistan/Bangladesh.

But first, we must consider the communities, to which these women belong. Coincidentally, *Midnight's Children* came out at the same time as Benedict Anderson's *Imagined Communities*. In this work, Anderson proposed "the following definition of the nation: it is an imagined political community—and imagined as both inherently limited and sovereign" (Anderson 5–6). Anderson's reasoning behind this concept of the nation is that: "It is *imagined* because the members of even the smallest nation will never know most of their fellow-members, meet them, or even hear of them, yet in the minds of each lives the image of their communion" (Anderson 6, emphasis original). The parallel "kind of collective failure of imagination," as Rushdie puts it regarding the Sinais' inability to view Saleem as anyone other than their child/brother/grandson (*MC* 158), is played out in this novel also as a failure to imagine on a grand scale, as it makes a close scrutiny of the first thirty years of the new India and its problems, its fragmentation, as Saleem puts it ruefully: "our ancient national gift for fissiparousness" (*MC* 557).

Through the different communities both men and women find themselves belonging to, Rushdie pays tribute to the idea that belonging to a nation exists only in the mind: the concept of the community involved exists in the imaginations of its citizens, not in the pragmatics of their daily lives. The new India is a perfect example of how a nation has to be brought into being mentally as well as physically, when:

> a nation which had never previously existed was about to win its freedom, catapulting us into a world which, although it had 5000 years of history, [...] was nevertheless quite imaginary; into a mythical land, a country which would never exist except by the efforts of a phenomenal collective will—except in a dream we all agreed to dream; it was a mass fantasy (*MC* 150).

Appeals have to be made to the many millions of citizens in terms of their geographical location, history, religion, culture, and language. In this case, Partition and the birth of Pakistan, came about as a result of appeals to the citizenry in terms of their spiritual devotion, even if those appeals came after a form of imposition without consultation. The Sinai family saw themselves obliged to leave India.

Through Saleem's meditations, Rushdie gives historical depth to the novel, and attempts to give geographical and cultural breadth through the device of the midnight's children. This is the ancient and multifaceted India that the children inherit, and they become "a mirror of the nation" (*MC* 354). Let's examine the roles played by women in the life of the protagonist, from the historical character of Indira Gandhi, through the females of his "adopted" family, his real family, and other females.

The Women of Saleem's Nurturing

As Saleem and Shiva grow up, they are shaped within their families. Shiva, with no mother, becomes rebellious and gives into "surliness" and anger (*MC* 176). Saleem, then, receives the care and nurturing that Shiva should have enjoyed by birth, and he is brought up by a "two-headed mother" (*MC* 170), not one mother but two: Amina Sinai and the ayah, Mary Pereira, who offered her services to the family out of remorse over having swapped the babies. She accepts the title "mausi, little mother", and she and Amina try to outdo each other in "demonstrations of affection" for Saleem (*MC* 174), nurturing him into being a utopian, which he expresses as follows: "The thing is, we must be here for a *purpose,* don't you think? I mean, there has to be a *reason,* you must agree. So what I thought, we should try and work out what it is, and then, you know, sort of dedicate our lives to ..." (*MC* 306, emphasis original). It is interesting to note that Mary does not offer her services to Wee Willie Winkie, although his "son" had no mother as a result of the switch.

For the women of Saleem's grandparents' generation, life had meant secluded life in purdah. There were, however, notable exceptions. Aadam Aziz's mother had come out of purdah to work, while he was studying in Germany. The modernization of the Indian woman is discontinued in her daughter-in-law, Naseem. Naseem is the girl whose body is famously viewed part by part through the hole in a sheet by Dr. Aziz, who falls in love with her and eventually marries her. Natarajan sees the national scale latent in the domestic synecdoche: "As he treats her in parts he begins to imagine her as whole. This coincides with his imagining a 'whole' Indian identity for himself instead of his regional Kashmiri one" (Natarajan 400). Naseem represents Indian woman through her body and through tradition. She refuses to comply with her husband's urging to come out of purdah by protesting: "You want me to walk naked in front of strange men," and she is uncooperative in bed, she will not be "a bad word woman" (*MC* 38). Natarajan calls this "refusing to do his sexual bidding" (*MC* 402), and Aadam never wins the battle of the bed. On the national level, this signifies the challenges facing anyone who tries to bring traditional India into the modern world.

Saleem's putative mother will have two names: Mumtaz and Amina Sinai. Her adultery proves to be hard for Saleem, who disapproves of such behavior. Natarajan conceives of such an example of divided allegiances metaphorically on the national level as "national anxiety":

Read against the cultural politics of the Bombay film industry, the spectacle of Amina as Mother India in *Midnight's Children* yields interesting ironies. The conflations of mother with origin, land, family, and Rule of Law, upheld in the Bombay cinema, are exposed in Rushdie's text. Amina is mother but not to her own son (Natarajan 405).

When the Sinais discover that Saleem is not their son, they do not reject him. Nurture comes to mean more than blood, which means little. Even when the crime of Mary Pereira is discovered, he is still loved: "we all found that it *made no difference*! I was still their son: they remained my parents. In a kind of collective failure of imagination, we learned that we simply could not think our way out of our pasts" (*MC* 158, emphasis original). Just as the community or the nation is collectively imagined, the domestic sphere also requires imagination. In this family, much is hidden, not the least of which is Amina and Ahmed's mutual infidelity and Saleem's mental activities.

Saleem's sister is called "the brass monkey" on account of her red hair. In her rebelliousness over the favoritism of her "brother" Saleem, she is in the habit of setting fire to shoes (*MC* 207). However, in her "sibling-loyalty" (*MC* 313), she fights the American tomboy Evie Burns, ostensibly over cats, but intrinsically and symbolically, over resistance to western impingement as women become "a site of East-West cultural battle so often depicted in Bombay cinema" (Natarajan 406–407). After moving to Pakistan, his sister changes completely (*MC* 406), becoming submissive, and at age fourteen is transformed into Jamila Singer, famous throughout Pakistan. In her fame, her face is protected by the Muslim veil. Eventually, she retreats not into purdah but into a Christian parallel, a convent. Jamila's major effect on Saleem's fate is that she betrays him, getting him sent into the army. As a result of the episode of the Sundarbans, Saleem loses his utopian optimism and is dogged by doubt about the possibility of improving the world: "In the midst of the rubble of war, I discovered fair-and-unfair" (*MC* 516). What is most unfair to him is that, as the most important midnight's child, he personally should have to *"bear the burden of history"* (*MC* 534, italics original).

Born in Old Delhi, the daughter of a conjurer, Parvati is one of the midnight's children. She possesses an important gift, that of sorcery, since she was born just seven seconds after midnight (*MC* 276–277). She is one of the female characters, who, on her marriage to Saleem, changes her name: to cover the shame of her pregnancy by Shiva (just like in Indian mythology, Parvati is the consort of Shiva), she converts to Islam and takes the name of Laylah ('night') (*MC* 580). So she gives birth to Shiva's son, but because he is adopted by Saleem and called Aadam Sinai, he returns to his true biological family—"He was the child of a father who was not his father" (*MC* 586) as a fortune-teller had prophesied—yet he is named after his true great-grandfather, Aadam Aziz. In another reference to mythology, he is described as follows "He was the true great-grandson of his great-grandfather, but his elephantiasis attacked him in the ears instead of the nose –because he was also the true son of Shiva-and-Parvati; he was elephant-headed Ganesh" (*MC* 587). Parvati disappears from the scene: the males of the midnight's children were sterilized and poorer females like Parvati no doubt were cast out when the Widow organized a purge on the slums. The son of Shiva and Parvati is the hope for the future, intelligence and prosperity being suggested by Ganesh, in spite of their working-class origins and outlook (Goonetilleke 40).

A crucial figure for the narrative is Padma, whom Saleem meets towards the end of his short life. Because she is his audience or interlocutor, her presence is, however, felt from the beginning of the novel. She is plump, illiterate, strong, jolly, and works for Saleem in Mary Pereira's chutney factory. She is not beautiful like Emerald, Pia, or Jamila Singer, indeed, she is "thick of waist, somewhat hairy of forearm" (*MC* 24). Her name is not the most beautiful either, as she is named after the lotus goddess "The One Who Possesses Dung" (*MC* 24). Her purpose here, however, is not a love relation. With *Midnight's Children* as one of her examples, Emilija Dimitrijevic correctly asserts: "One brand of post Second World War literature has continued in the footsteps of modernist literature in that it also gives more space to formal rather than traditional organization of experience and, more often than not, treats the question of intimacy and identity with irony" (Dimitrijevic 26). She goes on to refer to postmodern practice as being behind the emphasis on how the tale is told; that "love in these novels is not so much a theme but is a metatheme, what is foregrounded is not the relationship between the characters in the text but that between the text and the reader" (Dimitrijevic 26). Sterne's methodology of deliberate, perverse straying from the point or the chronological time-line in Tristram's telling of his lifestory is referenced: "But here is Padma at my elbow, bullying me back into the world of linear narrative [...]. 'At this rate,' Padma complains, 'you'll be two hundred years old before you manage to tell about your birth'" (*MC* 44).

Shiva never learned that Saleem had enjoyed the sheltered nurture that should have been his, and but for Mary Pereira, he might have been equally like Saleem: "Mushy, like overcooked rice. Sentimental as a grandmother" (*MC* 355). Shiva communicates to Saleem, not in as many words, more through their telepathic minds, that he believes that "children are the vessels into which adults pour their poison, and it was the poison of grown-ups which did for us" (*MC* 355). Thus the generation of midnight's children has been filled with different poisons, some have been brought up to believe that a better world can exist and that they should be optimistic and work to implement it, only to be disappointed, while others, like Shiva, cheated of his rightful education and nurture, are left pessimistic and only driven by selfish ends.

Both Saleem and Padma are fragile: Saleem needs to replace the cushioning of his childhood after the death of his "mother" Amina and the flight of Mary Pereira. He finds solace in Padma, but the relationship has its vicissitudes. Saleem has been sterilized, caught in the net thrown around the midnight's children by the Widow, and thus cannot be stirred physically by Padma, however much he appreciates her performing in *Kama Sutra* positions. She runs out on him because he has mentioned the word "love" (*MC* 206) and later gives him a love-potion that makes him ill (*MC* 270). But she remains with Saleem to the end, supposedly marrying him before he disintegrates. Finally, as Dimitrijevic comments on the role of intertextuality and censorship, she reminds us that, although

Saleem and Padma have been together since the beginning of their relationship with the reader, complementing each other, their love story is not there for its own sake and not at all central to the narrative: "The same goes for *Midnight's Children,* whose narrator, Saleem, and whose listener, Padma, represent a couple with problems of their own, but whose story melts into the background of the history of a new national India" (Dimitrijevic 175).

The women of Saleem's adopted family have a symbolic role in the metafictional dimension of the novel. Natarajan identifies three moments of nationalism in which women function as signifiers: "(1) the movement from regional to national in the 'modernizing process,'" and in this, Naseem played a role. The second moment she identifies is "(2) the threat of communal or civil rupture within the body politic", and here, we see Amina "as 'Bharat Mata' or 'Mother India,' a site for mythic unity in the face of fragmentation". Finally, "(3) the rise of fundamentalism, "which is particularly apparent in the transformation of the Brass Monkey: when she goes to Pakistan, she becomes: "a 'daughter of the nation', a site for countering the challenge posed by 'Westernization', popularly read as 'women's liberation'" (Natarajan 400).

The final figure to be discussed here is the Widow, a pseudonym for Prime Minister Indira Gandhi. As Saleem's antagonist in the novel, she, no doubt, set out with good intentions like her father, Nehru, one of the founders of the new nation. However, somewhere in the development of her mandate, she ordered measures to be carried out with "tyrannical powers" (Rushdie 2006) that Rushdie sees as detrimental to the nation. Rushdie draws upon negative connotations from East and West: on the one hand, "a widow is a figure of ill-omen in Indian culture" (Goonetilleke 34) and on the other, Rushdie acknowledges his debt to the green-skinned witch of *The Wizard of Oz* (Rushdie 33).

Rushdie's narrative strategy of equating Saleem with India makes Indira Gandhi his rival, and a much more powerful one:

Unpalatable, awkward queries: did Saleem's dream of saving the nation leak, through the osmotic tissues of history, into the thoughts of the Prime Minister herself? Was my lifelong belief in the equation between the State and myself transmuted, in 'the Madam's' mind, into that in-those-days-famous phrase: *India is Indira and Indira is India*? Were we competitors for centrality—was she gripped by a lust for meaning as profound as my own—and was that, was that why ...? (*MC* 587, emphasis and ellipsis original).

Saleem, with all his supernatural mental powers, cannot compete with the Widow, and the only hope is in the next generation, although, as D. C. R. A. Goonetilleke reminds us, Rushdie's own optimism ran out when his own life came under threat: "By 1988, this seemed to Rushdie 'absurdly, romantically optimistic'" (Goonetilleke 40; see also Rushdie, "Midnight's Real Children" 25). Catherine Cundy feels that Rushdie has been unduly harsh with the figure of Indira Gandhi in presenting her "in such relentlessly misogynist terms" (37).

Changed View of Women in *Midnight's Children*

In his ambitious project to portray in *Midnight's Children* the hopes and fears surrounding the birth of his new countries, India and Pakistan, and monitor them for their first thirty years, Rushdie lays himself open to accusations of short-sightedness. Of course, he could only sketch the future by extrapolating from the past. That Rushdie believes one *can* extrapolate is evident when he has Saleem assert: "What you were is forever who you are" (*Midnight's Children* 513). And, one might add: who or what you and your country are going to be. An individual's make-up is complex, and how much more so that of a country as diverse as India, where every facet may come to have a more or less relevant role. Saleem's questioning of his identity as he writes his account, thinking back to his anger upon internment in the widows' hostel after his sterilization, leads to his conclusion "*you'll have to swallow a world*":

Who what am I? My answer: I am the *sum total* of everything that went before me, of all I have been seen done, of everything done-to-me. I am everyone everything whose being-in-the-world affected was affected by mine. I am anything that happens after I've gone which would not have happened if I had not come. Nor am I particularly exceptional in this matter; each 'I', every one of the now-600 million-plus of us, contains a similar multitude. I repeat for the last time: *to understand me, you'll have to swallow a world* (*MC* 535).

The end of *Midnight's Children* is essentially pessimistic. In the early 1980s, when the novel was written and published, India had already gone to war with Pakistan at least three times: in 1947, bringing about Partition, and in 1965 and 1971, which saw the birth of Bangladesh. What Saleem cannot foresee with clarity is that India would become one of the fastest-growing major economies of the world by the end of the millennium and that one of the wars with Pakistan would be over Kashmir and nuclear rivalry. Although Rushdie could not foresee Indira Gandhi's death, he was right in anticipating the influence of the Gandhi family, indeed, her daughter-in-law, Sonia Gandhi, is still wielding power.

Midnight's Children opens in Kashmir with Dr. Aadam Aziz and ends there, coming full circle, as Saleem goes out with Padma to disintegrate and die. There is a sense of circularity, too, in the relations with womenfolk in Saleem's life, especially the one who affected it most, Mary Pereira. If she set him on track as a changeling baby and brought him up, she takes him under her wing at the end, as he manages her Braganza Pickle factory and meets Padma. Thus in Saleem's life, there have been plenty of powerful women like the Widow, who have wrought havoc in his life, and less powerful women, like the servant Mary Pereira, who could also wield power within the domestic sphere.

Rushdie has portrayed women from the top of the socio-economic scale to the bottom, from the rich "Widow" to the poor widow, Resham Bibi, who dies of cold in her hut (*MC* 578). Foreigners are used for cultural contrast, for example, when Ilse Lubin is widowed, her suicide is like a western version of sati, the difference being that for the western woman, death is freely chosen. Rushdie has shown how the middle of the twentieth century saw women's struggles to resist tradition and enter the modern world, sometimes with the help of their menfolk, and sometimes without. On the individual level, there are scales of benevolence and resentment, and these qualities have been "poured into" or have "leaked into" the new generation. The result is an unevenness, a perpetuation of the unfairness paradigm. As Goonetilleke suggests: "Perhaps the hope of a modern, integrated nation lay in the liberal intellectuals, the haves, with their hybrid culture, but the haves denied, ignored, suppressed the need to share their inheritance of India with the non-intellectual but practically and *physically* powerful masses, the dispossessed, the true heirs (Goonetilleke 35, emphasis original).

And finally, Goonetilleke sums up Rushdie's use of women's roles in the novel to express this fairness/unfairness, optimism/ pessimism debate, showing how the new mixture expresses the complexity and ambiguity of the new India:

> In *Grimus,* Rushdie's portrayal of women was seemingly feminist, yet subverts feminism. *Midnight's Children* marks a mixed kind of advance. His portrayal offers a greater range and positiveness, yet incorporates a curious negativity as well. [...] The preponderance of women, powerful yet exerting a certain attraction, suggests the altered view of women in *Midnight's Children* (Goonetilleke 42–43).

Works Cited

Anderson, Benedict. *Imagined Communities: Reflections on the Origin and Spread of Nationalism.* 1982. London: Verso, 2006.

Bewernick, Hanne. *The Storyteller's Memory Palace.* Bern, Switzerland: Peter Lang, 2010.

Cundy, Catherine. "Rushdie's Women." *Wasafiri* 18 (1993): 13–17.

_____. *Salman Rushdie.* Manchester, UK: Manchester UP, 1997.

Dell'Aversano, Carmen. "Worlds, Things, Words: Rushdie's Style from *Grimus* to *Midnight's Children.*" *Coterminous Worlds: Magic Realism and Contemporary Postcolonial Literature in English.* Eds. Elsa Linguanti, Francesco Casotti, and Carmen Concilio. Amsterdam & Atlanta, GA: Rodopi, 1994. 61–69.

Dimitrijevic, Emilija. *Intimacy and Identity in the Postmodern Novel.* Bern: Peter Lang, 2008.

Goonetilleke, D. C. R. A. *Salman Rushdie.* Basingstoke and London: Macmillan Press, 1998.

Natarajan, Nalini. "Woman, Nation and Narration in *Midnight's Children.*" 1994. *Feminist Theory and the Body: A Reader*. Eds. Janet Price & Margrit Shildrick. Edinburgh, UK: Edinburgh UP, 1999. 399–409.

Rushdie, Salman. "His Own Mt Sinai." *The Guardian* 5 May (2006). *The Guardian.* Web. 20 Dec. 2013.

————. *Midnight's Children.* 1981. London: Vintage, 2006.

————. "Midnight's Real Children." *The Guardian.* 25 March (1988): 25.

————. *The Wizard of Oz.* London: British Film Institute, 1992.

Sterne, Laurence. *The Life and Opinions of Tristram Shandy.* 1760. Oxford, UK: Oxford UP, 1983.

Verma, Charu. "Padma's Tragedy: A Feminist Deconstruction of Rushdie's *Midnight's Children.*" *Feminism and Recent Fiction in English*. Ed. Sushila Singh. New Delhi, India: Prestige Books, 1991. 154–160.

RESOURCES

Chronology of Salman Rushdie's Life————

1947	Rushdie is born on June 19 in Bombay (India).
1961	Rushdie joins Rugby School (UK).
1965	Rushdie joins King's College, Cambridge (UK).
1968	Rushdie receives MA in history from King's College; moves to Karachi (Pakistan).
1969	Rushdie returns to London.
1975	*Grimus* is published.
1976	Rushdie marries Clarissa Luard (divorces her in 1987). Rushdie becomes executive member of the Camden Committee for Community Relations (until 1983).
1979	Son Zafar is born.
1981	*Midnight's Children* is published. Rushdie receives Booker-McConnell Prize and James Tait Black Memorial Prize (for *Midnight's Children*).
1983	*Shame* is published. Rushdie becomes Fellow of Royal Society for Literature.
1984	Rushdie receives Prix du Meilleur Livre Étranger, France (for *Shame*).
1987	*The Jaguar Smile* is published.
1988	Rushdie marries Marianne Wiggins (divorces her in 1993). *The Satanic Verses* is published.

	Rushdie receives Whitbread Novel Award (for *The Satanic Verses*).
1989	Ayatollah Khomeini of Iran declares a *fatwa* on Rushdie on February 14; Rushdie goes into hiding.
1990	*Haroun and the Sea of Stories* is published.
1991	*Imaginary Homelands* is published.
1992	*The Wizard of Oz* is published.
1993	Rushdie is nominated as honorary professor of the humanities at MIT, Cambridge, Massachusetts. Rushdie receives Booker of Bookers Prize (for *Midnight's Children*).
1994	*East, West* is published.
1995	*The Moor's Last Sigh* is published. Rushdie receives Whitbread Novel Award (for *The Moor's Last Sigh*).
1996	Rushdie receives the European Union's Aristeion Literary Prize.
1997	Rushdie marries Elizabeth West (divorces her in 2004). *The Vintage Book of Indian Writing*, co-edited with Elizabeth West, is published.
1998	Rushdie returns to public life as the threat from Iran is lifted. Rushdie is nominated Doctor honoris causa, University of Tromsø (Norway).
1999	Son Milan is born.

The Ground Beneath Her Feet is published.

Rushdie is appointed Commandeur de l'Ordre des Arts et des Lettres (France).

Rushdie is nominated Doctor honoris causa, Freien Universität Berlin (Germany).

2000	Rushdie moves to New York City. Rushdie is nominated Doctor honoris causa, University of Liège (Belgium).
2001	*Fury* is published.
2002	*Step Across This Line* is published.
2003	Rushdie is nominated Doctor honoris causa, L'Universite de Paris (France).
2004	Rushdie marries Padma Lakshmi (divorces her in 2007). Rushdie is nominated as President of PEN American Center until 2006.
2005	*Shalimar the Clown* is published.
2006	Rushdie is nominated Distinguished Writer in Residence at Emory University, Atlanta, Georgia, until 2011. Rushdie is nominated honorary Doctor of Humane Letters at Nova Southeastern University, Florida.
2007	Rushdie is knighted as Knight Bachelor (Kt) by Queen Elizabeth II.
2008	Rushdie receives Best of the Booker Prize (for *Midnight's Children*). *The Enchantress of Florence* is published. Rushdie is nominated Doctor of Humane Letters, honoris causa at Chapman University, California.

Rushdie is elected as a Foreign Honorary Member at the American Academy of Arts and Letters.

2010	*Luka and the Fire of Life* is published.
2011	Rushdie is nominated University Distinguished Professor at Emory University. The Salman Rushdie Archive at Emory University opens.
2012	*Joseph Anton: A Memoir* is published. Deepa Mehtai's film *Midnight's Children* is released, with Rushdie as the narrator's voice.

Works by Salman Rushdie

Novels

Grimus, 1975

Midnight's Children, 1981

Shame, 1983

The Satanic Verses, 1988

Haroun and the Sea of Stories, 1990

The Moor's Last Sigh, 1995

The Ground Beneath Her Feet, 1999

Fury, 2001

Shalimar the Clown, 2005

The Enchantress of Florence, 2008

Luka and the Fire of Life, 2010

Short Stories

East, West, 1994

Nonfiction

The Jaguar Smile: A Nicaraguan Journey, 1987

Imaginary Homelands: Essays and Criticism 1981–1991, 1991

The Wizard of Oz, 1992

The Vintage Book of Indian Writing, co-edited with Elizabeth West [in the US as *Mirrorwork: 50 Years of Indian Writing 1947–1997*], 1997

Step Across This Line: Collected Nonfiction 1992–2002, 2002

Joseph Anton: A Memoir, 2012

Bibliography

Batty, Nancy E. "The Art of Suspense: Rushdie's 1001 (Mid-)Nights." *Ariel* 18:3 (1987): 49–65.

Bharat, Meenakshi, ed. *Rushdie the Novelist: From* Grimus *to* The Enchantress of Florence. Delhi: Pencraft International, 2009.

Booker, M. Keith. *Critical Essays on Salman Rushdie.* New York: G. K. Hall, 1999.

Brennan, Timothy. *Salman Rushdie and the Third World: Myths of the Nation.* London: Macmillan, 1989.

Byrne, Eleanor. "Salman Rushdie and the Rise of Postcolonial Studies: *Grimus, Midnight's Children* and *Shame." Salman Rushdie: Contemporary Critical Perspectives.* Eds. Robert Eaglestone & Martin McQuillan. London: Bloomsbury, 2013. 22–33.

Cundy, Catherine. *Salman Rushdie.* Manchester: Manchester UP, 1996.

Fletcher, M. D., ed. *Reading Rushdie. Perspectives on the Fiction of Salman Rushdie.* Amsterdam & Atlanta, GA: Rodopi, 1994.

Frank, Søren. *Salman Rushdie: A Deleuzian Reading.* Copenhagen: Museum Tusculanum Press, 2011.

Goonetillike, D. C. R. A. *Salman Rushdie.* New York: St. Martin's Press, 1998.

Grant, Damian. *Salman Rushdie.* Plymouth: Northcote House, 1999.

Gurnah, Abdulrazak, ed. *The Cambridge Companion to Salman Rushdie.* Cambridge: Cambridge UP, 2007.

Harrison, James. *Salman Rushdie.* New York: Twayne Publishers, 1992.

Hassumani, Sabrina. *Salman Rushdie: A Postmodern Reading of his Major Works.* Madison, NJ: Fairleigh Dickinson UP, 2002.

Hennard Dutheil de la Rochère, Martine. *Origin and Originality in Rushdie's Fiction.* Bern: Peter Lang, 1999.

Jani, Pranav. *Decentering Rushdie: Cosmopolitanism and the Indian Novel in English.* Columbus: Ohio State UP, 2010.

Kanaganayakam, Chelva. "Myth and Fabulosity in *Midnight's Children." Dalhousie Review* 67:1 (1987): 86–98.

Kuortti, Joel. *Fictions to Live In: Narration as an Argument for Fiction in Salman Rushdie's Novels*. Frankfurt/M: Peter Lang, 1998.

Mittapalli, Rajeshwar and Joel Kuortti, eds. *Salman Rushdie: New Critical Insights*, 1–2. Delhi: Atlantic Publishers, 2003.

Morton, Stephen. *Salman Rushdie*. Houndmills: Palgrave, 2008.

Mukherjee, Meenakshi, ed. *Rushdie's* Midnight's Children: *A Book of Readings*. Delhi: Pencraft International, 1999.

Parnell, Tim. "Salman Rushdie: From Colonial Politics to Postmodern Poetics." *Writing India 1757–1990: The Literature of British India*. Ed. Bart Moore-Gilbert. Manchester: Manchester UP, 1996.

Petersson, Margareta. *Unending Metamorphoses: Myth, Satire and Religion in Salman Rushdie's Novels*. Lund: Lund UP, 1996.

Ray, Mohit Kumar and Rama Kundu, eds. *Salman Rushdie: Critical Essays* 1–2. New Delhi: Atlantic Publishers, 2006.

Reynolds, Margaret and Jonathan Noakes. *Salman Rushdie :* Midnight's Children, Shame, The Satanic Verses. London: Vintage, 2003. Vintage Living Texts Ser.

Sangari, Kumkum. "The Politics of the Possible." *Cultural Critique* 7 (1987): 157–185.

Reder, Michael, ed. *Conversations with Salman Rushdie*. London: UP of Mississippi, 2000.

Smale, David, ed. *Salman Rushdie.* Midnight's Children. The Satanic Verses: *A Reader's Guide to Essential Criticism*. Houndmills: Palgrave Macmillan, 2001.

Joel Kuortti is Professor of English at the University of Turku. He is also Adjunct Professor of Contemporary Culture at the University of Jyväskylä, Finland. His research is on postcolonial theory, Indian literature in English, transcultural identity, hybridity, and cultural studies. His most important publications include *The Salman Rushdie Bibliography* (1997), *Place of the Sacred: The Rhetoric of the Satanic Verses Affair* (1997), *Fictions To Live In: Narration as an Argument for Fiction in Salman Rushdie's Novels* (1998), *Indian Women's Writing in English: A Bibliography* (2002), *Tense Past, Tense Present: Women Writing in English* (2003), and *Writing Imagined Diasporas: South Asian Women Reshaping North American Identity* (2007). He has co-edited such books as *Changing Worlds/ Changing Nations: The Concept of Nation in the Transnational Era*, with Om Prakash Dwivedi (2012); *Reconstructing Hybridity: Postcolonial Studies in Transition*, with Jopi Nyman (2007); and *Salman Rushdie: New Critical Insights*, 1–2, with Mittapalli Rajeshwar (2003). His articles have appeared in several anthologies and in such journals as *Textual Practice*, *Contemporary South Asia*, *Atlantic Literary Review*, *Kunapipi*, *Journal of Commonwealth Literature*, *Indian Journal of World Literature and Culture*, and *Transnational Literature*.

Contributors

Marianne Corrigan teaches literature at Keele University, UK, where she is finishing her PhD on globalization in the later novels of Salman Rushdie. She has published, or has forthcoming articles in *Textual Practice* and *Alluvium*. The book chapters she has written include "Rushdie as an International Writer" in Eaglestone and McQuillan (eds), *Salman Rushdie: Contemporary Critical Perspectives* (2013) and "Playing With Fire: Gaming, Cybernetics and Fictional Form in *Luka and the Fire of Life* and *The Cybergypsies*" in Gylphi's forthcoming collection on twenty-first century fiction. She recently co-organized the conference "Rushdie in the Twenty-First Century," which took place at the IES in London in June 2013. This event drew together leading Rushdie scholars to discuss the significance of his twenty-first century writings.

Ágnes Györke is a lecturer at the University of Debrecen, Hungary. Her academic interests include contemporary British and postcolonial literature, gender studies, and urban studies. She gained her PhD in 2009; the title of her dissertation was *Postmodern Nations in Salman Rushdie's Fiction:* Midnight's Children, Shame *and* The Satanic Verses. Györke has written scholarly articles about Salman Rushdie, Martin Amis, Tibor Fischer, Géza Gárdonyi, nationalism studies, and cultural studies. Her book on Rushdie, based on her dissertation, was published in 2012. She has been a visiting scholar at Indiana University; a fellow at Central European University and the Institute for Advanced Study, Budapest; and, currently, her work is supported by the EU-funded Zoltán Magyary Fellowship.

Tuomas Huttunen currently teaches literature in the Department of English at the University of Turku, Finland. Previously, he has worked as a researcher in several projects involving various aspects of postcolonial literatures. His recent interests have focused on the possibilities of combining narrative ethics and deconstruction. It was around this theme in the fiction of Amitav Ghosh that he compiled his doctoral dissertation in 2011. He has published articles on Amitav Ghosh, V. S. Naipaul, and M. G. Vassanji, as well as co-edited the 2008 volume *Seeking the Self – Encountering the Other: Diasporic Narrative and the Ethics of*

Representation, with Kaisa Ilmonen, Janne Korkka, and Elina Valovirta. His new research project involves examining new Indian English literatures from the 2000s within the framework of contemporary delineations of cosmopolitan, or post-postcolonial, approaches.

Liani Lochner is assistant professor of postcolonial and Anglophone world literature in the Department of English at Concordia University, Canada. Educated in South Africa and in England, her research interests are in the field of world literature, especially literary and theoretical refutations of the interlocking networks of position and power that mark contemporary life. She is working on a book on the political promise of literature—particularly works by Kazuo Ishiguro, Salman Rushdie, J. M. Coetzee, and Aravind Adiga—to disrupt the processes by which discourses on biotechnology, fundamentalism, state racism, and neo-liberal globalization position and interpellate the subject. She has published essays on *Never Let Me Go* and scientific discourse and ethics.

Anuradha Marwah is associate professor in the Department of English, Zakir Husain Delhi College, Delhi University, India. She has written three novels—*The Higher Education of Geetika Mehendiratta* (1993), *Idol Love* (1999), and *Dirty Picture* (2007)—and short stories, poems, and three plays. Her academic publications include the co-authored books *Creative Writing: A Manual for Beginners* (2008); *Srijan-I*, the NCERT textbook for Class XI for the course: Creative Writing and Translation (2009); and articles "The Tattered Burqa and the Peeling Palimpsest of Rushdie's Shame," in *Rushdie the Novelist: from Grimus to The Enchantress of Florence*, ed. Meenakshi Bharat (2009); "The Making of Global Success: Roy and Lahiri's Authentic Indian Fictions," in *South Asian Review* 33:2 (2012); and "Transnational Transactions and the Indian Woman: Interrogating Jhumpa Lahiri's Universalism" (forthcoming).

Raita Merivirta completed her PhD at La Trobe University in Melbourne, Australia in 2013. Her doctoral thesis is entitled *Representations of History in Post-Emergency Indian English Novels: Nation, State and Democracy in Indira Gandhi's India*. Currently, she works as University Lecturer in English Literature at the University of Tampere, Finland. Dr. Merivirta has published articles on Indian English literature as well as Irish cinema

---

and history, and she is the author of the book *The Gun and Irish Politics: Examining National History in Neil Jordan's Michael Collins* (2009). She is a co-editor of the collection *Frontiers of Screen History: Imagining European Borders in Cinema 1945–2010* (2013).

Jūratė Radavičiūtė is currently working as a lecturer at Vilnius University, Lithuania. She received her doctoral degree in 2011 after defending her dissertation *Postmodernism in Salman Rushdie's Novels* Midnight's Children *and* Shame. Her articles on the works of Salman Rushdie include: "Mimic Men of Salman Rushdie's *Midnight's Children*," in *Žmogus kalbos erdvėje* 5:2 (2008); "Undermining of the Traditional Usage of Synecdoche in Salman Rushdie's Novel *Midnight's Children*" in *American and European Studies Yearbook 2008–2009* (2010); and "Reality Preceded by Simulacra in Salman Rushdie's Novel *Shame*" in *Žmogus kalbos erdvėje* 7 (2013). Radavičiūtė's scientific interests include postmodern English literature, postcolonial literary theory, and deconstruction.

Jenni Ramone is senior lecturer in postcolonial studies and co-director of the Centre for Colonial and Postcolonial Studies at Nottingham Trent University. She is an executive board member of the Postcolonial Studies Association. Ramone is the author of *Salman Rushdie and Translation* (Bloomsbury, 2013) and *Postcolonial Theories* (Palgrave, 2011); she is coeditor of *The Richard and Judy Book Club Reader* (Ashgate, 2011) and of a double special issue of *Life Writing* journal, on women's life-writing in the postcolonial diaspora. Her research interests are in the literatures of South Asia and the Middle East and their diasporas, postcolonial and translation theories, postcolonial readerships, and postcolonial adaptation and translation. Her current project explores readers and reading in postcolonial literature.

Madan M. Sarma is currently a professor in the Department of English and Foreign Languages at Tezpur University, Tezpur, Assam, India. His areas of interest are critical theory, applied linguistics, translation studies, fiction, and folk literature. He is an eminent creative writer and critic in Assamese and also a translator. His papers on J. M. Coetzee, Amitav Ghosh, Salman Rushdie, and Shakespeare in translation have been published in critical anthologies such as *Salman Rushdie: Critical Essays* 1 (2006) and *Rethinking Modernity* (2005). He has published papers on translation studies and performing arts in Indian and international journals. He is presently working on a book about a traditional theatrical form and editing a volume on one of the leading modern Assamese writers.

Lotta Strandberg defended her doctoral dissertation "Embedded Storytelling and Gender Negotiations in Githa Hariharan's First Three Novels" at the University of Helsinki, Finland in 2011. She has published two articles on Salman Rushdie's novel *Shame*. The first is entitled "Images of Gender in Salman Rushdie's *Shame*" and it is published in *NORA: Nordic Journal of Feminist and Gender Research* (2004). The second Rushdie-related article is a book chapter in Finnish and deals with metafictional aspects and the authorial voice. The chapter is entitled "Dialogia tekijän kanssa: Salman Rushdien *Häpeä*" (Dialogue with the Author: Salman Rushdie's *Shame*) and is published in the book *Tekijyyden tekstit* (2006). She is currently a research scholar at New York University and is working on a monograph on South Asian fiction.

John J. Su is professor of contemporary Anglophone literatures at Marquette University in Wisconsin. He is the author of two books, *Ethics and Nostalgia in the Contemporary Novel* and *Imagination and the Contemporary Novel* (Cambridge University Press, 2005 and 2011 respectively). He is also author of over a dozen articles on aesthetics, ethics, memory, postmodernism, and postcolonial theory. Su has examined Rushdie's work in both books and in the article "Epic of Failure: Disappointment as Utopian Fantasy in Salman Rushdie's *Midnight's Children*." He is currently writing a book on representations of neoliberalism in literatures of the new millennium.

Celia Wallhead holds PhDs in Spanish and English from the Universities of London and Granada, respectively, and a BA in Spanish and French from the University of Birmingham. She currently works as a senior lecturer in English language and literature at the University of Granada, Spain. She has taught Spanish at the University of Auckland, New Zealand, and the University of Wales at Aberystwyth. She was working for the British Council in Granada, Spain, when Salman Rushdie visited. Since 1990, she has taught English language and literature at the University of Granada.

She has published articles on Salman Rushdie's books *East, West*; *The Moor's Last Sigh*; *The Ground Beneath Her Feet*; *Fury*; *Shalimar the Clown*; and *Joseph Anton: A Memoir*.

Index
